MW01142103

VISUAL INTELLIGENCE

VISUAL

W. W. NORTON & COMPANY

NEW YORK — LONDON

DONALD D. HOFFMAN

INTELLIGENCE

HOW WE CREATE WHAT WE SEE

Copyright © 1998 by Donald D. Hoffman

For information about permission to reproduce selections from this book,
write to Permissions, W. W. Norton & Company, Inc., 500 Fifth Avenue,
New York, NY 10110

The text of this book is composed in Garamond #3
with the display set in Trade Gothic
Desktop composition by Gina Webster
Manufacturing by Quebecor Printing Book Group
Book design by Judith Stagnitto Abbate

Library of Congress Cataloging-in-Publication Data

Hoffman, Donald David.
Visual intelligence : how we create what we see / Donald D. Hoffman.
p.   cm.
Includes bibliographical references and index.
ISBN 0-393-04669-9
1. Visual perception. 2. Vision. 3. Human information processing. 4.
Neuropsychology. I. Title.
BF241.H56   1998
152.14—dc21   98-6181
                            CIP

W. W. Norton & Company, Inc., 500 Fifth Avenue, New York, N.Y. 10110
http://www.wwnorton.com

W. W. Norton & Company Ltd., 10 Coptic Street, London WC1A 1PU

2 3 4 5 6 7 8 9 0

for Gery and Melissa

CONTENTS

PREFACE

After his stroke, Mr. P still had outstanding memory and intelligence. He could still read and talk, and mixed well with the other patients on his ward. His vision was in most respects normal—with one notable exception: he couldn't recognize the faces of people or animals. As he put it himself, "I can see the eyes, nose, and mouth quite clearly, but they just don't add up. They all seem chalked in, like on a blackboard. . . . I have to tell by the clothes or by the voice whether it is a man or a woman . . . The hair may help a lot, or if there is a mustache. . . ." Even his own face, seen in a mirror, looked to him strange and unfamiliar. Mr. P had lost a critical aspect of his visual intelligence.

We have long known about IQ and rational intelligence. And, in part because of recent advances in neuroscience and psychology, we have begun to appreciate the importance of emotional intelligence. But we are largely ignorant that there is even such a thing as visual intelligence—that is, until it is severely impaired, as in the case of Mr. P, by a stroke or other insult to visual cortex. The culprit in our ignorance is visual intelligence itself. Vision is normally so swift and sure, so dependable and informative, and apparently so effortless that we naturally assume that it is, indeed, effortless. But the swift ease of vision, like the graceful ease of an Olympic ice skater, is deceptive. Behind the graceful ease of the skater are years of rigorous training, and behind the swift ease of vision is an intelligence so great that it occupies nearly half of the brain's cortex. Our visual intelligence richly interacts with, and in many cases precedes and drives, our rational and emotional intelligence. To understand visual intelligence is to understand, in large part, who we are.

It is also to understand much about our highly visual culture in which, as the saying goes, image is everything. Consider, for instance, our entertainment. Visual effects lure us into theaters, and propel films like *Star Wars* and *Jurassic Park* to record sales. Music videos usher us before surreal visual worlds, and spawn TV stations like MTV and VH-1. Video games swallow kids (and adults) for hours on end, and swell the bottom lines of companies like Sega and Nintendo. Virtual reality, popularized in movies like *Disclosure* and *Lawnmower Man*, can immerse us in visual worlds of unprecedented realism, and promises to transform not only entertainment but also architecture, education, manufacturing, and medicine. As a culture we vote with our time and wallets, and at least in the case of entertainment, our vote is clear. Just as we enjoy rich literature that stimulates our rational intelligence, or a moving story that engages our emotional intelligence, so also we seek out and enjoy visual media that challenge our visual intelligence.

Or consider marketing and advertisement, which daily manipulate our buying habits with sophisticated images. Corporations spend millions each year on billboards, packaging, magazine ads, and television commercials. Their images can so powerfully influence our behavior that they sometimes generate controversy—witness the uproar over Joe Camel. If you're out to sell something, understanding visual intelligence is, without question, critical to the design of effective visual marketing. And if you're out to buy something, understanding visual intelligence can help clue you in to what's being done to you as a consumer, and how it's being done.

This book is a highly illustrated and accessible introduction to visual intelligence, informed by the latest breakthroughs in vision research. Perhaps the most surprising insight that has emerged from vision research is this: Vision is not merely a matter of passive perception, it is an intelligent process of active construction. What you see is, invariably, what your visual intelligence constructs. Just as scientists intelligently construct useful theories based on experimental evidence, so your visual system intelligently constructs useful visual worlds based on images at the eyes. The main difference is that the constructions of scientists are done consciously, but those of your visual intelligence are done, for the most part, unconsciously.

The constructive power of visual intelligence has long fascinated vision researchers. How can vision conjure up the endless panoply of colors and shapes and motions that we see about us in the "real" world?

How can it morph a mass of metal into a murdering maniac in the world of *Terminator 2*? How can it stretch before us a world in three dimensions when we watch, with special glasses, a 3D movie like *Dial M for Murder*? How can it "boldly go where no man has gone before," not just through the "strange new worlds" of *Star Trek* but through the stranger new worlds revealed by the cameras of the Hubble telescope and of probes like Voyager and Pioneer, worlds for which the eye has not obviously been adapted?

Vision, as we shall see, has divulged many of its secrets to physicists, neurobiologists, perceptual psychologists, and researchers in computer vision. But, as we shall also discover, many interesting secrets are yet to be unveiled. These secrets of your visual intelligence, both revealed and unrevealed, are sure to pique in you the same admiration and curiosity that animate vision researchers.

For some, science is like a "reaper binder" that methodically mows down wheat: science methodically mows down unanswered questions and leaves ever less room for wonder. But our exploration of visual intelligence will suggest that science is more like an island: "The larger the island of knowledge, the longer the shoreline of wonder," the preacher Ralph W. Sockman noted. For each question we answer, ten new ones arise, and for each new probe at nature, entire vistas arise.

Our island of knowledge about visual intelligence has grown immensely in the last two decades. A book-length tour of the new terrain can hit but a few of the interesting sights. *Visual Intelligence* hits those sights that may inspire you to linger on the shoreline of wonder.

Visual Intelligence has several tourists in mind. For those in marketing, advertising, and graphic design, *Visual Intelligence* will better acquaint you with your first client: visual intelligence. Your images must pass the scrutiny of customers' visual intelligence before they can go on to convince their rational intelligence of a need and their emotional intelligence of a desire for your product. Visual intelligence is your path to the head and heart of a customer, and understanding visual intelligence is key to successfully navigating that path.

For the reader of popular science, *Visual Intelligence* explains why your brain devotes billions of its valuable neurons and trillions of its valuable synapses to vision, why each of your eyes contains within it more computing power than the fastest supercomputers made today, why you can buy a chess machine that beats a Master but can't yet buy a vision machine that beats a toddler's vision, why computer vision is not only possible but is destined soon to be a multibillion-dollar industry that alters our day-to-day lives no less than the computer or the telephone. *Visual Intelligence* will leave you astonished at what happens when you simply open your eyes.

For the undergraduate with an undeclared major, beware: *Visual Intelligence* might lure you away from a high-paying career as a doctor or lawyer or CEO, and lure you into a career as a vision researcher. The unsolved puzzles of visual intelligence are a worthy challenge for the sharpest of minds (and the pay isn't half bad). There is much to be done, and the field could use your help.

For those building virtual worlds, *Visual Intelligence* documents that human vision (and touch and hearing) is the real creator of virtual reality (VR), and that the role of VR systems is to "trick" human vision into creating those realities that you, the VR designer, want created. To build compelling virtual worlds, one must understand visual intelligence and how it constructs visual realities.

For lawyers concerned with eyewitness testimony, *Visual Intelligence* conveys the latest scientific insights and perspectives on the visual processes that underlie such testimony. The visual reality of an eyewitness is a constructed reality. Understanding the rules by which eyewitnesses construct visual realities can be critical to the proper evaluation of eyewitness testimony.

For philosophers interested in the epistemological and ontological issues raised by perception, *Visual Intelligence* provides an accessible entrance into the latest empirical and theoretical literature on vision, and suggests that an idealist reading of this literature can be at least as compelling as the best physicalist readings.

For vision researchers, faced with a burgeoning literature from a variety of disciplines, *Visual Intelligence* provides a provocative synthesis. Unifying themes can be discerned in the diversity of our technical results, and contemplating these themes is not only worthwhile in its own right but can alter how we conceive and conduct our technical work.

For those who are just plain curious about how they see, or who aren't curious because they can't imagine there's that much to it, *Visual Intelligence* is for you.

That should include just about everyone.

As in many scientific fields, mathematics has cropped up everywhere in vision research—a help to researchers and a hindrance to laymen. Fortunately, the key discoveries about visual intelligence can be conveyed without mathematics. To that end, mathematics is banished to endnotes for those so inclined. This approach is, of course, not new. The

Greek physician Galen (A.D. 130–200), for instance, adopted it when he wrote about vision:

> I have explained nearly everything pertaining to the eyes with the exception of one point which I had intended to omit . . . since it necessarily involves the theory of geometry. . . . [But] I felt impelled to take up again what I had omitted and add it to the end of this book.

Also banished to the back are all notes and citations. These are listed by page number. If you find an intriguing fact or picture or quote on page 73 and want to know more, chances are you'll find more in Note 73 at the back of the book.

Many people have helped in the development of *Visual Intelligence*: Laura Andes, Joe Arpaia, Margaret Atherton, Kimberley Babb, Bruce Bennett, Francis Crick, Alan Gilchrist, Heiko Hecht, Dieter Heyer, David Hoffman, Loretta Hoffman, Nicole Huber, Stan Klein, Larry Maloney, Rainer Mausfeld, Brian McLaughlin, Alan Nelson, Chetan Prakash, Whitman Richards, Scott Richman, Craig Sauer, Armin Schwegler, Stan Schein, Robert Schwartz, Greg Seyranian, Manish Singh, Carol Skrenes, Dejan Todorović, Vanessa Vollmer, and many students in my class on the mind-body problem at UC Irvine, and in Stan Schein's class on sensation and perception at UCLA, who read an earlier version of this book for the class and gave helpful feedback. My editor at Norton, Angela von der Lippe, expertly helped me to streamline the text and broaden its appeal. My agents Katinka Matson and John Brockman encouraged me early on, and guided me through the proposal process. Dee Yox and Ashley Barnes assisted with figure permissions, and Sydney Cohen compiled the index. Thank you all for your help.

Work on this book was supported in part by a sabbatical leave from the University of California, Irvine, by a grant from the UC Irvine Committee on Research, and by a grant from the Zentrum für interdisziplinäre Forschung of the University of Bielefeld, Germany. Thank you for your support.

VISUAL INTELLIGENCE

ONE

A CREATIVE GENIUS
FOR VISION

Y ou are a creative genius. Your creative genius is so accomplished that it appears, to you and to others, as effortless. Yet it far outstrips the most valiant efforts of today's fastest supercomputers. To invoke it, you need only open your eyes. This might sound like the mantra of a new therapy, or the babble of a fortune cookie. But it is, instead, the reasoned conclusion of researchers in the field of cognitive science. What happens when you see is not a mindless process of stimulus and response, as behaviorists thought for much of the twentieth century, but a sophisticated process of construction whose intricacies we are now beginning to understand. In a fraction of a second your visual intelligence can construct the strut and colors of a peacock, or the graceful run of a leopard, or the fireworks of an ocean sunset, or the nuances of light in a forest at dusk, or any of countless other scenes of such subtlety and complexity. In repertoire and speed you far surpass the greatest of painters.

You are a visual virtuoso. Perhaps, though, you are unaware of or flatly disbelieve in your innate talent. My goal is to persuade you otherwise, to present you with the evidence uncovered by researchers in the cognitive sciences, evidence that, quite frankly, has come as a surprise to the researchers themselves. Indeed, rumor has it, an early researcher at MIT so underestimated vision that he assigned it to a graduate student as a summer project, a mere warm-up for more substantial forays into human and artificial intelligence. Now, a few decades later, thousands of researchers in a variety of disciplines work full-time to explore the genius of vision. What they have found will, I suspect, prod even the most jaded of viewers to awe.

Your visual prowess is nowhere more impressive than when you view a natural scene. But to appreciate that prowess it is best to begin with something far simpler. This is, after all, the method of science: study first the simple, then the complex. Try arithmetic before calculus. In this spirit, let's look first at a simple figure, a mere trifle for the constructive powers of your visual intelligence. Here is the "ripple":

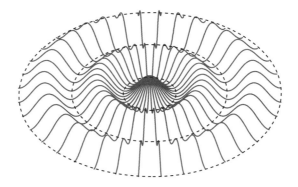

This figure is of course a drawing on a flat—or, more precisely, two-dimensional (2D)—surface. You can check this, should you wish to, by touching it. But the figure also appears to be, as the name "ripple" suggests, a surface that is far from flat, and that undulates in space like waves on a pond. You can check this by viewing the figure. Indeed, *try* to see the ripple as flat; I have never succeeded.

Logic dictates that the ripple cannot be at once flat and not flat, so either the hand or the eye (or both) must be in error. Everyone to whom I have shown the ripple has opted to believe the hand. So assume for now that the hand is right and the figure is flat. Then your visual system has made a serious error: it has constructed an elaborate ripple in space despite ample evidence that this construction is unwarranted. And it perseverates in this error, ignoring your better judgment that the figure must be flat. This might not seem the virtuoso performance I mentioned a moment ago.

There is, as we shall see, method to this visual madness. But for now, look again at the ripple and note that it has three parts: a bump in the center, a circular wave around the bump, and another circular wave on the outside. As an aid to discuss the figure, I drew dashed curves along the boundaries of these parts.

We have gone from bad to worse. Your visual system not only fabricates the ripple, it then endows it with parts. But could it be that the dashed curves—and not your visual system—are the real culprits here, and that without the dashed curves you would see no parts? You can check that this is not so. Simply turn the figure, or your head, upside down. You now see an inverted ripple with new parts: the dashed curves now lie on crests of waves and not, as before, in the troughs between waves. Turning the figure upright restores the original parts. And if you turn the figure slowly you can catch it in the act of flipping from one set of parts to the other. So the dashed curves aren't the culprits, since the parts you see in the inverted ripple don't always respect those curves.

Has your visual system gone off the deep end? It constructs from whole cloth a ripple in space and then proceeds to embellish it with mutable parts. Shall we henceforth distrust the witness of vision, knowing now its penchant to perjure?

This last conclusion is of course too hasty. Our evidence, so far, suggests only a single mistake, not inveterate fabrication. To establish the harsher verdict, we must consider more evidence. That we shall do through much of this book. In the process we shall find that your construction of the ripple and its parts follows a beautiful logic. But for now consider next the "magic square":

Magic Square   Magic Square   Almost Gone!

The middle figure consists of sixteen lines at random orientations. You might see, in addition, four edges that form the boundary of a square. And the square itself might look a brighter white than the rest of the page. But a photometer, a device which measures light intensity by catching and counting light particles, would discern neither the edges nor the brighter interior of this square.

Logic again dictates that the figure cannot at once contain and not contain a bright square, so either the photometer or your visual system (or both) must be in error. Everyone to whom I have shown the magic square has opted to believe the photometer. So assume for now that the photometer is right and the figure has no bright square. Then your visual system has again made a serious error, and of the same type it did with the ripple: elaborate fabrication.

The magic square appears as well in the figure on the left. But when I superpose the left and middle figures to obtain the figure on the right, the magic square almost disappears. This seems to make no sense. If the left figure and the middle figure each prompt your visual system to construct a square, then we should expect, if anything, that superposing them would prompt your visual system to construct another, more salient, square. After all, there is now twice the "evidence" for a square, since there are now twice as many lines that terminate along its presumed boundary. Why build a square based on small evidence, and yet refuse to build one when there is more? This example, and the ripple, suggest that your visual system not only fabricates, it does so willy-nilly.

This charge is again too hasty. We will find that your visual system fabricates, and does so chronically—but not willy-nilly. There is a compelling logic to your construction, and deconstruction, of the magic square.

Now consider the "devil's triangle," a fiendish figure devised in 1934 by Oscar Reutersvärd:

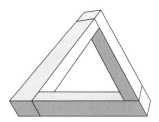

Once again we catch vision in the act of perjury. Its testimony to a solid triangle extended in depth is flatly contradicted by evidence from the hand. But this time we also catch vision in that joy of opposing counsel: self-contradiction. The triangle that is so confidently fabricated by vision, and which vision will not retract despite the witness of the hand, is not consistent. You could not build it with lumber and nails, which is why it's sometimes called the "impossible triangle."

This is striking. It suggests that vision not only fabricates, it does so, at times, unconstrained by reality. Constrained fabrication we might endure, but fabrication unconstrained goes well beyond the pale. Perhaps, though, the devil's triangle is exceptional. Perhaps the visual system fabricates an inconsistency simply because there is no way, given this figure, to fabricate anything else. If so, we might excuse the visual system on grounds that it must, by nature, fabricate and that no consistent fabrication could be had. This explanation is attractive because it would avoid accusing vision of gratuitous inconsistency, and would confine all inconsistencies to such rarities as psychology labs and exhibitions of Escher.

An admirable try, but it won't work. There are, as it happens, many (infinitely many!) different objects one can build with lumber and nails that, if photographed from the proper angle, give the same image as the devil's triangle. The psychologist Richard Gregory has taken the time to build one. His construction looks something like this:

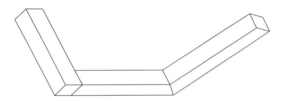

If you construct this with wood and view it from just the right angle, you can see the devil's triangle. Of course, what you construct with wood is not the devil's triangle itself, since that is impossible. Instead what you construct with wood is another object which, when viewed from the appropriate angle, leads you to see the devil's triangle.

So we can't excuse the visual system on grounds it had no consistent options; it had them, all right, and either ignored or discarded them. But, as we shall find, there is no need to excuse the visual system at all. Its fabrication of the devil's triangle is governed by elegant principles, and knowing these principles we can predict when its fabrications will be consistent or inconsistent.

And this, we shall find, is typical of your visual intelligence. Its nature is to construct, and to do so according to principles. Without exception, everything you see you construct: color, shading, texture, motion, shape, visual objects, and entire visual scenes. The three examples we just considered—the ripple, the magic square, and the devil's triangle—are simple demonstrations of your visual intelligence and its genius to construct.

But wait. If you construct all you see, then since you see this book, you construct it as well. And if that's so, then why should you buy it and why should I get royalties? What right have I to copyright your construction?

This question has more than passing interest to me as an author, and I shall have to raise a distinction to rescue my royalties. We use the phrase "what you see" in at least two ways. Sometimes we use it to mean "the way things look to you," "the way they visually appear to you," "the way you visually experience them."

Philosophers call this the *phenomenal* sense. Someone with delirium tremens may see, in the phenomenal sense, a pink elephant in the room, even though the rest of us do not. Someone normal may see, in the phenomenal sense, the devil's triangle, even though what is seen can't be built with wood. You see the depth and parts of the "ripple" in the phenomenal sense. You also see the edges and brightness of the magic square in the phenomenal sense. Photometers can't discern what you see in this sense of "see," and so they can't discern the magic square.

We also use the phrase "what you see" to mean roughly "what you interact with when you look." This is the *relational* sense. Someone with delirium tremens can, simultaneously, see a pink elephant in the phenomenal sense and fail to see a pink elephant in the relational sense—if there is in fact no pink elephant. A thing must exist to be seen in the relational sense. Suppose you are the only thing that exists (a strange idea called *solipsism*). Then you could never see anything else in the relational sense, since there would be nothing else to interact with. You might still, of course, continue to see in the phenomenal sense, since you might continue to have visual experiences.

So when I say that your visual intelligence constructs what you see, I mean "see" in the phenomenal sense: you construct your visual experience. When you look at this book, everything you see, i.e., everything you visually experience, is your construction: the thickness of the spine, the white color and rectangular shape of the pages, the black color and curved shapes of the letters—no less than the ripple, the magic square, and the devil's triangle.

But when you see this book there is also, I hope you will agree, something that you see relationally, something with which you interact. If so, that thing is something I helped to create (by typing at a computer terminal), and therefore I get to keep my royalty. Philosophical distinctions can indeed be of practical value!

This distinction, however, might cost you more than money, it might cost you worry. Just what are these things that we interact with when we see, and how do they relate to our visual experiences? Interesting issues lurk here, but we shall have to postpone them until later. But here, in brief, is a metaphor I find useful. The relation between what you see phenomenally and what you see relationally is like the relation between icons and software on a computer. When you use, say, that neat paint program or word processor on your PC, you interact with megabytes of software of such complexity that its creation took talented programmers many months of concerted effort. Fortunately for you, they made their software "user-friendly" so you don't need to know its grisly innards. They gave you colorful icons and clever graphical tools that make it easy to get your work done. As a result, you can be an expert user of that paint program without knowing how to write a program—indeed, without even knowing about or believing in programs. But every time you click an icon or drag a paintbrush you in fact interact with a complex unseen world of software (and hardware). The relation between icons and software is systematic but arbitrary; those icons could take many different forms and colors, as they often do from one paint program to the next, and still have the same function. Similarly, our visual experiences serve as our user-friendly icon interface with those things we relationally see (whatever they are). Experienced chairs, books, cars, trees, and stars are all icons of this interface.

We'll explore this "icon metaphor" in more detail later. For now, however, and for most of the book, we'll explore the genius of your visual intelligence to construct visual experiences—that is, to construct your icon interface.

"The only difference between genius and stupidity," said an unknown wag, "is that genius is limited." This is precisely the finding of cognitive science. You are a genius at a few things, like vision and language, whether or not you have a high IQ. One must be severely retarded (or have a special handicap) before failing to see or talk. Your genius at vision, like your genius at language, is innate, safely wired into your brain under the influence of your genes. (However, the brain itself, with its neurons, is part of the icon interface. It is the icon we see when we peek inside skulls.)

But vision, unlike language, is a genius we share with many other animals. Of course, vision varies widely from species to species, and in many respects it's a mistake to think that vision in other species resembles vision in humans. To underline this point, the biologist Adrian Horridge prefers to call the vision of insects *semivision*. But the vision, or semivision, of other species is impressive in its own right. Goldfish have color vision—in fact they have four color receptors, compared to our three—and "color constancy": they can continue to find, say, green objects despite changes in color of the ambient light in their tank. Honeybees have color constancy and can see the magic square. They can also navigate using the sun as a compass, even if it's hidden behind a cloud: they find it via the polarization of ultraviolet light from blue patches of sky. The fly uses visual motion to compute, in real time, how and when to land on a surface and how to alter its trajectory to intercept another fly. Day-old chicks discriminate spheres from pyramids, and peck preferentially at the spheres (most seeds are shaped like spheres, not pyramids). The praying mantis uses binocular vision to locate a fly in space and then, when the fly is at just the right distance, flicks out a foreleg to catch the fly in its tarsal-tibial joint. The mantis shrimp has ten color receptors, can find the range to a prey with just a single eye, and accurately stuns its prey with a quick strike of its raptorial append-age. Macaque monkeys see "structure from motion": with just one eye open they can construct the three-dimensional (3D) shape of a moving object. And the story that holds for our visual genius holds, in every case, for theirs as well: vision is construction.

Of course some visual constructions display less genius than oth-ers. For newly hatched goslings, whose first priority is to find Mom and safety, the first big moving object they see becomes "Mom." When Konrad Lorenz arranged to be that first big moving object, he instantly became "Mom" to several goslings, who faithfully followed him there-after and, in adolescence, found him attractive as a possible mate.

The ethologist Niko Tinbergen found that for blackbird nestlings, "Mom" (or "parent") can be as simple as two adjacent disks, one having a diameter about a third that of the other. The absolute size of the disks matters little, but if the ratio of their diameters deviates much from one third, or if there are extra disks around, then they are not "Mom":

"Mom"   Not "Mom"   Not "Mom"

Hungry blackbird nestlings will gape to a cardboard copy of "Mom," but not to copies of the other two figures.

Tinbergen also found that for chickens and ducks, a harmless "goose" can be a cross moving in the direction of its long end, and a feared "hawk" can be a cross moving in the direction of its short end:

"Goose"   "Hawk"

A cardboard "hawk" flown overhead by mischievous ethologists sends chickens running for cover. A cardboard "goose" is ignored.

Jörg-Peter Ewert found that for the common toad *Bofu bofu*, a "prey" can be a stripe moving in the direction of its longer axis, and a "predator" can be a stripe moving along its shorter axis:

"Prey"   "Predator"

A cardboard "prey" moved around by other mischievous ethologists triggers the toad to orient, approach, fixate, snap, gulp, and wipe—only to find that cardboard just can't satisfy like a juicy slug or a crunchy beetle. Gary Larson catches the humor of all this in a cartoon showing a frog stuck to the bottom of a jumbo jet by its outstretched tongue.

What's so funny in each case is how easily the animal is duped. Simple figures trigger fantastic visual constructions. But as we laugh at these foibles we laugh at ourselves, for we too cannot help but create visual fantasies, as shown by the ripple, magic square, and devil's triangle. Perhaps we aren't taken in by our creations as badly as is the gosling. Yet, despite our better judgment, a simple figure triggers us to construct a ripple, just as a large moving object triggers a gosling to construct "Mom." In this respect there is no difference in principle between us and goslings. There is a difference in practice: we're not duped by some visual figures that dupe goslings. But then it's likely that they aren't duped by some figures that trigger visual fantasies in us.

So we share with all sighted animals a genius to construct and, in consequence, a chance to err. This raises questions. When should we trust what we see? If the ripple and magic square are false constructs, what further falsehoods might we see? And if our "genius" to construct can mislead, then why not dispense with it and just see the world as it is?

The sobering fact is that we cannot dispense with construction. To construct is the essence of vision. Dispense with construction and you dispense with vision. Everything you experience by sight is your construction. This is, as we shall see, more than brute fact; it is a dictate of logic.

This was recognized by Ptolemy in the second century A.D. in his *Optics*, and since then by many other students of vision. For instance, the Islamic scholar Alhazen (965–1039) described the perception of most visual properties as being due to a process of unconscious inference:

> . . . For the shape or size of a body, or the transparency of a transparent body, and such like properties of visible objects, are in most cases perceived extremely quickly, and not immediately, since they are perceived by inference and discernment. . . .

The second volume of Alhazen's seven-volume *Optics* describes in detail how we infer visual properties, such as the distance, size, and shapes of visible objects, or the beauty of the human face. In this he anticipates the spirit of modern researchers who use Bayesian inference to model visual constructions.

It's easy to underrate these inferences, since vision feels so easy. But anyone who studies them soon discovers their sophistication. The philosopher Nicholas Malebranche (1638–1715) became so impressed that he decided we couldn't do these inferences alone, and that they must be done for us, on the fly, by God:

> . . . God through this general law gives us precisely all those perceptions we would give ourselves a) if we had an exact

knowledge, not only of what takes place in our brain and in our eyes, but also of the situation and movement of our bodies, b) if in addition we knew optics and geometry perfectly, and c) if we could, on the basis of this actual knowledge . . . instantaneously produce an infinity of precise inferences. . . .

Major advances in our understanding of visual inferences came from the German physicist and physiologist Hermann von Helmholtz (1821–1894), who described vision as a process of unconscious inference (*unbewusster Schluss*):

The psychic activities that lead us to infer that there in front of us at a certain place there is a certain object of a certain character, are generally not conscious activities, but unconscious ones. In their result they are equivalent to a *conclusion*, . . . it may be permissible to speak of the psychic acts of ordinary perception as *unconscious conclusions*, thereby making a distinction of some sort between them and the common so-called conscious conclusions.

Helmholtz took care to describe visual inferences as unconscious, and to contrast them in this respect to conscious inferences as they arise in science and in everyday life. The term "inference," however, still carries the connotation of a conscious activity. For this reason I prefer to use "construct" rather than "infer" to describe the creative processes of visual intelligence.

The British neurophysiologist David Marr (1946–1981) described visual constructions by analogy to information processing in computers:

Vision is a process that produces from images of the external world a description that is useful to the viewer and not cluttered with irrelevant information. . . .

Marr thought of vision as an active process that produces useful descriptions. Much of his book *Vision* describes in detail how this active process constructs perceived shapes, textures, motions, and entire objects.

This active process of vision, this penchant to construct, is key to the success of great paintings. From one perspective a painting is just dabs of pigment on canvas. But the cooperative viewer sees more: a landscape with jagged mountains and blue streams, a still life with green grapes and a black fly, a woman with long brown hair and an inscrutable smile, a saint peppered with darts, looking to heaven. The genius of the artist places pigments so that the genius of the viewer can thus interpret them; or, as with cubists, so that the genius of the viewer meets contradictions in its every attempt to interpret. The essential ambiguity of paintings, and their constructive interpretation by viewers, is the central theme of art historian Ernst Hans Gombrich (b. 1909) in his book *Art and Illusion*. Gombrich notes that viewers interpret paintings by processes of construction which are unconscious and automatic, which he calls "projection," and by processes of construction which are conscious and more labored, which he calls "inference" or "knowledge." This power of construction was well known to Leonardo da Vinci (1452–1519), and used by him for "quickening the spirit of invention" of the artist, as he describes in his book *Treatise on Painting*:

> You should look at certain walls stained with damp, or at stones of uneven colour. If you have to invent some backgrounds you will be able to see in these the likeness of divine landscapes, adorned with mountains, ruins, rocks, woods, great plains, hills and valleys in great variety; and then again you will see there battles and strange figures in violent action, expressions of faces and clothes and an infinity of things which you will be able to reduce to their complete and proper forms. In such walls the same thing happens as in the sound of bells, in whose stroke you may find every named word which you can imagine.

Among the most amazing facts about vision is that kids are accomplished geniuses at vision before they can walk. Before age one, they can construct a visual world in three dimensions, navigate through it quite purposefully on all fours, organize it into objects, and grasp, bite, and recognize those objects. As the psychologist Philip Kellman puts it, the challenge facing a newborn is "SPACE: THE FIRST FRONTIER." By about the age of one month, kids blink if something moves toward their eyes on a collision course. By three months they use visual motion to construct boundaries of objects. By four months they use motion and stereovision to construct the 3D shapes of objects. By seven months they also use shading, perspective, interposition (in which one object partially occludes another), and prior familiarity with objects to construct depth and shape. By one year they are visual geniuses, and proceed to learn names for the objects, actions, and relations they construct. By age eighteen, typical high school graduates know about sixty thousand words, and a quick computation shows that during the previous seventeen years they must have learned, on average, one word every ninety waking minutes.

Kids aren't taught how to see. Parents don't sit down with their kids and explain how to use motion and stereo to construct depth, or how to carve the visual world into objects and actions. Indeed, most parents don't know how they do this themselves. And yet it appears that each normal child comes to construct visual depth, shape, colors, objects, and actions pretty much the same way as any other normal child. Each normal child, without being taught, reinvents the visual world; and all do it much the same way. This is remarkable, because in so doing each child overcomes the fundamental problem of vision:

The fundamental problem of vision. The image at the eye has countless possible interpretations.

By "image at the eye" I mean the retinal image, i.e., the image cast on light-sensitive tissue at the back of the eye.

So, for instance, each child constructs a visual world with three spatial dimensions—height, width, and depth. But an image has just two dimensions—height and width. It follows that, for a given image, there are countless 3D worlds that a child could construct, each of which is compatible with the image in this sense: if you view that 3D world from the right place, then you will obtain the same image. This has been understood at least since William Molyneux (d. 1698) published in 1692 the first English text on optics, *Dioptrika Nova*, where he states:

> For *distance* of it self, is not to be perceived; for 'tis a line (or a length) presented to our eye with its end toward us, which must therefore be only a *point*, and that is *invisible*.

This point was developed by George Berkeley (1685–1753) in his *New Theory of Vision*:

> It is, I think, agreed by all that distance, of itself and immediately, cannot be seen. For distance being a line directed endwise to the eye, it projects only one point in the fund of the eye, which point remains invariably the same, whether the distance be longer or shorter.

Berkeley wasn't denying the obvious, namely, that we do see depth the instant we open our eyes. He was pointing out that the depth we see is but one of countless depths we could see for a given image at the eye.

This ambiguity holds not just for depth, but for all aspects of our visual constructions, including motion, surface colors, and illumination. This is not to deny that images are rich in information, and that moving images are richer still. The psychologist James Gibson (1904–1979) clearly demonstrated this fact. Yet despite the richness of images, the fundamental problem of vision still holds: there are still countless visual worlds that kids could, in principle, construct from them.

This makes the task sound impossible. How could a child sort through countless possible visual worlds and arrive at much the same answer as every other child?

It is impossible. Unless, of course, kids come to the task with innate rules by which they learn to construct visual worlds. If they are born with rules which determine the visual worlds they can learn to construct, and if these rules are universal in the sense that all normal kids have the same rules, then although these rules must blind them to many possibilities, these rules can also guide them to construct visual worlds about which they have consensus. Two toddlers, from opposite ends of the earth, can both be shown the same novel image and see, in consequence, the same visual scene. We take this for granted. But it is magic unless they both share the same innate rules that guide their visual constructions. These innate rules, which grant visual mastery to the child by age one and lead to consensus in the visual constructions of all normal adults despite the infinite ambiguity of images, I call *the rules of universal vision*.

The argument here for rules of universal vision parallels a well-known argument, devised by the linguist Noam Chomsky, for rules of universal grammar that permit the acquisition and exercise of language:

> The language each person acquires is a rich and complex construction hopelessly underdetermined by the fragmentary evidence available [to the child]. Nevertheless individuals in a speech community have developed essentially the same language. This fact can be explained only on the assumption that these individuals employ highly restrictive principles that guide the construction of grammar.

These principles are, according to Chomsky, a genetically determined part of the cognitive structure of the child. Without them, the acquisition of language would be impossible. With them, it is not just possible, but inevitable, given adequate exposure to any human language. As the psycholinguist Steven Pinker puts it:

> The crux of the argument is that complex language is universal because children actually reinvent it, generation after generation—not because they are taught, not because they are generally smart, not because it is useful to them, but because they just can't help it.

Similarly, complex vision is universal because children actually reinvent it, generation after generation—not because they are taught, not because they are generally smart, not because it is useful to them, but because they just can't help it.

Without innate rules of universal vision, the child could not reinvent vision and the adult could not see. With innate rules of universal vision, we can construct visual worlds of great subtlety, beauty, and practical value.

The rules of universal grammar allow a child to acquire the specific rules of grammar for one or more specific languages. These specific rules are at work when the child, having learned a language, understands or utters sentences of that language.

Similarly, the rules of universal vision allow a child to acquire specific rules for constructing visual scenes. These specific rules are at work when the child, having learned to see, looks upon and understands specific visual scenes. These rules I call *rules of visual processing*. The innate rules of universal vision are part of the child's biology, and allow the child to acquire, through visual experiences that might vary from one culture to another, the rules of visual processing. The rules of visual processing, in turn, allow the visually competent child or adult to construct specific visual scenes by looking.

This construction process is multistaged. You don't construct a visual scene in one step, but rather in a multiplicity of stages. Typically the construction at one stage depends upon, and takes as its starting point, the results of constructions at other stages. Your construction, for instance, of the shape of a book in three dimensions might take as its starting point the results of your constructions of motion, lines, and vertices in two dimensions.

With this multiplicity of stages is associated a multiplicity of rules of visual processing. These rules of visual processing, and their many and varied interactions, are central to your visual intelligence. They work so quickly and effectively that normally you are unaware of them. Getting to know them will enhance your mastery and appreciation of your visual intelligence. The rules are the key.

And they are the theme of this book.

INFLATING AN
ARTIST'S SKETCH

urgery without anesthesia is no fun. So before the advent of anesthesia many patients understandably put a premium on speed in their choice of surgeon. Among the most celebrated and rapid surgeons of the preanesthetic era was the Englishman William Cheselden (1688–1752), who pioneered several surgical procedures and cared for Sir Isaac Newton in his last illness.

In 1728, Cheselden published in the *Philosophical Transactions of the Royal Society* what became the most famous case study in the history of science prior to Freud. The study was titled "An Account of some Observations made by a young Gentleman, who was born blind, or lost his Sight so early, that he had no Remembrance of ever having seen, and was couch'd between 13 and 14 Years of Age." It reported a new surgery, in which Cheselden made an "artificial pupil" in each eye of a thirteen-year-old boy who had congenital cataracts. The surgery worked, and the big question was, what would the boy see? Cheselden gives this tantalizing account:

> When he first saw, he was so far from making any Judgment about Distances, that he thought all Objects whatever touch'd his Eyes, (as he express'd it) as what he felt, did his Skin. . . . One Particular only (tho' it may appear trifling) I will relate; Having often forgot which was the Cat, and which the Dog, he was asham'd to ask; but catching the Cat (which he knew by feeling) he was observ'd to look at her stedfastly, and then setting her down, said, So Puss! I shall

know you another Time. . . . We thought he soon knew what Pictures represented, which were shew'd to him, but we found afterwards we were mistaken; for about two Months after he was couch'd, he discovered at once, they represented solid Bodies; when to that Time he consider'd them only as Party-colour'd Planes, or Surfaces diversified with Variety of Paint; but even then he was no less surpriz'd, expecting the Pictures would feel like the Things they represented, and was amaz'd when he found those Parts, which by their Light and Shadow appear'd now round and uneven, felt only flat like the rest; and ask'd which was the lying Sense, Feeling, or Seeing?

The boy asked a natural question. If a picture, like the ripple in Chapter 1, looks "round and uneven" but feels "flat like the rest," then sight and touch contradict and it's natural to wonder if one, or both, is lying. You might think the answer is obvious: touch is surely never wrong, so if sight contradicts touch then sight is lying. But we shall see later that you construct all that you experience through touch, and that your touch constructions can go very wrong, leading to bizarre illusions.

The boy also answered, to Berkeley's satisfaction, a question posed several decades earlier by Molyneux to the philosopher John Locke (1632–1704). Locke records the question in *An Essay Concerning Human Understanding*:

"Suppose a man *born* blind, and now adult, and taught by his *touch* to distinguish between a cube and a sphere of the same metal, and nighly of the same bigness, so as to tell, when he felt one and the other, which is the cube, which the sphere. Suppose then the cube and sphere placed on a table, and the blind man be made to see: *query*, whether *by his sight, before he touched them* he could now distinguish and tell which is the globe, which the cube?" To which the acute and judicious proposer answers, "Not. For, though he has obtained the experience of how a globe, how a cube affects his touch, yet he has not yet obtained the experience, that what affects his touch so or so, must affect his sight so or so; or that a protuberant angle in the cube, that pressed his hand unequally, shall appear to his eye as it does in the cube."—I agree with this thinking gentleman. . . .

Berkeley also agreed with this prediction, and said so in his *New Theory of Vision* nineteen years before Cheselden published his case. For Berkeley thought that, strictly speaking, we don't see shape and space, we feel them; that we see only colored patches, and then associate these patches, through experience, with the shapes and spaces we feel. The association becomes so strong and quick that we're fooled. So Berkeley predicted that one born blind could not, upon being cured, immediately recognize shapes, since it takes time to associate the colored patches we see with the shapes we feel. Instead, he said, "the sun and stars, the remotest objects as well as the nearer, would all seem to be in his eye, or rather in his mind."

The Cheselden case confirmed, for Berkeley and most of his peers, this prediction; the boy, after all, "thought all Objects whatever touch'd his Eyes . . . as what he felt, did his Skin," and he had to see a cat while touching it before he could recognize it by sight alone. This success led to widespread acceptance of Berkeley's theory and its central principle of association.

For two months after his surgery, the Cheselden boy saw no solid shapes or depth in pictures. Then he saw in them "solid Bodies" some of which were "round and uneven," and was surprised that they felt flat. Berkeley explained this new 3D perception of pictures as due to learned associations between vision and touch. We now understand better the principles that underlie our construction of visual shapes, and can now tell a more adequate and interesting story.

A good place to begin is the "Necker cube," a famous figure published in 1832 by the Swiss naturalist Louis Albert Necker:

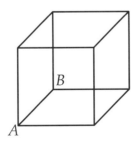

This picture feels flat but looks like a cube. For convenience, I've labeled one vertex *A* and another *B*. If you stare at the figure you may notice that you see not just one cube, but two, and that you flip between seeing one and the other. For one cube, vertex A is behind B, and for the other B is behind A.

Now consider this question: Which vertex is behind when you don't view the figure? Is it A or B? Or is it neither? These seem to be the only possible answers. But all three answers are puzzling.

If, when you look at the figure, the cube you see has A behind, does the cube still have A behind when you look away? Well, to answer this you could get a friend to help out. First you look at the figure until you see a cube with A behind. Then you look away and have your friend look at the figure. Your friend can report which vertex is behind, A or B or neither, and settle the matter.

But unfortunately this won't do. Here's the problem. Ask your friend to look at the figure *at the same time you do*, and then both of you report which vertex is behind. What you'll find is that sometimes you agree, and sometimes not. Sometimes you'll see A behind when your friend sees B. In this case, who is right?

To settle this, you could bring in other friends. But about half of them will agree with you, and half with your friend. So this won't help either.

And for that matter, you don't always agree with yourself. You look at the cube and see, say, vertex A behind. Then, zap, something happens and now B is behind. Shall we say that you are right both times? Wrong both times? Neither? Both? Or perhaps we should ask the question this way. Let's call the cube with vertex A in front "cube A" and the other one "cube B." Now suppose that you see cube A for a while, and then suddenly flip to seeing cube B. What happened to cube A? Where did it go? And where did cube B suddenly come from?

Many puzzling questions pop up from this simple figure. Let's summarize them, and then write down some possible responses. Maybe then we can find evidence that will narrow things down. The main questions are these:

1. Where is cube B when you are seeing cube A?
2. Where is cube A when you are seeing cube B?
3. Where are cubes A and B when you look away from the figure?
4. When you see cube A and your friend at the same time sees cube B, who's right?

And here are possible responses to this set of questions:

1. Don't worry. The Necker cube occurs only in psychology labs, not in nature, and therefore is not "ecological." It tricks the eye

in unnatural ways, and reveals nothing about normal vision. The questions are thus pointless.

2. Cubes? What cubes? I don't feel any cubes when I touch that figure.

3. *You* construct the cubes you see. You aren't aware, perhaps, of your construction process. But you are aware of the *result*.

Let's consider these responses. The first one says "Don't worry." The figure is, after all, unnatural. It's concocted to cause trouble. When you look at the natural world, rather than at a contrived figure, these troubles just don't arise. Vision is adapted to nature, not to the tricks of psychologists. If you use a device in ways it was not intended, of course you'll have trouble.

The problem with this response is that it's not clear what, in principle, separates the natural and ecological from the unnatural. Shall we say, for instance, that any image for which our perception flips back and forth is not "natural"? This is, of course, arbitrary and tantamount to just saying, "Don't study these things." Maybe, then, situations that are man-made are unnatural; or maybe flat things. It's just not clear what should count.

But even if a principled distinction could be made, there is another, deeper problem with this response. It denies us a powerful tool of science: the study of simple systems. Ultimately, of course, we want to understand nature in her full glory and complexity. But between here and there we have much to do, and one way to make progress, many times, is to study simple, and therefore perhaps unnatural, systems.

The second response—"What cubes? I don't feel any cubes"—points to a principle we discussed before. In general, if I see a cube nearby, then I can touch it as well. I can confirm what I see by what I feel. But with the Necker cube my perceptions disagree. I see a cube but don't feel one. In this case, one, or both, of my perceptions must be wrong, since they disagree. Agreement, of course, does not prove them right; they could both be wrong. But disagreement guarantees, it would seem, that at least one is wrong. And if I had to bet, I'd place my money, this time, on touch not sight.

Fine. Perhaps the cubes are illusory. But shall I dismiss them from further study? This still seems the wrong strategy. My visual system confidently reports that there is a cube, indeed two cubes, each time I view the figure, despite the contradictory report of my hands. This persistence, this confidence, should not be overlooked. If we probe further, the system may here reveal secrets of its operation.

The third response is common among cognitive scientists and

researchers in computer vision: What you see is what you construct, and what a computer with video cameras "sees" is what its software constructs. Why do you see a cube when you view the figure? Because the figure triggers your visual intelligence to construct a cube. When you look from the figure to, say, your hand, you stop constructing a cube and start constructing a hand. When you look back to the figure, you again construct a cube.

Where, then, are cubes *A* and *B* when you look away? When you don't view the figure you don't construct the cubes, so they are *nowhere*.

Where is cube *B* when you see cube *A*? This is tricky. If when you see *A* you construct *A* but not *B*, then the answer is, again, that *B* is nowhere. But it may be that when you see *A* you also construct *B* but don't see it. Then *B* is somewhere unseen.

If what you see is what you construct, then how do you construct the cubes?

First, notice the leap you make when you see cube *A*: you view a page with two dimensions but see a solid with three. Nothing on the page *demands* that you see cube *A*. It's likely, for instance, that many sighted species wouldn't see cube *A*; and there are countless shapes, besides cube *A*, that you could see instead. For instance, you could see all those lines in the drawing not as straight edges of cube *A*, but as curves bending and wiggling in depth. Of course, all such curves would bend and wiggle in a direction perpendicular to the page of the figure, so that each curve still projects to a line in the page. But this leaves room for infinite variation.

So you go out on a limb in two ways: you see a solid, although the figure feels flat; and of the countless solids you could see, you see but two. You discard, it would seem, the countless set of other options.

It gets worse. The psychologist Hertha Kopfermann discovered in 1930 that we are picky, in strange ways, about which figures we will see as cubes. Consider these, for example:

 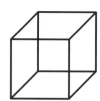 

In the middle is the Necker cube. On the left and right are line drawings that, to most viewers, look flat; but each depicts a possible view of a cube. It might take a minute to see these "Kopfermann cubes."

You easily see the Necker cube in three dimensions, but not the Kopfermann cubes. Why?

You have good reasons, but they'll take a minute to spell out. To begin with, why is it easy to see three dimensions in the Necker cube? In part because you see three dimensions in images that have but two *each time you open your eyes.* The Necker and Kopfermann drawings are not, in this respect, artificial. For the image at each eye, like a drawing on paper, has but two dimensions—no matter where you are or what you view. Whether walking in woods, driving a car, or sitting with friends at a party, you never get three dimensions at the eye, only two. So you face a principled ambiguity each time you need to see depth. This ambiguity is a special case of the fundamental problem of vision:

> **The fundamental problem of seeing depth.** The image at the eye
> has two dimensions; therefore it has countless interpretations
> in three dimensions.

This is as true of two eyes as of one, and of dynamic images as of static: they have countless interpretations in three dimensions. It follows that *anytime* you see depth you construct it, not just when you view strange drawings like Necker's and Kopfermann's but also in everyday life. There are no exceptions. You construct the depth you see on the street, in your office, at a football game, or from the top of a mountain. If this bothers you, if it strikes you as strange, then I think you understand. I still recall my shock the first time I understood: I construct all the depth I see.

You construct depth each time you open your eyes. By now you're an expert. You do it well enough to walk, drive, play tennis, and perform a host of other activities which require that you quickly and effectively construct visual depth. This explains, in part, why you easily construct depth in flat figures like Necker's: you construct depth from 2D images all the time; Necker's is just one more 2D image.

But why not construct depth in Kopfermann's figures? If you construct depth from 2D images all the time, why stop here? The answer is: You don't construct depth willy-nilly, you construct it according to rules. These rules direct you to construct depth in Necker's figure, but deter you in Kopfermann's figures. They decree which 3D structure, of the countless possibilities, you will construct.

Quite simply, your visual system is biased. It constructs only those 3D worlds that conform to its rules. Most others it simply ignores. These rules are powerful. They prune the possible depths you can see from infinity down to one or two. This is useful, for if you saw all options then you would see depth flip or distort with your every glance. And that would be bad for tennis.

We'll consider in a moment a concrete rule that helps us construct the Necker cube, and that hinders us from constructing the Kopfermann cubes. But let's pause briefly to consider, in greater generality, the role of rules.

Rules of construction are critical to vision. You employ, as we shall see, many rules. They are not inviolable. Sometimes one rule overrides another, sometimes they compromise, often they are not black and white, but deal instead in probabilities. They are not explicitly written down in your mind, as one might write down instructions for assembling a bicycle, but are implicit in its workings, just as the laws of physics are not explicitly written down in nature, but are implicit in its workings. You are not, in general, aware of these rules or of their role in constructing what you see. In fact, it has required clever work from many researchers to uncover them. And there are, undoubtedly, many more yet to be uncovered. Finding the rules occupies many vision researchers, and describing them occupies much of this book. Their centrality to vision deserves a highlight.

> **The fundamental role of visual rules.** You construct visual worlds from ambiguous images in conformance to visual rules.

No one teaches you these rules. Instead, you acquire them early in life in a genetically predetermined sequence that requires, for its unfolding, visual experience. Just as a child acquires the grammar of its language without being taught, but simply by being exposed to linguistic experience, so also a child acquires the rules for constructing visual worlds without being taught, but simply by being exposed to visual experience. And just as an adult, using rules of grammar, can understand countless sentences (in principle if not in practice), so also an adult, using rules of vision, can understand countless images (again, in principle if not in practice). Indeed, it is this infinite capacity to understand that provides a strong argument for rules both in language and in vision. We are finite creatures without the memory to store countless sentences or images, so learning a language or learning to see can't just be a matter of storing sentences or images. It must instead be a matter of acquiring a finite set of rules that endow an infinite capacity. It is these rules that allow you to understand sentences or images you have never before encountered. These rules put the intelligence in visual intelligence.

Here is our first concrete example. One rule you use to construct the Necker cube, and that deters you from constructing the Kopfermann cubes, is the rule of generic views.

> **Rule of generic views.** Construct only those visual worlds for which the image is a stable (i.e., generic) view.

To understand the rule, consider this drawing of a vertex:

Suppose you wish to give this drawing a 3D interpretation. That is, you wish to construct an object in 3D that, if viewed from some direction, would give you this image.

You could simply construct a V. This would work, in the sense that there are views of a V that give the vertex image; and in fact a V is probably what you see. But you could also construct a different 3D interpretation, which I'll call "chopsticks": Two straight lines in space that do *not* meet at their tips to form a V. Instead there is a gap between their tips. This construct will also work, in the sense that there are views of it that give the vertex image. In such a view the tip of one line lies directly in front of, but does not touch, the tip of the other, so that the tips appear to meet in a vertex.

Chopsticks is consistent with the vertex image, but it's not nearly as plausible as the V. And here's why: if you were viewing chopsticks, and moved your head just a little bit in almost any direction, then a gap or a crossing would appear, like this:

This means that for the chopsticks it's an *accident of viewpoint* if the tips of the two lines appear to coincide. *Almost every* view of the chopsticks gives an image in which these tips do not coincide. But for the V it's not an accident that the tips coincide; they do so in every possible view. So the vertex image is a typical view of a V, but an accidental view of chopsticks.

And here's the punchline. Accidental views are hard to come by. You have to work hard to get your eye in the right place. So the probability that any given image falling at your eye is an accidental view is almost zero. Therefore you reject any interpretation, like chopsticks, that requires that your current image be an accidental view.

And that, in essence, is the rule of generic views. It is indeed powerful and, as we have just seen, well justified.

Let's use it. Consider an image having but a single line:

There are countless 3D interpretations you could give. For instance, it could be a circle seen from the side, or a semicircle, or a wiggly curve, and so on. But the rule of generic views eliminates *all* these candidates. The only interpretations it allows are *straight lines*!

The argument is simple: Only by an accident of viewpoint will any other curve look straight. Only straight lines project to straight lines from almost every view.

Think of it this way. Suppose the 3D object you view is not straight but is instead, say, a wiggly curve, and suppose the image at your eye is a straight line. If you move your eye slightly, then suddenly the line in the image will become wiggly. A wiggly curve looks wiggly from almost every view. A straight line, and only a straight line, looks straight from almost every view. The only exceptions are end-on views, in which the line projects to a point. But perturb such a view in almost any way and the point will change into a short line. Which is why we see points as points and not as lines viewed end on.

A wiggly curve almost always betrays its wiggles if you move your view a bit. Thus, by the rule of generic views, straight lines in an image cannot be interpreted as wiggly lines, or as anything else except straight lines. We can summarize all this in the form of two simple rules:

Rule 1. Always interpret a straight line in an image as a straight line in 3D.

Rule 2. If the tips of two lines coincide in an image, then always interpret them as coinciding in 3D.

These are simple but powerful rules that prune countless 3D interpretations. Let's use them on this Kopfermann figure:

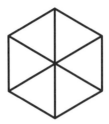

Here's why it's hard to see this as a cube. Note that it has three lines running through its middle, joining the six vertices. According to Rule 1, each line must be interpreted as a straight line, without any corners, in space. This precludes interpreting the figure as a cube.

If we change our view of this Kopfermann cube ever so slightly, then we obtain a generic view and find it easy, once again, to see a cube:

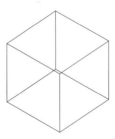

Rule 1 no longer keeps you from constructing a cube, and in fact Rules 1 and 2 together explain, in part, why you do construct one. But an alternative might already have occurred to you. Perhaps it's not the rule of generic views that keeps you from seeing the Kopfermann cubes, but merely the fact that Kopfermann's drawings have simple and symmetric interpretations as plane figures. Since they have such interpretations in 2D, there's no reason to construct something in 3D.

Symmetry and simplicity are indeed important rules of visual construction. This was recognized by Gestalt psychologists in the first half of this century and incorporated in their principle of *Prägnanz*, or precision.

So we have two competing explanations: generic views and symmetry. Both account for our failure to see Kopfermann's cubes. To decide which prevails here, we can check, in a style typical of science, cases for which they differ in predictions. First we check a view that is symmetric and generic. Symmetry predicts that since the view is symmetric, you should see it as 2D; but the rule of generic views predicts that since the view is generic, you can see it as 3D. Here is such a case:

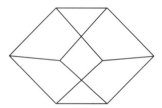

This figure is symmetric about a vertical axis and presents a generic view of a 3D shape. If you see a 3D shape, then this suggests that the rule of generic views, rather than symmetry, here dominates your visual construction.

As a second test, we can check a view that is unsymmetric and nongeneric, and compare it with a nearby view that is unsymmetric and generic. Symmetry predicts no clear difference, since neither is symmetric. The rule of generic views predicts a big difference: the generic view should more easily be seen as 3D. Here is such a case, first devised by the psychologist Gaetano Kanizsa:

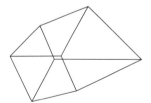 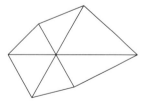

On the left is a generic view of a 3D shape, and on the right a nearby view of the same shape, chosen to be nongeneric and unsymmetric. If you more easily see three dimensions on the left, then this suggests that the rule of generic views, not symmetry, here dominates your construction.

Now we can understand our trouble with the devil's triangle, and how to fix it:

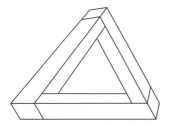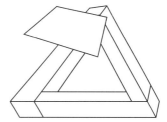

By Rule 1 you see each line in this figure as a line in space. By Rule 2 you see each vertex as a vertex in space. But the triangle on the left depicts a nongeneric view, and Rules 1 and 2 work only for generic views. So you get it wrong. It is an accident of view that the leftmost line, which goes from the left corner to the top, appears unbroken. Change the view slightly and a break will appear (at the "T" intersection near the top), revealing that you were wrong to interpret it as a single unbroken line. Once you've made this wrong turn, you're on the road to trouble. But your commitment to the rule of generic views is so strong that even when you discover your trouble you faithfully stick to the rule. You construct an impossible 3D interpretation rather than violate the rule. If I cover the nongeneric parts, as in the triangle on the right, then you are no longer misled: you construct, as the psychologist Irvin Rock pointed out, a legitimate 3D interpretation.

This shows the power and problem of visual rules. They let us construct visual worlds of great diversity and beauty. They endow us with the capacity to understand countless images, even ones not yet seen by any person at any time. In short, they permit us to see. But at the same time they blind us—to the countless possibilities we can never see because our rules forbid them. Many times I have seen the wooden object which, when photographed from just the right viewpoint, gives an image of the devil's triangle. And yet I can't help but see an impossible object each time I view the image. I can imagine the possible object, but my visual rules forbid me to see it.

Although I cannot, by dint of will, overcome the rule of generic views, other visual rules can. Consider, for instance, the "trading towers":

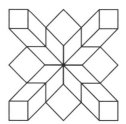

Notice the long diagonal lines passing through the middle of the figure. When you see the tall thin towers, then these diagonals seem to bend once, right at the center of the figure. But this breaks Rule 1, which says that straight lines in an image must be seen as straight lines in 3D (no bends allowed!). When you see the short fat towers, then the vertical and horizontal lines that form a cross in the middle also seem to bend right at the center, again breaking Rule 1. Your visual intelligence dislikes breaking this rule: its processes of construction automatically search for alternatives that don't break the rule. This may explain the extraordinary instability of this figure. Note how briefly you see each interpretation before flipping to the other.

We also break the rule of generic views in our interpretation of a figure devised by Whitman Richards and Allan Jepson, the "attached boxes":

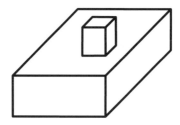

Here we see a small box resting atop a big box. Notice the vertical line on the front right edge of each box. These two lines are colinear in the figure, but they probably don't look colinear to you in 3D: the front face of the small box appears to sit well behind that of the big box. In this case, your interpretation breaks the rule of generic views, because that rule entails the following:

> **Rule 3.** Always interpret lines colinear in an image as colinear in 3D.

The reason is simple. If two lines in space are not colinear, then only by an accident of view can they appear colinear; almost any small change in view will destroy the apparent alignment. You can check this for yourself with two pens. Hold one a few inches behind the other, and move them until, when viewed with just one eye, they appear colinear. Now move your head a bit and you'll see them instantly misalign.

Why do we break this rule of generic views when we construct the attached boxes? You might guess that vision also has rules of construction based on gravity: objects under gravity don't float in midair. For us to see the colinear edges of the two boxes as colinear in space, we'd have to see the little box floating in midair above the big one. To avoid this we're willing to violate the rule of generic views.

This is an interesting idea, and the psychologist Irvin Rock found that vision does at times use rules about gravity. But gravity doesn't seem to be the main rule here. You can check this by inverting the figure or turning it on its side. The small box still looks attached to the big one, breaking Rule 3, even though gravity no longer requires this.

Perhaps instead we use *proximity*, as illustrated by the "Necker cube with bubbles," devised by the psychologist Marc Albert:

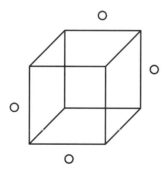

The four bubbles appear to have different depths, two in front and two a bit behind. The depth of each bubble is about the same as the depth of that edge of the cube nearest to it. When the cube reverses in depth, so too do the bubbles. If you cover the cube but not the bubbles, then the bubbles all appear coplanar. Uncover the cube and once more the bubbles assume distinct depths. They inherit their depths from the cube, and the rule of inheritance is proximity: each bubble inherits its depth from the portion of the cube nearest to it in the figure.

Rule 4. Interpret elements nearby in an image as nearby in 3D.

Applying this to the attached boxes, consider the bottom right edge of the smaller box. It is closest, in the image, to the upper right edge of the larger box. As long as you focus on these two edges, the rule of proximity assigns the two edges similar depths, so that the small box sticks to the top surface of the large box. But now focus on the upper back edge of the small box. It is nearest, in the image, to the upper back edge of the large box. Now the rule of proximity assigns these two edges similar depths, and you may see the small box rest inside the large box, such that their two top surfaces have the same depths. By flipping your focus between these two cases you can get the small box to flip from being on top to being inside the large one. Both percepts violate the rule of generic views, but both are predicted by the rule of proximity.

Of course, both also violate the rule of proximity: seeing the small box on top, for instance, entails seeing its top edge at a different depth from the top edge of the large box. So in this figure we not only pit proximity against generic views, we also pit proximity against proximity. What you see depends in large part on the portion of the figure to which you attend. If you attend at once to the top and bottom edges of the small box, thus directly pitting proximity against itself, then you may see the small box hover halfway between being inside and being on top of the large box. We resolve the conflict, in this case, by a judicious compromise. By contrast, we resolve the conflict between proximity and generic views, in this figure, by *vetoing* generic views and giving proximity what it wants. This process of adjudication between conflicting rules of interpretation is called "cue integration" by perceptual psychologists and "sensor fusion" by researchers in computer vision.

So far we've studied figures made of straight lines. But you are, of course, equally adept with curves. Consider, for instance, the "doughnut":

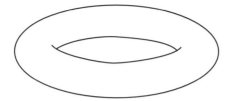

Here you see a 3D shape similar to a doughnut. You can sense how this shape curves in space, not only along the drawn contours, but also in blank regions between them. You can tell how to orient your hand in space to grasp it and take a bite. But there are no straight lines, colinear lines, or lines with coinciding tips in this figure, so Rules 1–3, which helped in previous figures, can't help you construct the doughnut.

But the rule of generic views, which dictates Rules 1–3, also dictates other rules that can help with the doughnut. It dictates, for instance, the following:

Rule 5. Always interpret a curve that is smooth in an image as smooth in 3D.

The reason is again simple. If you interpret such a curve as not smooth in 3D, as having gaps or cusps in 3D, then a slight change of view would, almost surely, destroy its smooth appearance. Suddenly a gap or cusp would appear, and the image curve would no longer be smooth.

Your construction of the doughnut respects this rule. You see curves that are smooth in the figure as smooth in 3D on the doughnut.

This is fine so far as it goes. But notice that the two curves in the middle of the figure meet at two points. Each point of meeting is not smooth; it is a cusp called, for obvious reasons, a "T-junction." Each T-junction is circled in the doughnut below. It just so happens that in this figure each T is upside down, with its cap below its stem.

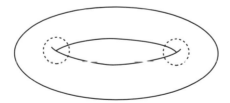

The stem and cap of the T are coplanar in the figure, but notice that they don't appear coplanar on the 3D doughnut. The stem appears to lie behind the cap, and to pass invisibly underneath it, as though occluded by the opaque body of the doughnut. This is often how we interpret T-junctions, not only in the doughnut but in images more generally.

Why don't we interpret a T the other way, with the stem in front and the cap behind? As you might guess, this would violate the rule of generic views: a small change of view would, almost surely, make a gap appear between the stem and cap, or else make the stem cross over the cap. This is much like the problem with the chopsticks interpretation we discussed earlier.

Then why not interpret the stem and cap as having the same depth, so that they meet to form a real T? This satisfies the rule of generic views, since a real T looks like a T from almost any view. The stem and cap can, of course, appear to change in length and in the angle they form, but the tip of the stem will always lie on the cap. So why not take this flat interpretation?

The answer to this follows from another powerful rule, the rule of projection. This rule describes how three dimensions can be smashed into two. Since the 3D world you construct and the 2D image at your eye are related by such smashing, the rule of projection is central to many of your processes of visual construction. In the case of a T-junction, this rule dictates that you interpret it just as you do—with the stem behind and the cap occluding. To show this will take a minute.

The rule of projection, like the rule of generic views, is what we might call a "megarule." It's general and powerful, and dictates a host of specific rules for special cases. Various of these specific rules of projection have been discovered by painters over the centuries, opening greater possibilities for realism in art. Perhaps most famous is the discovery of linear perspective by Filippo Brunelleschi (1377–1446), its transformation to a practical method of painting by Leon Battista Alberti (1404–1472), and its formal statement by Leonardo da Vinci. Also famous is the discovery of natural perspective by the Greeks, reported by Euclid about 300 B.C. in his *Optics*. Natural and linear perspective are intimately related: natural perspective tells why the moon can just eclipse the much larger but more distant sun; linear perspective tells how properly to render natural perspective onto a painter's canvas (or any surface). Before the discovery of linear perspective, painters at times ran into trouble from which the only escape was an artistic "fig leaf." An example is "The Whipping Punishment," a panel from the *Middle Rhein Altarpiece* painted about 1410, now at the Museum Catharijneconvent in Utrecht:

In this panel, the tiles on the left clash in perspective with the tiles on the right; they fail to have a common vanishing point. To avoid an eyesore the artist placed a fig leaf, in this case a column, over the offending region where the tiles would meet. This neatly solved the problem, only to raise another: the soldier on the right whips the column, not Christ. Again a problem of perspective.

Linear perspective and natural perspective are powerful rules to create and interpret images. Both follow from the rule of projection, but they are not alone. The rule of projection also dictates specific rules to interpret the silhouettes of smooth objects. It is these rules that can properly interpret a T-junction, and to which we now turn.

If you were to walk around on a typical smooth surface, such as a sphere, you would notice that the surface changes orientation as you walk. Imagine that you take a pouch of arrows with you, each arrow the same length, and every so often you push the tail of an arrow into the surface, so that the arrowhead sticks straight up from (i.e., perpendicular to) the surface. After you had done this until you were bored, the sphere might look something like this:

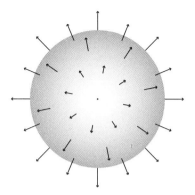

Notice that the arrows are not parallel, but stick out like the spines on a porcupine. Since each arrow sticks straight out of the surface, the direction it points depends on the *local* orientation of the surface. So the direction of each arrow is a convenient way to describe this local orientation. In fact it is so convenient that geometers, and vision researchers, use such arrows all the time. Of course, they don't call them arrows; they use a fancier term: *surface normals* (or just *normals*).

The surface normals on a sphere point, literally, in all directions. If you hold up a sphere and look at its normals, you'll find that one points directly toward your eye, one directly away, and one in every other direction. Let's call the direction that your eye is looking your *line of sight*. You can think of this direction as defined by an arrow with its tail at your eye and its head at the point where you are looking. Then, as you can check with the sphere, the projected length of a normal (its length in the drawing) depends on its angle with your line of sight: normals with smaller angles have shorter projected lengths; the shortest is the normal in the center, which points right along the line of sight and so projects to just a dot. This effect is called *foreshortening*, and was discovered by Greek painters in the fifth century B.C. You can play with foreshortening using a pen. Close one eye and hold the pen at arm's length with the tip pointing at your eye. Its projected length is small. Now slowly rotate the tip away; the projected length grows until the pen is perpendicular to your line of sight. Continue to rotate the pen; now its projected length shrinks. This shows that any line, including a normal line, has its longest projection when it is perpendicular to your line of sight.

To discuss normals and T-junctions further, we need some geometrical intuitions and terms. These are illustrated here:

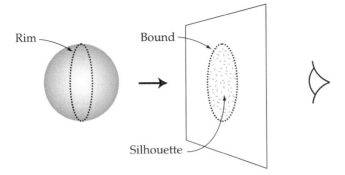

On the right is your eye, on the left a sphere, and in the middle a projection of the sphere onto an image plane. If the sphere is opaque, then your eye cannot see all of it at once; the boundary between what's visible and invisible, indicated by the dashed contour on the sphere, is called the *rim*. If you move your eye then you move the rim, since different portions of the sphere become, for you, visible and invisible. The image depicts the portion of the sphere that is, for you, visible. Since the rim surrounds this visible portion, the projection of the rim, called the *bound*, surrounds the image of the sphere. The entire projected image of the sphere is called its *silhouette*.

The projection of the sphere onto the image is by linear perspective. For simplicity I have just portrayed this projection by a large arrow. However, a much better job was done in 1525 by the artist Albrecht Dürer (1471–1528) in his famous woodcut *Man Drawing a Lute*:

On the right, where the string attaches to the wall, is the assumed position of the viewer's eye; on the left is a lute to be rendered; and in the middle is a canvas onto which the lute is to be rendered (the artist has kindly rotated back the canvas so we may see it). The string indicates a line of sight. It remains attached to the same spot on the wall, but attaches to different spots on the lute, thus rendering the lute onto the canvas in proper linear perspective.

With the help of Dürer's woodcut, we can see that for points of the rim, the line of sight just grazes the surface of the sphere (or lute, or whatever). For at these points the string just touches the sphere and can continue without passing into it; but for other points the string hits the sphere and cannot continue without passing into it.

Since the line of sight just grazes the sphere at points of its rim, the surface of the sphere at each such point, as represented by its normal, must be oriented precisely at a right angle to the line of sight. To help your intuitions here, you can look back at the sphere with arrows protruding from it; note how the normals rotate away from your line of sight as your eye scans from the center of the sphere toward its rim, and how the normals at the rim are all perpendicular to your line of sight. Indeed, we can define the rim as being those visible points on the surface whose normals are perpendicular to your line of sight. This turns out to be equivalent to defining the rim as those points which divide the visible from invisible.

And now we're almost ready to understand why we interpret T-junctions as we do. Let's refer again to the doughnut:

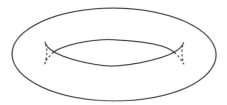

The solid curves are intended to depict the doughnut's rim. This depiction works, in the sense that you do see these curves as being the rim of a doughnut. And it works because your visual system constructs its 3D interpretations with a bias toward interpreting image curves, where possible, as rims of smooth objects. We can state this as another powerful rule of visual construction.

Rule 6. Where possible, interpret a curve in an image as the rim of a surface in 3D.

You might be wondering about the dashed curves on the doughnut. These too indicate points where the line of sight grazes the surface. They just don't happen to be visible from the current view. But at each of these points, as with points on the rim, the surface normal is perpendicular to the line of sight. So it is natural to group them all together, and call them the *full rim*. Then the rim is simply the visible part of the full rim.

What we can now see in this figure is that the T-junction is the point where one part of the full rim, namely the cap of the T, starts to conceal another part of the full rim, namely the stem. The dashed contours show this concealed portion of the full rim.

This is not only true of T-junctions on the doughnut, it's also true, as H. Whitney proved in 1955, for T-junctions formed by projecting any smooth surface: the cap conceals the stem at the T. This theorem underwrites a rule for interpreting T-junctions.

Rule 7. Where possible, interpret a T-junction in an image as a point where the full rim conceals itself: the cap conceals the stem.

Together, Rules 5–7 predict much about the 3D shape you construct when you view a drawing like the doughnut. Much, but not all. Consider, for instance, the richness of shape you see in the 1959 painting *The Rites of Spring* by Pablo Picasso (1881–1973):

These silhouettes convey a remarkable sense of curved shapes in 3D. Why they do so puzzled Marr and other vision researchers. And naturally so, for this painting is, after all, quite simple: it has no texture, no shading, no literal motion, and no color but black.

A key piece of the puzzle was discovered in 1984 by the physicist Jan Koenderink. It explains how you can construct curved shapes, and why it's legitimate to do so, when you view silhouettes like Picasso's. To understand this key, we need some simple concepts about surfaces and how they curve.

Imagine that you're a bug standing on the surface of a drinking glass:

As you look around, you notice that the surface of the glass curves away from you, and that how quickly it does so depends on which direction you look. If you look in the direction labeled 2, you find that the surface curves most quickly; and in direction 1 it doesn't curve at all. Between these two directions it smoothly changes from curving much to curving little.

These two directions, in which the surface curves most and least, are called *principal directions*; the corresponding curvatures of the surface are called *principal curvatures*. The principal curvature in direction 1 is zero, because the surface doesn't curve at all in that direction. The principal curvature in direction 2 is just the curvature of the circle depicted at the top of the glass.

In the case of the glass, it's pretty clear that the principal directions, namely directions 1 and 2, are perpendicular to each other. What is not so clear, but is true nonetheless, is that the principal directions are always perpendicular to each other at every smooth point on any surface, no matter how complicated that surface may be. This remarkable fact was discovered by the mathematician Leonhard Euler (1707–1783).

Actually, surfaces aren't too complicated. They can curve in only three basic ways:

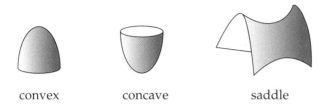

convex   concave   saddle

At a convex point a surface curves like an egg, at a concave point it curves like the inside of an egg, and at a saddle point it curves like a horse's saddle. The principal curvatures differ in each case. If you're a bug standing on a convex point, you'll see that the surface curves downward from you in both principal directions, and in every other direction. If you stand instead in a concave point, you'll see that the surface curves upward from you in both principal directions, and in every other direction. And if you stand on a saddle point you'll see that the surface curves downward in one principal direction (where your legs would hang down the saddle) and that it curves upward in the other principal direction (toward the front and back).

Convex regions of a surface bound the material of objects, concave regions bound pockets of air, and saddle regions bound nothing, but instead provide a transition between convex and concave regions. As a result, saddle regions are easily overlooked, by artist and layman alike. Alberti, for instance, in his 1435 text of academic art theory, *On Painting*, sums up the possible surface shapes as follows:

> We have now to treat of other qualities which rest like a skin over all the surface of the plane. These are divided into three sorts. Some planes are flat, others are hollowed out, and others are swollen outward and are spherical. To these a fourth may be added which is composed of any two of the above. The flat plane is that which a straight ruler will touch in every part if drawn over it. The surface of the water is very similar to this. The spherical plane is similar to the exterior of a sphere. We say the sphere is a round body, continuous in every part; any part on the extremity of this body is equidistant from its centre. The hollowed

plane is within and under the outermost extremities of the spherical plane as in the interior of an eggshell. The compound plane is in one part flat and in another hollowed or spherical like those of the interior of reeds or on the exterior of columns.

Alberti omits the saddle from his list, and this omission is repeated by others well into the twentieth century. Kurt Badt, for instance, in his important 1963 book on plastic art writes:

There are three basic possibilities: plane, convex, and concave curvatures. Of these three only the convex is—as a sign and expression of the visibly surging vital force—fundamentally plastic.

Though artists and others may neglect the saddle, your visual intelligence doesn't: when you view a silhouette, like Picasso's, you construct shapes with convexities *and* saddles. Your rule for constructing saddles is simple and elegant, as is your rule for constructing convexities. Both rules were discovered by Koenderink. Intuitively, they say this: Interpret convexities in a silhouette as convexities in 3D; interpret concavities in a silhouette as saddles in 3D. We'll check this out with a picture in a moment. But first I'll state the rules more precisely, using the terms "bound" and "rim" that I just defined.

Rule 8. Interpret each convex point on a bound as a convex point on a rim.

Rule 9. Interpret each concave point on a bound as a saddle point on a rim.

You are right to use these rules, for they too follow from the rule of projection. As Koenderink proved, convex points on a rim project to convex points on a bound, and saddle points on a rim project to concave points on a bound.

What about concave points on the rim? Why don't Rules 8 and 9 mention them? Not to worry. From almost every view, concave points of the full rim simply aren't visible. Only its convex and saddle points are visible.

Koenderink's rules greatly constrain how you interpret the doughnut:

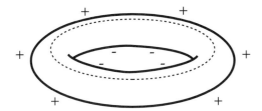

The outer bound of the figure is, at each point, convex. So by Rule 8 you interpret it as a convex rim. I indicate this by labeling it with + signs. The inner bound of the figure is, at each point, concave. So by Rule 9 you interpret it as saddle points on a rim. I indicate this by labeling it with − signs. And now we're almost done with the doughnut. We need only one more rule:

Rule 10. Construct surfaces in 3D that are as smooth as possible.

Just what "smooth as possible" means and why it's justified are technical issues that we'll skip here. Instead we'll use the rules to explain the doughnut, as follows.

By Rules 8 and 9, the doughnut is convex on the outside and saddle-shaped in the center. In between you construct a surface which, by Rule 10, changes smoothly from convex to saddle. The points where it switches, where convex meets saddle, are indicated by the dashed contour. At these switch points the surface is neither convex nor saddle, but is shaped instead like a drinking glass: curved in one principal direction, straight in the other. Why? Because to switch from convex to saddle, one of the two principal curvatures must switch from curving downward to curving upward; so it must, at the switching point, be straight.

In sum, the outer portion of the doughnut is convex, the inner portion is saddle, and the dashed contour, where the convex and saddle portions meet, is shaped like a drinking glass. Nowhere is the surface of the doughnut concave.

And that, in short, is how you see so much 3D shape in the doughnut. It is also how you see so much 3D shape in Picasso's silhouettes, or in any silhouettes. You use simple but sophisticated rules. Only recently have researchers discovered them, but you've used them expertly since infancy to construct the richly curved shapes that you see.

Your expertise goes much further. The silhouettes and line drawings of this chapter are, for you, mere trifles. Your powers of construction are not yet fully engaged. And yet these figures, by their very simplicity, most clearly reveal your constructive genius at work. A small part of this genius is in the ten rules we discussed. A larger part is in orchestrating these rules to produce masterpieces of visual composition.

It's fun to use these rules to make visual surprises. Here's one by the psychologist Roger Shepard:

Both tabletops are precisely the same shape, just rotated. You can check this with a ruler. But they certainly don't look the same. One looks long and narrow, the other short and squat. What you see here, as always, is what your visual intelligence constructs.

Compare your visual intelligence to that of the $6 million Imager for Mars Pathfinder (IMP), the visual system of the Mars Pathfinder that landed in Ares Vallis, on the surface of the planet Mars, on July 4, 1997. IMP has two camera "eyes" that allow scientists to create 3D images of the terrain around the Pathfinder, and thereby to guide the explorations of the rover. IMP also has twenty-four filters by which it takes color images critical to the study of Mars's geology, atmosphere, and magnetic properties. The pictures IMP sent back are spectacular, and so popular that more than two dozen mirror web sites were set up to handle all the internet visitors wanting to take a peek.

The pictures indicate that the Mars Pathfinder, after parachuting to the surface and then tumbling around on inflated air bags, came to rest in an old flood plain that, at some point in Mars's history, was deluged with water. Rocks are strewn here and there, embedded in silt much as one might see in a dried-up streamed here on earth. Some of the more notable rocks near Pathfinder were given memorable names, such as Wedge, Yogi, and Casper.

IMP was a great success, a monument to the sophistication of modern technology, and a tribute to the central role in that technology of imaging and vision. Through the eyes of IMP, we can see a bit of Mars and infer something of its history. We can tell how much dust is in its atmosphere and what minerals are in its soil and rocks, and we can even examine its two moons, Deimos and Phobos.

Although we see a lot through the eyes of IMP, you might be surprised at how little IMP sees through its own eyes. We see Yogi, Casper, the rover, the deflated airbags, and silt that has been disturbed by the retraction of the airbags. IMP sees none of this. To give you an idea of what IMP does see, I downloaded one of its gray-level images of Yogi, kindly provided free of charge on the internet by NASA and the Jet Propulsion Laboratory at the California Institute of Technology:

In this image we see a rock in the lower right, Yogi at the top casting a shadow, and silt in between. Here is what IMP sees:

```
              •
              •
              •
    147 138 145 156 142 141
    133 130 138 145 145 157
• • • 140 130 141 158 170 184 • • •
    157 150 154 164 169 180
    174 174 178 184 180 186
    172 178 187 196 193 195
              •
              •
              •
```

To IMP a picture is just an array of numbers indicating, roughly, the brightness of the picture at each point. The numbers displayed here are a small portion of the numbers in the Yogi picture. IMP gets these numbers by focusing light from its camera eyes onto two charge-coupled device (CCD) arrays that measure the quantity of light at each point.

When you look at those numbers, how much insight do you gain about Mars, Yogi, silt, and shadows? For me, none. They're in the wrong format to engage my visual intelligence, so they just sit there as an uninteresting array of numbers. However, the same numbers reformatted in lights and darks, as in the photograph, do engage my visual intelligence and thereby trigger me to construct rocks and silt and shadows.

These numbers, in any format, trigger nothing comparable in IMP, since IMP has no visual intelligence. Six million dollars of taxpayer money endowed IMP with fantastic optics and filters and CCD arrays, but no visual intelligence whatever. The visual intelligence of IMP is less than that in the retina at the back of your eye.

The line drawings scattered throughout this chapter, though simple, engage your creative genius to construct shapes in three dimensions. The same line drawings presented to IMP would be translated into an array of numbers, much like that shown above, and there would be the end of it. For IMP there is no insight, no 3D conception, and no comprehension. These require visual intelligence, and, even with its impressive optics and filters, IMP without visual intelligence is, frankly, blind.

So you can sit back and relax, secure in the knowledge that the visual intelligence you display when viewing the figures in this chapter is something that IMP, with all its high technology, can't duplicate.

And you have more visual intelligence to explore.

THREE

THE INVISIBLE SURFACE
THAT GLOWS

Carbon monoxide poisoning is a good thing to avoid. Now and then someone doesn't and the result, if not death, is often brain damage. Such was the fate of Mr. S, whose name is hidden to protect his privacy. He ended up in the hands of two neurologists, Frank Benson and John Greenberg, who diagnosed him to have "visual form agnosia." If it sounds bad, it is. Mr. S had normal vision in most respects. He had fine acuity, could discriminate colors properly, and could easily see even small motions. But he couldn't see objects. He couldn't take the colors and motions and edges that he saw and put them together to experience the forms of objects. The result was devastating, as Benson and Greenberg report:

> He was unable to select his doctor or family members from a group until they spoke and was unable to identify family members from photographs. At one time he identified his own image in a mirror as his doctor's face. He did identify his own photograph, but only by the colour of the military uniform. After closely inspecting a scantily attired magazine "cover girl," he surmised that she was a woman because "there is no hair on her arm." That this surmise was based on flesh colour identification was evident when he failed to identify any body parts. For example, when asked to locate her eyes he pointed to her breasts.

He still knew what objects were, and still identified objects by sound; he just couldn't see them. The visual processes which, for him before the poison and for you even now, construct an experience of objects out of colors, lines, and motions were selectively destroyed.

This way of putting it might still strike you as odd. *Construct* objects? Isn't that going a bit far? Do I really wish to claim that Mr. S, before the poison, and you right now construct books, chairs, trees, cars, the sun, moon, and people?

I admit it sounds outlandish, but I want to claim it nonetheless— with one proviso: As I mentioned in Chapter 1, you construct the objects that you see in the *phenomenal* sense. That is, you construct your visual experience of objects. You also construct, though I shall spend less time defending this claim, your perceptual experience of objects by touch, taste, smell, and sound. To experience is to construct, in each modality and without exception.

But experience is also the main reason this claim seems outlandish. When you look at objects you don't experience yourself as constructing them. It feels more like this: The objects are there, whether you look or not, and when you look you just see the objects that were there all along. That's certainly the way it feels to me.

But it feels that way because we're fast and expert at construction. Were you slow and inexpert, like Mr. S, you might more readily buy the story on construction. The inference from "it doesn't feel like construction" to "therefore it's not construction," while plausible to most of us, lacks the force of logic. Compare: Would you want to argue from "it doesn't feel as if I, and the earth on which I stand, rotate at hundreds of miles per hour" to "therefore I and the earth don't so rotate"? This was plausible to many prior to Copernicus, but wrong. Sometimes things are the way they feel, sometimes not.

But this, of course, is no positive defense of construction. For such defense I will try two things in this chapter. I will try to change how it feels for you to see objects; to have you feel that at least in some cases, you construct the objects you see. I will also show concrete evidence, apparent to your own eyes, that you in fact construct visual objects. This evidence is *subjective contours* and *subjective surfaces*.

Consider first these subjective triangles devised in 1955 by G. Kanizsa:

In each figure you see a white triangle which lies atop disks and lines. Each triangle has a clear border and is brighter than the background.

But these triangles, which are evident to you, are invisible to a photometer or image scanner. If you run a sensitive photometer over each figure, it will detect neither the borders of the triangle nor the increased brightness of its interior. Similarly, if you scan each figure into a computer and examine the scanned image, pixel by pixel, with your favorite image software, you'll find no change in pixel values as you go from outside the triangle to inside.

And if you carefully cover, with paper or fingers, just the disks and lines in each figure, the white triangle disappears. Uncover them, and the triangle reappears, because you reconstruct it. For it's clear that the triangle, with its borders and brightness, is entirely your construction. I drew no triangle in this figure. The triangle depends entirely on your visual intelligence for its existence.

Your talents of construction aren't limited to triangles. You're also great with disks, as the psychologist Walter Ehrenstein showed in 1941 with these figures:

Here you see two disks with clear circular borders. The disk on the left looks whiter than white, and the disk on the right looks blacker than black. But again, photometers and scanners would fail to find a disk: they, unlike you, aren't designed to construct disks or triangles from figures like these. Some devices have been built that, like you, find such disks and triangles; but each of these devices embodies a complex process of construction, sometimes patterned after the neural processes in the visual brain, and each disk, triangle, or other shape that the device finds it in fact constructs.

You can construct borders without also constructing changes in brightness. A disk devised by Theodore Parks in 1980, a wiggly border by Kanizsa in 1976, and a square by Slava Prazdny in 1983 all illustrate this:

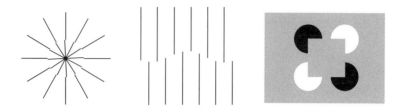

Conversely, you can construct changes in brightness without also constructing borders, as a display by John M. Kennedy illustrates:

But typically you construct both together, as in Kanizsa's triangles and Ehrenstein's disks, and you use the borders to contain the brightness.

Our prowess at such constructions first attracted scientific study in 1900, with the work of psychologist Frederich Schumann. But artists knew about it and used it to advantage centuries, even millennia, before. Japanese ukiyo-e artists of the seventeenth and eighteenth centuries, working in woodcuts, used subjective contours and surfaces to depict hair, feathers, and flowers. An engaging example is *Crow and Heron in the Snow*, produced in the 1770s by Isoda Koryusai. A detail of the heron shows how Koryusai used subjective contours to create its shape and enhance its whiteness:

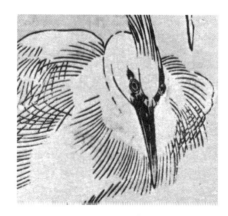

Notice how the tips of black strokes are carefully aligned; this induces you to construct subjective contours and enhanced whiteness. In like manner, but with white lines over black surface, Koryusai enhanced the blackness of a crow. The crow and heron were commonly used to contrast black and white. Koryusai accented this contrast with his clever use of subjective surfaces.

Many medieval and Renaissance woodcuts created "glowing" suns, moons, and highlights with subjective surfaces. Dürer, for instance, used them in his 1505 woodcut *The Satyr Family* to form highlights on the legs and arms of the satyrs. In 1515 he reworked this woodcut into a pattern for wallpaper, and numerous wallpapers since have sported subjective surfaces and contours.

But examples of subjective figures go back much earlier. A Buddhist cave temple at Dunhuang, Gansu province, in China has a drawing of a lion from the ninth century A.D. with subjective contours on its legs and face. A cylinder seal from Mesopotamia from about the first half of the second millenium B.C. shows two lions, each with a subjective contour down the center of its mane. The prize for oldest might go to a bracelet made of mammoth ivory discovered in Mezin, Ukraine, and dating from 22,000 B.C. Its zigzag motif shows striking subjective contours along the corners:

Runner-up might go to Paleolithic cave drawings of bison, rendered between 10,000 and 30,000 B.C. In some of these drawings the bodies of bison are defined by subjective contours, as you can see in this detail from a photograph by Jean Vertut:

Again, as in Koryusai's heron, it is the careful alignment of tips of strokes that induces you to construct the subjective contours.

These examples are, of course, by no means exhaustive. They are instead a small selection from among those rare pieces that have survived the ravages of time. As such they show all the more that subjective figures have captured the interest of artists and others for a long time.

That interest is, if anything, more intense now than ever: literally thousands of papers have, in this century, explored subjective figures, looking for rules and principles that might explain their construction. As a result we can now, with confidence, point to many rules that aren't used; we can point to far fewer that are. Looking at both is a great way to better appreciate your sophistication at constructing subjective figures.

A rule that once seemed plausible is symmetry. Consider these figures:

The two on the left give strong subjective squares, but the one on the right does not. What's the difference? Gestalt psychologists, in particular Kanizsa, noted that creating a subjective square in the two left figures lets you see each black Pac-Man as a complete disk, partially occluded by the subjective square. It lets you transform unsymmetric Pac-Men into symmetric, but partly occluded, disks. And you like symmetry a lot. So you go for it. You construct the subjective square, stick it in front, and complete the Pac-Men to disks underneath it.

But the figure on the right is different. If you construct a subjective square, stick it in front, and complete the crosses underneath, you destroy the beautiful symmetry of the crosses and transform them into unsymmetric shapes. Why bother doing that? So you keep the symmetry you have already with the crosses, and forgo constructing a square.

In a nutshell, then, the story is this: You create subjective figures only if by doing so you can transform unsymmetric shapes into symmetric ones that are partly occluded.

It's a nice story, but not the whole story, as Kanizsa himself later pointed out. Consider these counterexamples:

The figure on the left, by Marc Albert, has curved crosses that are symmetric, indeed just as symmetric as the straight crosses. But most observers nonetheless see a subjective figure, this time in the shape of a pillow and disks. So here's a case where you destroy an existing symmetry to create a subjective figure.

The figure on the right starts off with unsymmetric shapes, and creating a subjective surface doesn't let you transform them into symmetric ones. But this doesn't stop you. You still create a subjective surface, and stick it in front of asymmetric blobs.

Another rule that once seemed plausible was based on simultaneous brightness contrast. Consider this figure:

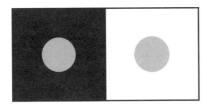

Which of the two gray disks is darker? Most observers say the disk on the right. In fact, however, both are printed with the same ink, and a photometer would declare them the same. But you aren't a photometer. You construct, as we'll discuss later, all the levels of gray that you see, and you do so by comparing different regions of the image. You compare the disk on the right to its surrounding white region, and the disk on the left to its surrounding black region, and the different grays you see result from these different comparisons. This effect is called *simultaneous brightness contrast* (or SBC for short).

Now the subjective figures we've seen have, in most cases, an obvious feature: they're white regions surrounded by black blobs or lines. So perhaps it's SBC that makes subjective figures. The black inducers surround white regions, and make them look brighter by contrast. If so, then more black should, by contrast, lead to brighter whites.

Again a nice story, but not the whole story. Counterexamples are easy. Consider, for instance, these figures by Marc Albert:

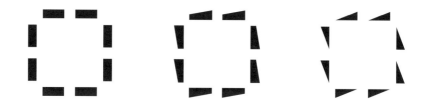

The left figure has the most black, the right the least. So SBC predicts that the left figure should have the brightest subjective square and the right the least. But most observers see just the opposite.

Or try these figures by Kanizsa and D. Varin:

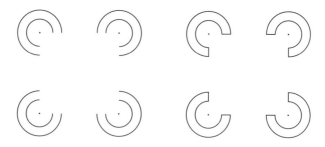

The right figure is just the left figure with little black line segments added, so the right figure has more black than the left. SBC predicts then that the right figure should have the brightest subjective square. This prediction fails.

Many other principles have been proposed to explain subjective figures. Perhaps the most explicit and interesting is by the psychologists Thomas Shipley and Philip Kellman:

> . . . all good subjective figure displays appear to have inducing elements with abrupt changes in the slope of their outer boundaries.

Some examples should help make their point:

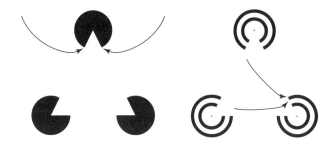

On the left, notice the points on the Pac-Man indicated by arrows. At these points its border isn't smooth. Instead it has, as Shipley and Kellman put it, an abrupt change in slope. Similarly on the right, the points indicated by arrows aren't smooth, but have an abrupt change in slope. Let's call such points *cusps*. Cusps come in two basic types: convex and concave. A convex cusp points out of an object, a concave cusp points into it, as you can see in this Pac-Man:

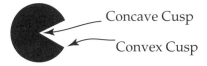

Concave Cusp

Convex Cusp

If you look back over the subjective figures in this chapter you will see that Shipley and Kellman are on to something. In each case there are convex cusps on the lines or blobs that induce you to see the subjective figure. If you round off these cusps, look what happens:

The subjective disk that is so clear on the left, where there are convex cusps, almost disappears on the right, where these cusps have been smoothed. You can do this in figure after figure with similar results.

Shipley and Kellman's rule is almost right. It needs just one small change. Careful experiments, by Shipley, Kellman, and Albert, show that we can, in some cases, still see subjective figures even without convex cusps. Often these figures are stronger if there are cusps. But they can be pretty strong without cusps, as you see in the "smooth square":

Smooth Square   Jumbled Pac-Men

And in some displays with convex cusps, as in the jumbled Pac-Men, subjects see no subjective figures. So convex cusps are neither necessary nor sufficient to see subjective figures. But they're still relevant.

The key is this: If there are convex cusps, then any subjective figures that you see will appear to occlude; otherwise they won't. If you look back at Kanizsa's triangles or Ehrenstein's disks you'll see that they appear to occlude their inducers. But the smooth square doesn't occlude its inducers; instead the inducers look like blobs pushed up against its side. They crowd around it but aren't occluded. This casual observation is confirmed in more careful experiments by Albert.

So we can state one rule that guides your construction of subjective figures:

Rule 11. Construct subjective figures that occlude only if there are convex cusps.

Why should this be a rule? So far I have only given examples, not justification. The justification comes from two familiar sources: the principle of generic views and the principle of projection. This is illustrated here:

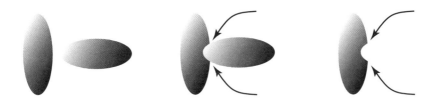

On the left are two objects, seen from a view in which they appear separate. The middle shows a different view, in which one occludes the other. Arrows show where one rim covers the other, creating T-junctions. Such T-junctions are generic: if, from some view, one rim occludes another, then that view and each nearby view almost surely has a T-junction at the point of occlusion. This justified Rule 7, which says to interpret a T-junction as one rim occluding another.

Here we need one more step, as shown by the figure on the right. If the object in front disappears, perhaps because of camouflage or lighting, then T-junctions turn into convex cusps (indicated by arrows).

So the upshot is this: If the rim of one object occludes the rim of another then there is, almost surely, either a T-junction or a convex cusp. Only by an accident of view would one rim occlude another without leaving one of these telltale signs. If the occluder is visible you get a T-junction; if it's invisible you get a convex cusp.

So Rule 11 is justified entirely on logical and mathematical grounds. If the rim of an invisible surface occludes another rim, then there is, almost always, a convex cusp. So only if you see a convex cusp should you construct a subjective surface that occludes.

This rule nicely captures part of your prowess at subjective figures. But only part. For it only states when you won't construct, not when you will. You won't construct a subjective figure that occludes if there aren't convex cusps. Fine. But will you construct one if there are? Not necessarily. Consider for instance these figures:

Both have convex cusps, and these cusps are equally well aligned. Yet you construct a strong subjective square on the right, but not on the left. Why? Symmetry can't be the answer here, since completing inducers on the left would lead to symmetric squares.

Nor can gap size be the answer. In both figures the white gaps, through which a subjective border must pass, are the same size. You don't have to construct a longer border on the left than on the right.

And the ratio of gap length to total length, sometimes called the *support ratio*, can't be the answer. Not only are gaps the same length, so are the black borders. The mouths of Pac-Men on the right are no longer than the inner angles of L's on the left. So subjective borders have the same support ratio in both figures. Experiments by Shipley and Kellman suggest that the support ratio affects the clarity of some subjective borders. But that's not the difference here.

Consider also these figures devised by Albert:

Again both have convex cusps, and these cusps are equally aligned. Both have identical support ratios. Yet on the right you construct a strong subjective ellipse that occludes, but not on the left. Why?

The best answer so far comes from a principle of "nonaccidental relations" described by psychologists Andrew Witkin and Marty Tenenbaum. Suppose two curves are parallel in an image. Then you will, by the rule of generic views, see them as parallel curves in 3D space. But now consider this. How likely is it that two random curves in space will happen to be parallel? Not very. In fact the probability is precisely zero. And that's a pretty good hint that these aren't just two *unrelated* curves, generated independently and tossed into space, but that they are *related* curves, generated by the same cause or process. Their nonaccidental relation in space suggests a nonaccidental relation in genesis. And you take that suggestion seriously. You group the curves together and assert that they derive from the same source. You often call that source an *object*, and the parallel curves its edges, as the psychologist S. Morinaga showed with figures like these:

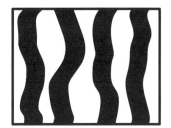 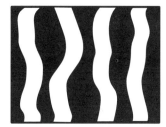

On the left you see black objects over a white ground, and on the right white objects over a black ground. In both cases you group parallel curves together to form objects.

Parallel curves are, of course, just one type of nonaccidental relation. There are many others, including colinear line segments, symmetric curves, and skew symmetric curves. What they have in common is this: A given structure replicates or continues with little or no change. A pair of parallel curves is the simplest case; one curve replicates and translates with no change in shape to yield the other. For a pair of symmetric curves, one curve replicates, translates, and undergoes a symmetry transform to yield the other. And so on for other nonaccidental relations. When you see curves, or visual structures more generally, in any of these nonaccidental relations, you group them and assign them to a common origin. This is a general rule that guides your visual constructions.

Rule 12. If two visual structures have a nonaccidental relation, group them and assign them to a common origin.

So, for example, if we modify Morinaga's display so that pairs of curves aren't parallel, but nonetheless bear a nonaccidental relation, you still group them:

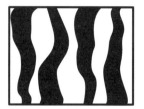 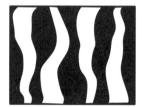

Here you still see on the left black figures over a white ground, and on the right white figures over a black ground. Yet the curves that bound the individual figures are clearly not parallel. The distance between the curves at one end is more than twice that at the other. But the relation between the curves is nonaccidental: one is related to the other by replication without change in shape, followed by translation and rotation. You note this relation and group curves accordingly.

Albert recognized that nonaccidental relations can answer our question about subjective figures. Consider again this example:

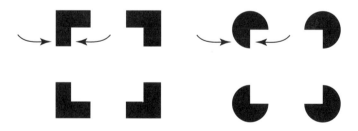

On the left, two arrows point to two edges of a black inducer. These edges are parallel. By Rule 12 you group them together as edges of a single object, namely the L. This means that both edges, the outer and inner, belong to the L. Since the inner edge belongs to the L it can't also, except by an accident of view, belong to another object as well. In particular it can't, except by an accident of view, be the edge of an occluding rectangle. And that's why you don't construct a subjective rectangle on the left.

On the right, two arrows also point to two edges of a black inducer. These edges are far from parallel. Nor do they enjoy any other nonaccidental relation. So you don't, a priori, group them into a single object. Since the inner edge doesn't belong, a priori, to the Pac-Man you are free to determine if it might better belong to a different object. Ultimately you decide yes, and make it belong to an occluding rectangle. This has the advantage, again, of grouping parallel edges.

The same account applies to Albert's ellipses:

On the left two arrows point to two edges of an inducer. These edges are parallel, so you group them. The inner edge then is not free to belong to another object. But on the right the two edges indicated by arrows are not parallel, so you don't group them initially. This leaves the inner edge free to belong to another object. Ultimately you decide it does, and make it belong to an occluding ellipse.

These examples show that the principle of nonaccidental relations guides your construction of objects generally, and of subjective figures in particular. This principle is distinct from the principle of generic views. You use the principle of generic views to find stable interpretations, to construct 3D worlds for which your current image is a stable view. You use the principle of nonaccidental relations to decide which parts of your interpretation should be grouped together into objects. Both principles use probability, but they do so to different ends.

Remember the magic squares from Chapter 1? I promised to explain them later, and now it's time to deliver. Here they are again:

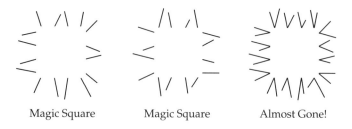

Magic Square   Magic Square   Almost Gone!

In the left and middle you construct occluding squares, but not on the right. Yet the figure on the right is just the first two superposed. So why don't you see an even stronger occluding square? (This is a tad tricky, but you now have the tools to answer it. Since I'm about to tell all, you might want to pause and try your hand first.)

The answer follows from generic views, which underwrites this rule:

Rule 13. If three or more curves intersect at a common point in an image, interpret them as intersecting at a common point in space.

If they didn't intersect at a common point in space, then only by an accident of view would they appear to intersect at a common point in the image. A slight change of view would displace the curves away from this common intersection.

This applies to the squares as follows. Constructing an occluding square on the left and middle does not violate the rule of generic views. A slight change of view, under this interpretation, would cause some image lines to grow a bit and some to shrink a bit, but it would not cause any qualitative changes, such as straight lines turning wiggly or points of intersection disappearing. So you're free to construct an occluding square in these figures.

But if you construct an occluding square on the right, then at each point where its edge meets the tips of the V's, you have three curves intersecting at a common point in the image. By Rule 13 you must interpret these three curves as intersecting at a common point in space. And that precludes putting the square in front where it could occlude. The best you could do, without violating the rule of generic views, is to construct a square and put it at the same depth as the V's. Sometimes I find myself doing just that when I view this figure. More often I find myself not bothering to construct a square at all.

Another long-standing puzzle can be seen in these figures:

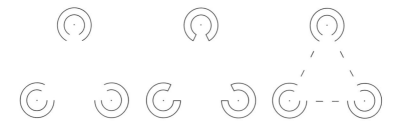

On the left and right you construct an occluding triangle, but not in the middle. Why? The only difference between left and middle is little line segments that are added to the middle. Something about these segments blocks your construction. The same segments on the right, differently placed, don't block you, suggesting that placement of segments is critical.

And indeed it is. For the segments in the middle are placed so that their tips coincide with tips of the circular arcs. Recall Rule 2: If the tips of two lines coincide in an image, then interpret them as coinciding in 3D. Accordingly, you interpret the segments and arcs to have the same depth.

Now if you construct an occluding triangle you must choose whether or not to attach the segments to its border. If you attach them, then the triangle, segments, and arcs have the same depth, so the triangle cannot occlude the arcs. If you don't attach them, then you violate the rule of generic views: change view slightly and the triangle must occlude some segments. Given these options, you don't bother to construct a triangle at all.

I've spent quite some time in this chapter demonstrating that it's your visual intelligence that constructs subjective borders and surfaces. Kanizsa's triangle is really your triangle. Kanizsa's drawing simply gives you the context you need to construct it. If you don't look, then there is no triangle. The same holds for all subjective borders and surfaces in this chapter. You create them all.

You're probably willing to grant me this point. Sure, subjective figures are a clear case where you construct what you see. But you know I'm after a bigger point: I want to claim that you construct everything you see. Not just subjective figures. Everything.

And you might not be willing to grant me that. Look, you say, I agree that Kanizsa's triangle is my construction. But Kanizsa's *drawing* is surely his. There is, I admit, no triangle on the paper when I don't look, but there are surely black lines and blobs on that paper whether or not I look. Those lines and blobs aren't my construction. They're just there. And if they weren't, there would be no context for me to construct the triangle. So the drawings that support your smaller claim—that subjective figures are my construct—are the very drawings which refute your larger claim—that everything is my construct.

If you're thinking along these lines, I'll admit your argument has some appeal. But it's wrong. Even the black lines and blobs on the paper are entirely your construction. They aren't there unless you put them there. Indeed, the very forms of the letters and words you are reading right now are all your construction. They're on the page because you put them there (with all due respect to the publisher and printer).

The easiest way to make this point is to look for a moment at the structure of your eye, and in particular at its light-sensitive tissue, the *retina*. The punchline will be this: The image at your eye is *discrete*. You can think of it as like a Pointillist painting by Georges Seurat, composed entirely of tiny and separate daubs of color. Your image, like Seurat's painting, has neither curves nor surfaces—only dots. But you see more than dots; you see curves and surfaces. Logic dictates, then, that you are their source. You construct each curve and surface you see. That entails, in particular, that you construct each line and blob of Kanizsa's drawing. (You also construct the dots!)

This conclusion is strong and, for most, unintuitive, so let's look at the physiological evidence. This will detour us for a few pages, but the detour is interesting in its own right, and is necessary to secure this unintuitive conclusion. We begin first with the gross structure of the eye:

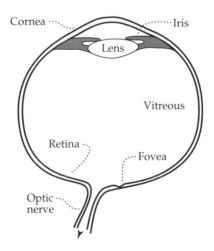

This structure has been known since before Galen (A.D. ca. 129–ca. 199). Its function was not well understood until Kepler published in 1604 his theory of the retinal image. But several interesting theories were proposed prior to Kepler.

The Greek atomists held that objects send, in all directions, material replicas of themselves, in the form of thin films composed of atoms. These films, called *eidola* or *simulacra,* enter the eye and cause vision by their impact. Sight, on this theory, is a kind of touch. Epicurus (ca. 341–270 B.C.) put it this way:

> For particles are continually streaming off from the surface of bodies. . . . And those given off for a long time retain the position and arrangement which their atoms had when they formed part of the solid bodies. . . . We must also consider that it is by the entrance of something coming from external objects that we see their shapes and think of them. For external things would not stamp on us their own nature of colour and form . . . so well as by the entrance into our eyes or minds, to whichever their size is suitable, of films coming from the things themselves.

This is an "intromission" theory, so called because it requires that something enter the eye. But it has problems. How can films, emanating from all objects at all times, pass through each other without disruption? And how can films of big objects, say mountains, pass the tiny pupil of the eye?

An alternative that avoids these problems, an "extramission" theory, was proposed by Plato: Light or fire issues from the eye and coalesces with sunlight to form a medium which contacts both eye and object, thus making vision possible. As he put it in the *Timaeus*:

> For the pure fire within us is akin to this, and they caused it to flow through the eyes. . . . Accordingly, whenever there is daylight round about, the visual current issues forth, like to like, and coalesces with it [i.e., daylight] and is formed into a single homogeneous body in a direct line with the eyes, in whatever quarter the stream issuing from within strikes upon any object it encounters outside. So the whole [homogeneous body] . . . passes on the motions of anything it comes in contact with or that comes into contact with it, throughout the whole body, to the soul, and thus causes the sensation we call seeing.

Some version of extramission theory was held by many thinkers, including Euclid, Ptolemy, and, prior to 1492, Leonardo da Vinci. An argument in its favor was that nocturnal animals can see at night; to do so their eyes must emit light, and indeed one can often see their eyes glow in the dark.

But the extramission theory too has problems, as Leonardo himself later realized:

> It is impossible that the eye should project from itself, by visual rays, the visual power, since . . . this emanation would have to go forth to the object and this it could not do without time. And this being so, it could not travel so high as the sun in a month's time when the eye wanted to see it.

The eye and its function triggered much debate and many books over two millennia. Finally, in 1604, Kepler found the key: a proper theory of refraction by spherical lenses. Applying his new theory to the eye, Kepler showed that the eye has a clear function: to focus an image on the retina.

Kepler's insight remains to this day. You can think of the eye as like a camera. Just as the lens of a camera focuses an image on film, so the cornea and lens of an eye focus an image on its retina.

But your retina, unlike film, is not a passive recipient of images. Instead, it actively transforms them, using hundreds of millions of cells, called neurons, all working in parallel. The computing power of your retina dwarfs the most advanced supercomputers.

Your retina first transforms the image by capturing it with a discrete array of light-sensitive cells called photoreceptors. Near the fovea, the part of your retina with the best resolution, these cells are packed tightly together, as you can see in this photomicrograph by Christine Curcio and colleagues:

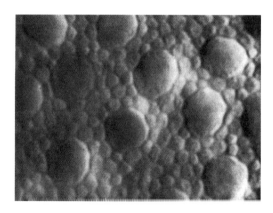

The smaller cells, called rods, work best in low light. At night in the dark you see with your rods. The larger cells, called cones, mediate color vision and work best in high light. During the day, when the light is bright, you see with your cones.

Each rod and cone changes its electrical activity when it catches light. The more it catches, the more it changes. Light itself comes in discrete packets called photons. Each rod and cone can capture zero, one, two, three, or more photons of light at a time, but it can't capture, say, one and a half photons or two and a third photons. If just one of your cones captures just ten photons, you will see light. Remarkable efficiency.

Your retina has about 120 million rods and 7 million cones. The cones cluster together primarily in the fovea and rods primarily outside. When you glance directly at an object, you move your eye so that the image of that object falls on the fovea and its cones. You might have noticed that sometimes at night if you look directly at a faint star you can't see it, but if you look slightly away then you can. This is due to the placement of your rods and cones. When you look directly at the star you cast its image on the cones in your fovea. But cones don't work well in low light, so you don't see the star. If you look slightly away, then you cast the image of the star on your rods. They work best in low light, so you do see the star.

With this background we can return to the punchline: You construct every curve or surface you see. This follows from the discrete packing of rods and cones at your retina. Here, for example, is the best they can do at capturing a straight line:

 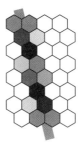

On the left is a patch of retina, with cones idealized as hexagons. Superimposed on these cones is an idealized line. On the right, cone responses to this line are indicated by color, with darker meaning more response. As you can see, the result is not a line. Instead it is a collection of distinct cone responses. However, from these responses it is possible, if you wish, to construct a line.

And that is what you do each time you see a line. You construct it from receptor responses. This is not so easy as you might think. Just ask researchers in computer vision. They have worked on "edge detection" or "line finding," an apparently simple problem, for decades. They have made progress, but their current solutions require much computation— on the order of tens of millions of multiplications and additions just to construct lines in one small image. Even so, their performance is no match to yours.

Our current understanding of visual anatomy and physiology suggests that you too put much effort into making lines. It may feel effortless, but in fact you employ millions of neurons. Your retina is just one step of the process. When it finishes processing an image, it sends its results to your brain through the optic nerve, an electric cable composed of one million wires called axons. Many of these wires go first to a structure in your midbrain called the *lateral geniculate nucleus* or, in brief, LGN:

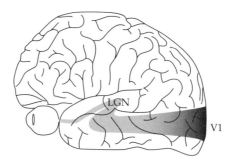

After more processing in the LGN, the results go out a new set of axons and arrive at *primary visual cortex*, also known as V1. Here, the physiology suggests, you first construct lines. I must emphasize the word "suggests." For, as physiologists like Alan Cowey point out, the physiology of a neuron does not unerringly indicate its function in perception. There is, nonetheless, consensus among physiologists that lines are first made in V1.

The evidence comes primarily from electrodes, poked near single neurons of monkey cortex, which physiologists use to measure *receptive fields*. The receptive field of a neuron is that part of the visual field to which the neuron responds by changing its rate of electric discharge. For example, many neurons in the LGN have receptive fields like this:

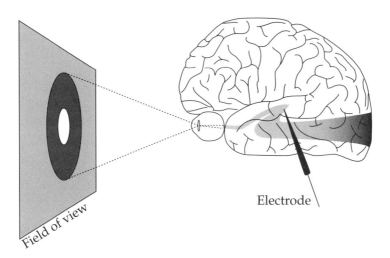

Electrode

Field of view

On the right an electrode records electric signals, called *spikes* or *action potentials*, from a neuron in the LGN. Each spike is a fluctuation in electric potential that travels down the long axon of the neuron. Each spike has the same size as all others, so the degree of electric activity of the neuron is measured not by the size of each spike, but rather by the number of spikes per second that travel down the axon.

On the left is a screen with a light stimulus of the type that best stimulates many neurons of the LGN and retina: a central bright disk, surrounded by a dark ring, or "annulus." If this stimulus is of the right size (usually much smaller than depicted here) and in the right position on the screen, then the neuron spikes quickly. If the stimulus is the wrong size, or moved slightly out of the best position, the neuron spikes slowly. In short, this cell is electrically excited by light in the central region, electrically inhibited by light in the annular surround, and indifferent to light elsewhere in the field of view. Other neurons in the LGN and retina prefer a stimulus just the reverse of this: dark in the central disk and bright in the surrounding annulus. Those that prefer a bright disk are called *on-center* and those that prefer a dark disk are called *off-center*. There are roughly equal numbers of both types. For each point of your field of view, there are neurons of both types "looking" for their optimal stimulus at that point. That takes a lot of neurons, literally a million in each retina and each LGN.

Now we move the electrode to V1:

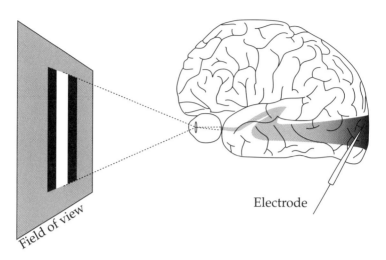

Field of view

Electrode

We again find many cells with on-center and off-center receptive fields. But, as David Hubel and Torsten Wiesel first discovered, we find something new as well: cells excited by lines. A typical stimulus is shown on the left of the figure. To optimally excite a given cell, the line must have the right position and orientation. Move the line or rotate it, and the cell spikes little or not at all. Shorten the line, and the cell spikes less; lengthen it, and the cell maintains its high spiking rate. In sum, the cell is excited by light in the bright bar region, inhibited by light in the flanking dark regions, and indifferent to light elsewhere. Such cells are called *simple cells*.

For each point of your field of view, there are simple cells in V1 "looking" for their optimal line. One cell wants a vertical line, another a horizontal, and another an oblique. All orientations of lines are represented at each point of your field of view. Again that takes a lot of neurons, literally hundreds of millions in V1.

Simple cells are not alone. *Complex cells*, like simple cells, look for oriented lines, but have larger receptive fields and no clear division between excitatory and inhibitory subregions. *Hypercomplex cells* also look for oriented lines, but care about their length. If a line is too long, the hypercomplex cell reduces its rate of spiking. And some simple cells themselves exhibit *direction selectivity*: they are excited best if a line moves in a certain direction.

What happens if you show a subjective border (or, more precisely, a display in which we see a subjective border) to cells in V1? This has been checked in macaque monkeys, and about half of the cells are excited, if the border has the right position and orientation. In area V2, which is next to V1, about a third of the cells are excited by subjective borders. Similar results obtain with cats.

These are just some highlights, but they are enough, I hope, to convince you that you take great efforts to construct lines.

My argument, in sum, is simple. Your retinal image is discrete, not continuous. So if you see continuous lines and surfaces (and you do), then you must construct them from discrete information. And if you construct them, then we should see evidence of this in the brain's activity. In species after species, we find clear evidence of great neural resources employed in constructing lines. So it's not just the subjective borders of Kanizsa's figures that you construct, it's every line and blob of his drawing as well. If you see it, you construct it.

This argument implies an interesting conclusion about neurons themselves. We can *see* neurons (with the help of stains and microscopes). In fact, here's a picture of some:

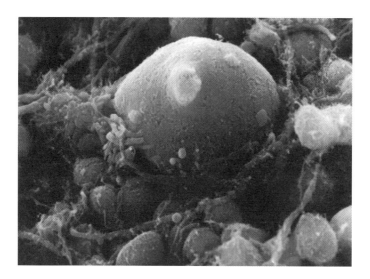

So if we construct all we see, then, since we see neurons, we construct neurons. Neurons, no less than the subjective triangles of Kanizsa, are the clever construction of your visual intelligence.

You are in fact more versatile at constructing subjective figures than I've let on. I've only shown you drawings for which you construct flat figures. But you can construct them in 3D as well. Consider, for instance, this figure:

This is a stereo display that you can "fuse" as follows. Cross your eyes slightly, so that the four disks on the left slide on top of the four disks in the middle. It may help to put a finger in front and look at it, while paying attention to the disks behind. When you get them fused, you will see two subjective cylinders curving in 3D. One appears to lie in front of black disks, and the other appears to be seen through black holes in white paper.

How does a stereo display work? The key is that the image at your left eye is slightly different from the image at your right eye. Check this out for yourself. Close your left eye and hold up your right index finger at arm's length. Using your right eye only, line up your right index finger with some object nearby, say a doorknob or a tree trunk. When your index finger looks like it's perfectly lined up with the object, then, without moving your finger, close your right eye and open your left. Notice that your index finger is no longer lined up with the object, but instead is a bit off to the right of it. This demonstrates that your left eye sees a slightly different image from your right.

Your visual intelligence uses the small disparities between the left- and right-eye images, and some trigonometry, to construct shapes in 3D. If you've ever seen a 3D movie, say at an IMAX theater, this is what's happening. The theater arranges to show slightly different images to your left eye and right eye, thereby triggering your visual intelligence to construct 3D shapes. One method makers of 3D movies use is liquid-crystal shutter glasses. You put on a helmet that alternately blocks off all light to one eye and then to the other, but does this so rapidly that you don't even know that half the time each eye is looking at total darkness. While the right eye is unblocked, they project onto the screen the image that they want the right eye to see. Then when the left eye is unblocked, they project onto the screen the image that they want the left eye to see. This happens more than sixty times a second, with the result that your left eye and right eye see sequences of images that are slightly different, and your visual intelligence goes to work to construct a 3D world from these small differences.

Using stereo, we can construct a version of Kanizsa's triangle that curves in 3D:

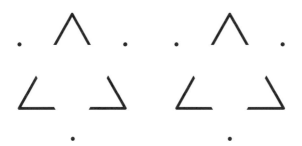

If you fuse this you will see the corners of the subjective triangle bending over and then behind the black lines.

Your versatility with subjective figures is not limited to drawings on paper. Several drawings in this chapter have been built out of wood and other solid materials. The report in each case is the same. One still sees a subjective figure, and it appears to float in space.

So subjective figures are not just part of picture perception. They are part of ordinary everyday seeing. And that should come as no surprise. You construct *every* figure you see. So, in this sense, every figure you see is subjective.

I said at the start of this chapter that, for most of us, it doesn't feel as if we construct objects, but that I hoped to change that feel. Subjective figures go a long way in that direction for me. But still two doubts might linger.

First, you might say, if this table or this tree is my construction, then why does everyone else see the same thing? If I construct them each time I look, then why do you see them too?

Let's call this the *argument from consensus*. I admit at once that it has considerable appeal. But it's fallacious all the same. We can see this if we spell it out:

Premise: We all see this table.
Conclusion: Therefore none of us constructs the table.

This is an *enthymeme*: an argument with a hidden premise. The premise is this: If we all see X, then none of us constructs X. We can call this the *premise of consensus*. So the full argument, including the premise of consensus, is this:

Premise: We all see this table.
Premise: If we all see X then none of us constructs X.
Conclusion: Therefore none of us constructs the table.

But the premise of consensus is just false. We've seen counterexamples to it throughout this chapter. Here are two more:

We all see subjective triangles with lines poking through them, and yet each one of us constructs the triangles. That is, we all see X and yet we *all* construct X. So the premise of consensus is false and so is the argument from consensus.

But then why do we all see the same thing? Is the consensus magic? No. We have consensus because we all have the same rules of construction. We see the same things because we construct the same things. And we construct the same things because we use the same rules of construction.

But a second doubt lingers. Look, you say, I admit that the argument from consensus fails. But I still don't buy that I construct this table. Here, watch. I'm trying to push my fist through the table and it won't go. No matter how hard I try, no matter how much I want it to, my fist won't go through the table. So I don't need the argument from consensus, I just need a table and my fist to prove that I don't construct the table. I refute you thus (pounding on table).

Let's call this the *argument from compliance*. Again, I admit that this argument has considerable appeal. But again it's fallacious. Let's spell it out:

Premise: I can't put my fist through this table.
Conclusion: Therefore I don't construct the table.

Again this is an enthymeme, and a hidden premise is this: If I construct X then X complies with my wishes. We can call this the *premise of compliance*. So the full argument, including the premise of compliance, is this:

Premise: I want to put my fist through this table.
Premise: If I construct X then X complies with my wishes.
Premise: I can't put my fist through this table.
Conclusion: Therefore I don't construct the table.

But the premise of compliance is just false. We have seen counterexamples to it throughout this chapter. Here is one more, the subjective Necker cube devised by Heywood Petry:

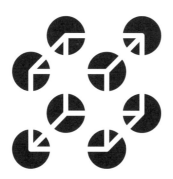

You construct the subjective edges of the cube and its 3D shape. But do the cube and its edges comply with your every wish? Not at all. Try to see the edges bend rather than be straight. I can't. Or notice that sometimes the black disks are behind the cube, but other times the black disks are holes through which you see the cube. Now try to switch the cube at will between these. I can't. Sometimes it switches when I want, but usually it takes its own sweet time, or doesn't switch at all. Here's a case where I construct X, but X does not comply with my wishes. Each subjective figure in this chapter is also a case. So the premise of compliance is false and so is the argument from compliance.

But then why don't your constructs comply with your wishes? Why can't you do with them whatever you wish? The answer, in part, is that you construct them according to rules. You can't do to them what you wish if what you wish violates your rules of construction. Your rules allow you to construct what you see, but they also restrict what you can construct and what you can do with your constructions. Similarly, the rules of chess allow you to play an endless variety of chess games, but they strongly restrict the moves you can make. If you wish to move your queen like a knight, you can't do what you wish, for that wouldn't be playing chess. If you want to play, you've got to play by the rules.

That's part of the answer but not, I think, the whole. The whole I shall have to defer to later. The fact remains, however, that the table before you is your construct. If you point to it, others will agree that they too see a table. There is consensus. And if you pound on it your fist won't go through, even if you wish it to. There is noncompliance. But it's your construct all the same.

We began this chapter with the case of Mr. S, who could not see objects even though he could see colors and motions. Since objects are the clever construction of your visual intelligence, it makes sense that certain impairments of your visual intelligence should render you unable to construct, and therefore unable to see, objects. Mr. S and many others with visual form agnosia provide sad confirmation of this surprising prediction.

It also makes sense that certain impairments of your visual intelligence might render you unable to *stop* constructing visual objects. If so, then you would see objects that others, with normal visual intelligence, do not see. Such is the case with those suffering from Charles Bonnet syndrome.

An example is Mrs. B, who, in her early sixties, had a right-hemisphere stroke that left her partially blind in her left visual field and partially paralyzed on her left side. After her stroke she could still read, see colors, and recognize faces. Her intelligence and memory were above average. But off and on for ten days she saw, while awake and in clear consciousness, vivid and realistic hallucinations of traffic, children, animals, relatives, and dripping water. These hallucinations usually lasted for several minutes.

Several times she saw two children in a doorway, laughing and dodging back and forth. They looked so lifelike that, as she put it, "I just wanted to chat to them . . . they kept disappearing and when the nurse came in I asked who the children were and I could tell by the look on her face that there weren't such things." On several occasions Mrs. B tried to talk with the children, but they just smiled and played and never talked back.

Mrs. B also saw two of her dogs that had died before her stroke. They came into her room, wagging their tails. One decided to go outside into the rain, and when it returned all wet Mrs. B got a towel to rub it dry. As she rubbed it, she felt the dog and its wet fur. In this case she created visual and tactile objects in coordination, a feat she did not always do. When, for instance, she hallucinated dripping water or puddles on the floor, she never reported feeling the wetness. Nor did she ever, in any of her hallucinations, report hearing sounds from the hallucinated objects.

Perhaps her most complex hallucination was of a street busy with traffic just outside her ground-floor window. Cars, people, and red double-decker buses appeared to pass by. The traffic was so realistic that Mrs. B commented on it to others on her ward: ". . . this morning we were having breakfast and I said to somebody where do the big red buses go from here and they said there aren't any red buses, and I said there are because there is one coming by now . . . 197 was the number." An unusual feature of her traffic hallucinations was that she saw the traffic below her, as though she were looking at it from a second-story window, even though the hospital where she was treated had, in fact, only one floor. The persistence and vividness of her traffic hallucinations, however, led her to believe that the hospital must have a second floor.

Mrs. B is a striking example of the creative powers of visual intelligence. Normally these powers are exercised subject to appropriate restraints. But a stroke or other insult to the visual system can eliminate some of these restraints, with the result that the creative powers run relatively unchecked, creating hallucinations of people, animals, and even traffic. The dogs you see are no less constructed than the hallucinated dogs of Mrs. B; the difference is that you construct them with more restraint than did Mrs. B.

FOUR

SPONTANEOUS
MORPHING

magine your plight if you could see just one object or one part of an object at a time, and even that one often faded from view. Such is the plight of patients suffering from dorsal simultanagnosia. They often have full visual fields; they can see as far up, down, left, or right as the rest of us, so their problem is not a restriction of view. Instead it seems to be a restriction of attention. They can attend to at most one, or on rare occasions two, objects or parts of objects, but even that one object or part will often suddenly slip from attention and fade away. This disorder usually occurs after a stroke or other damage to the parietal and occipital cortex of both hemispheres of the brain. In a sense, patients with dorsal simultanagnosia are better off than Mr. S, whose visual form agnosia prevented him from seeing any objects at all. He could see motions and edges with normal acuity, but he couldn't put them together into objects or parts. Patients with dorsal simultanagnosia, by contrast, can put them together, but for just one object or part at a time. This restriction is still so severe that they act as if they are blind.

Since these patients often see just one part of an object at a time, their attempts to recognize objects can go astray. One example is Ms. W, who was studied by the neuropsychologist H. Richard Tyler in the late 1960s. When Ms. W saw just one part of an object, she tried to guess what the whole object might be from that part:

> When shown a pitcher pouring water into a glass, she first noted the handle and said "suitcase." When asked to look

again she spotted the glass, and remembering the handle she kept looking until she perceived the pitcher (now with the handle on it).

Tyler showed Ms. W an American flag. She described her experience as follows:

> I see a lot of lines. Now I see some stars. When I see things like this, I see a lot of parts. It's like you have one part here and one part there, and you put them together to see what they make.

Tyler showed her this scene for six seconds:

Ms. W said that she saw "a mountain." He showed it to her for another two seconds; she said that she saw "a man." She didn't report the camel, and apparently didn't know that she was viewing the same picture as before. Tyler then let her look at the picture for thirty seconds, and she finally said, "It's a man looking at the mountains." The problem, she said, was that she never saw the "whole" but only parts that would "fade out."

Ms. W is not alone in seeing parts. You too carve your visual world into parts, as a critical step in your construction and recognition of visual objects. A big difference between you and her, though, is that you can quickly and effortlessly assemble many parts into many objects, whereas she is limited to one part or one object at a time.

Just what is a part? The question isn't easy to answer because you construct parts in many different ways—using color, motion, shape, texture, and prior experience. Here I'll focus on shape. Geometry might not have been your best subject in school, but your visual intelligence is an expert, cleverly using geometry to create parts of shapes, quickly and subconsciously.

We glimpsed your geometrical talents back in Chapter 1, when we looked at the ripple:

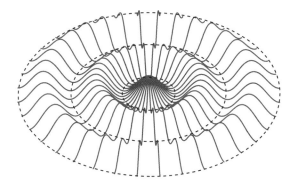

The ripple is an impressive feat of your construction. The curves you see on the page, and the ripply surface you see in 3D—you construct them all. You also organize the ripple into three concentric parts, which look like water waves; the dashed contours in the troughs mark roughly where one part stops and the next begins. You aren't a passive perceiver of parts, but their active creator. The three parts you see wouldn't be parts at all unless you constructed them. In fact, if you turn the figure upside down, you'll find that you choose to discard these three parts, and to construct different ones. You can check that they're indeed different: notice that the dashed contours no longer lie in troughs between parts, but on crests of the new wavelike parts that you have constructed. Now turn the figure right side up, and you chose once again to construct the original parts.

You're a master part maker. I'm going to tell you how you make them, and why. You'll find out how you make the parts of the ripple, and why you make different parts when you turn the figure upside down. In the process you'll learn the answer to a visual puzzle discovered in 1885 by the physicist Ernst Mach.

Tyler's picture of the desert (on previous page) is a good place to start. Notice that you easily recognize the scene and its objects even though the picture has no color, shading, or motion, and little texture. Although these cues can aid recognition, they are, as this picture shows, not necessary. In fact, experiments by the psychologists Irv Biederman and Ginny Ju show that you're just as fast at recognizing line drawings like Tyler's as you are at recognizing full-color photographs.

Tyler's picture also shows that context (i.e., place and time) isn't needed for recognition. Normally you can use where you are and what time it is to aid in recognition. You would be surprised indeed to see a polar bear in your bedroom or a freezer at the north pole. So context is normally a help, but not in Tyler's picture. Before you first looked at his picture you had no idea what it would be; it could have depicted anything. Where and when you happened to view the picture didn't constrain what it depicts.

But this posed no problem for you. With a glance you recognized the scene and its objects. What, then, did you use to do this? Just shape, and that mostly indicated by curves depicting the rims (outlines) of objects. You can, as we have discussed before, construct 3D shapes from 2D curves. Tyler's picture shows that you can easily take the next step— use the 2D curves and 3D shapes you construct to recognize objects. A key to your success is that you efficiently divide these shapes into parts, and describe both the parts and their spatial relationships. You can do this before you know what the objects are. Once you have the parts and their spatial relations you use this information to search the vast list of objects you know, until you find a match.

Why are parts so helpful to recognition? There are two main reasons. First, most objects are opaque. You can see the front of an object but not its back; you might not even see all of its front, if another object is in the way. Since you rarely see all of an object at once, you must recognize it from its visible parts. As you move or the object moves, new parts become visible and old parts disappear. By carving an object into parts, and using the visible parts to search your memory for a match, you can recognize it from many different views.

Second, many objects are not rigid. Your body, for instance, has many movable parts—arms, legs, fingers, toes. If they move, your body changes configuration. How shall you recognize a body despite such changes? Again parts come to the rescue. If you pick your parts prudently (and you do), then the parts won't change as the configuration does. This gives you a stable description of objects and an efficient index into your memory of shapes.

Notice that these arguments for parts hold both for 2D and 3D descriptions of shape. Psychologists and some researchers in computer vision now debate whether human vision uses 2D or 3D representations of shape for recognition. I suspect that you use both, their relative importance varying with the object you view. But that's a separate issue. The point here is that parts are useful in either case.

That is, if you choose the right parts. There are countless ways to carve shapes into parts: any subset of a shape is a possible part. But most of these are useless for recognition.

To be useful, your parts should satisfy at least four conditions. First, they shouldn't change if you move your view a bit. You need stable parts for stable recognition. Second, they shouldn't change if the object changes its configuration a bit. Again, stable description is the key. Third, you should be able to construct the parts from the retinal images at your eyes. If you can't do it from images you can't do it at all. Fourth, you should be able to construct the parts on a wide variety of objects; the larger the better. If your scheme for constructing parts is not general-purpose, then it might fail you at critical times. If you missed that tiger because you couldn't see its parts, it could ruin your whole day.

Suppose, for instance, that you choose parts to be cylinders, cones, spheres, cubes, and certain deformations of these basic shapes. Every time you see an object you try to decompose it into these basic shapes. It's a nice idea, and has been explored extensively by many researchers in human and computer vision. The problem is that no one has found a set of basic shapes that will do the job. Legs and arms can be approximated by deforming cones and cylinders, but how about shoes and faces and sunglasses? Objects come in all sorts of odd shapes, and no set of basic shapes has been found that can handle them all.

But you can recognize all sorts of odd shapes. So what do you do instead? You rely on another rule, similar in spirit to the rule of generic views. It is the rule of *transversal intersection*:

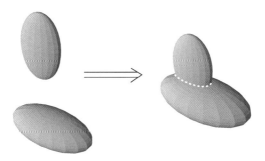

Suppose that you have two arbitrary objects as on the left of the figure. Their shapes needn't be ellipsoids; they could be anything. And suppose that you interpenetrate them at random to form a new composite object, as on the right. Then the original two objects, which are separate parts of the visual scene, are prime candidates for being parts of the new composite object. If we could just tell where they are and where they meet by looking at the shape of the composite object, we would have our parts.

Fortunately, it's a theorem of differential topology that if two arbitrary shapes interpenetrate at random then you can almost always tell where they meet.

Here's how. Differential topologists have found that in the generic case, two objects meet in a "transversal intersection": at points where the two objects intersect, indicated in the figure by a dashed contour, their surfaces form a concave crease. Concave creases are sharp edges in the surface that point *into* the object. It helps to contrast them with convex creases, like the edges of a cube, which point *out* of the object. So if you want to find parts, look for concave creases. They tell you where one part meets another. This motivates a first rule for dividing 3D shapes into parts:

Rule 14. *Rule of concave creases:* Divide shapes into parts along concave creases.

Now this rule can't help us find parts on the ripple, since the ripple is entirely smooth. We'll have to generalize the rule in a moment to handle smooth surfaces. But in its present form the rule explains some well-known visual effects. Consider for instance, these figures:

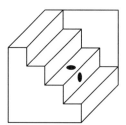 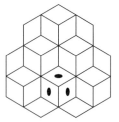

On the left is the famous Schröder staircase, published by H. Schröder in 1858. When you first view this figure you probably see the two dots as lying on a single step, one on its rise and the other on its tread. Notice that this step is bounded above and below by a concave crease. In fact, as predicted by the rule of concave creases, all the steps you see are bounded by concave creases.

If you keep looking at the staircase for a while you'll notice something else. The staircase reverses "figure" and "ground," which is why it is so famous. What was once empty space (the "ground") becomes steps (the "figure"), and what was once steps becomes empty space. If you don't see this, just turn the page upside down and it will reverse. Of course, you construct the staircase and you make it reverse. Your rules of construction create two staircases rather than just one, and you alternate between them.

But the rule of concave creases now makes a less obvious prediction. When you reverse the staircase, you reverse concave and convex as well. Each convex crease becomes concave, and vice versa. So, according to the rule, you should see new parts bounded by the new concave creases. You can check that this is so. When the staircase reverses, the two dots no longer lie on a single step, they lie on two distinct steps. And all the new steps are bounded by the new concave creases.

The rule is not, of course, limited to staircases. On the right of the figure is another example with stacked cubes. When you first view the figure you probably see the three dots as lying on a single cube. Notice that the cube is bounded on all four sides by concave creases. Again, if you look for a while, figure and ground will reverse and you'll see a new set of cubes, each bounded by the new set of concave creases. The three dots which before were on one cube will now lie on three distinct cubes.

Another prediction of the rule can be seen with "elbows":

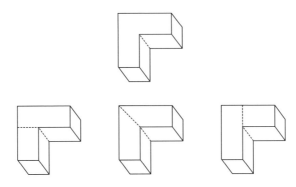

Consider first the elbow on top. All of its creases are convex except for the one depicted by a dashed line. But this concave crease doesn't encircle the elbow. So the rule of concave creases doesn't define the parts of an elbow; it does, however, constrain these parts to have a boundary that includes the concave crease. There are at least three natural ways that one might define the parts, which are depicted in the second row, and all three do include the concave crease. We'll see later that in cases like this you prefer to define parts so that boundaries are as short as possible. With a symmetric elbow, however, this preference can't help you choose between the left and right partitions depicted on the bottom row.

All these examples show that the rule of concave creases is key to your construction of parts in polygonal objects. It's not the only rule you use, but it is central.

However, many objects are smooth, like the ripple, and have no concave creases. Yet you have no trouble constructing their parts. Can we extend the rule of concave creases to handle smooth shapes as well?

This is easy enough. But first we need a few more ideas about smooth surfaces and the way they curve.

We earlier discussed surface normals and principal curvatures. Recall that normals to a surface are like arrows that stick straight out of the surface:

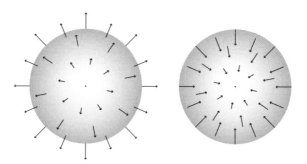

On the left is a sphere with its field of normals depicted pointing outward. But the field of normals can also point inward, as shown on the right. In fact most surfaces have, like the sphere, two distinct fields of normals, one pointing outward and one pointing inward. The only exceptions are some strange surfaces like the Möbius strip, which you can create by taking a long and narrow strip of paper, giving it a half twist, and then taping together its two ends. The result is a surface with only one side, not two. But we will ignore such unusual surfaces for now.

Most surfaces also have two possible choices of figure and ground.

That is, most surfaces have two sides, and either side can be taken as the object (the "figure") or as the background (the "ground"). Let's adopt the convention that the field of normals always points to the ground. So for the sphere on the left with outward normals, figure is inside the sphere and ground is outside, like a baseball. For the sphere on the right with inward normals, figure is outside the sphere and ground is inside, as though the sphere were a bubble under water (and water is taken to be figure). Reversing the choice of figure and ground on a surface entails, by this convention, a concomitant reversal in the field of surface normals.

Recall that a surface can curve differently in different directions. If you were a bug standing on the surface of a drinking glass you would find that the glass curved most quickly in one direction and not at all in another. These two directions, in which the surface curves most and least, are called the principal directions; the corresponding curvatures are called principal curvatures.

Suppose now that you glance around from where you stand on the glass until you find the direction of least curvature, and then take a step in that direction. If you do this repeatedly, leaving a trail of ink behind as you go, you trace out one of the lines shown in the figure on the left:

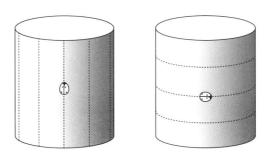

These are called lines of least curvature. If instead you always take a step in the direction of greatest curvature, then you trace out a line of greatest curvature. A few are shown on the right.

A principal curvature can be positive, negative, or zero. On the left, the principal curvature in the direction of the lines is zero; the surface doesn't curve at all along each line. On the right, the principal curvature in the direction of the lines is not zero; the surface does curve along these lines. But is this principal curvature positive or is it negative? That depends on the choice of surface normals and therefore, by our convention, on the choice of figure and ground, as illustrated here:

If the normals point outward, so that figure is inside the glass, then this principal curvature is positive. If the normals point inward, so that ground is inside the glass, then this principal curvature is negative. The key point here is that the choice of figure and ground determines the sign of the principal curvatures. Reverse figure and ground and you reverse the signs of the principal curvatures. We'll see the significance of this in a moment.

That's all the geometric background we need. Now let's see what happens if we smooth a concave crease. This will tell us how to generalize the rule:

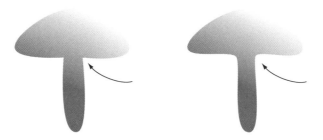

On the left we see a mushroom whose stem meets its top in a concave crease, indicated by the arrow. On the right this crease has been smoothed. As you can see, the crease turns into a point of high curvature. Indeed this point has, locally, the highest curvature. This is the key insight.

If we want to find parts of the mushroom, not of the background, then we choose the mushroom to be figure. This entails, by our convention, that surface normals are outward-pointing. And this entails, by a simple calculation, that the curvature at the smoothed crease is negative. Putting this all together, we find that smoothing a concave crease turns it into a negative minimum of a principal curvature. We have our new rule:

> **Rule 15.** *Minima rule:* Divide shapes into parts at negative minima, along lines of curvature, of the principal curvatures.

If we apply the minima rule to a tipped vase we get part boundaries as depicted by the dashed curves:

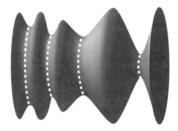

These boundaries nicely capture the parts that we in fact see.
The minima rule predicts the parts we see on the ripple:

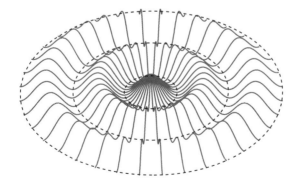

It partitions the ripple along the dashed contours. It also explains why the parts change when you turn the drawing upside down. Turning it upside down makes you flip your assignment of figure and ground on the ripple (apparently you prefer to see objects below rather than overhead). When figure and ground reverse, then, in accordance with our convention, so does the field of surface normals. And this, as we discussed a moment ago, flips the signs of the principal curvatures. So negative minima of the principal curvatures become positive maxima, and vice versa. Since you use negative minima for part boundaries, you see new parts. This is just like the story for concave creases: flipping figure and ground flips concave and convex, so you see new part boundaries at the new concave creases. Here, flipping figure and ground flips positive and negative curvatures, so you see new part boundaries at the new negative minima of curvature.

So far we've considered parts on 3D surfaces. But you see parts quite well on silhouettes, as Tyler's figure demonstrates. By studying how 3D shapes project to 2D silhouettes, which we won't pursue here, it's easy to extend the minima rule to silhouettes:

> **Rule 16.** *Minima rule for silhouettes:* Divide silhouettes into
> parts at concave cusps and negative minima of curvature.

The only new concept here is the curvature on a silhouette, and all you need to know is that this curvature is negative in concavities and positive on convexities. So the rule says to make a part boundary at each concave cusp, and at the point of highest curvature in each smooth concavity.

We can use this rule to explain an interesting effect noted by the psychologist Fred Attneave:

On the left is a disk with a curve scribbled down its middle. On the right, the two halves of the disk are pulled apart. Notice how different the halves look even though they have the same bounding contour.

The minima rule explains this difference in appearance as a difference in parts:

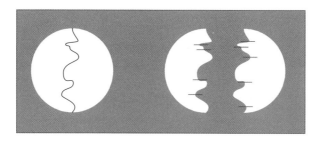

The parts boundaries defined by the rule are marked on each half-moon by dashes: each dash lies on the point of highest curvature within a concavity. Notice that the dashes differ in placement on the two half-moons. They differ because figure and ground, and therefore concave and convex, are reversed between the two. As a result, you break one half-moon into different parts than you break the other. Parts are central to your representation of shape and, therefore, to your judgments of appearance and similarity. So it's the difference in parts that makes the two half-moons, despite their identical contours, look so different to you.

The same explanation applies when the part boundaries are all cusps:

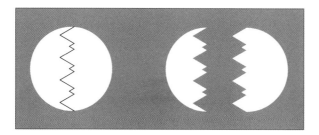

You see the right half-moon as tall and short mountains in alternating series, but the left half-moon as identical tall mountains with notches. The difference in appearance is again due to a difference in parts, as predicted by the minima rule.

My favorite test of the minima rule is the face-goblet illusion. The earliest example I've seen is this detail of the *Weeping Willow*, a picture puzzle from 1795:

Another example appears in 1819 on the frontispiece of *A Conchological Dictionary of the British Islands*, by William Turton. Not until 1915, with the work of Edgar Rubin, did it attract the serious attention of perceptual psychologists.

The minima rule works as follows:

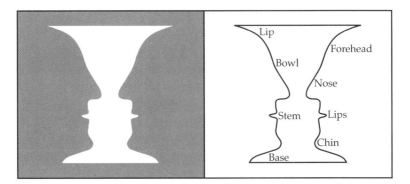

On the left is the standard illusion. For one choice of figure and ground you see a goblet. For the opposite choice you see two faces. On the right, dashes mark part boundaries defined by the minima rule.

Consider first the part boundaries you get if you see the faces. These are marked on the right side. As you can see, negative minima (points of highest curvature in concave regions of a curve) divide the face into a forehead, nose, upper lip, lower lip, and chin. Now consider the boundaries you get if you see the goblet. These are marked on the left side. As you can see, negative minima divide the goblet into a lip, a bowl, a stem with three parts, and a base. The change in figure and ground between the two interpretations leads to a change in part boundaries, and therefore to a change in parts.

What's striking about this example is that parts picked out by the minima rule are ones that you name with single words. To name regions of a shape other than these parts, you often require more complex descriptions. Consider, for instance, the bowl of the goblet. How would you describe this same region on the face? Something like "the lower half of the forehead and the upper half of the nose." The description is no longer a simple word, like "bowl." But then, according to the minima rule, this region is not a part *of the face*; it's just a region.

It should be no surprise that, in most cases, you use a single word to name a part picked out by the minima rule. If these parts are, as experiments now suggest, basic units of your visual description of shape, then you have good reason to make them basic units of your verbal description as well. The way you carve the world visually should affect how you carve it verbally. After all, for quick and clear communication you want units of discourse that match units of meaning used by you and your hearer. The way we carve up the world verbally is not arbitrary; it depends in part on how we carve it up visually. And the way we carve up the world visually is not arbitrary; it depends in part on fundamental principles of mathematics, such as transversality.

This match between words and parts has yet to receive systematic investigation. I predict interesting finds.

We have seen that the minima rule predicts some judgments of shape similarity. Its effect is stronger than you might think. Here's a little test. The next figure (don't look at it yet!) has a single half-moon on the left and two half-moons, one above the other, on the right. I want you to glance quickly at the half-moon on the left, and then at the two on the right. Without analyzing or scrutinizing, just decide which of the two on the right looks most similar to the one on the left. Okay, go ahead and look:

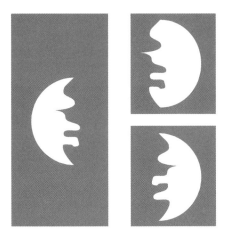

I hope you chose the bottom one. In a controlled experiment with similar stimuli, I found that subjects chose it, or the one corresponding to
it, 94 percent of the time.

Now let's look more carefully. The half-moon on top has exactly
the same bounding curve as the one on the left. They fit like pieces of a
jigsaw puzzle. So these two curves are identical. The half-moon on the
bottom has a bounding curve which I changed from that on the left in
two ways. First, I mirror-reversed it. And second, I cut two of the lower
parts at their negative minima, and swapped them. You can check this
for yourself.

The top curve is identical to the left one, and the bottom is not.
You might guess, then, that the top should look most similar to the left.
But it doesn't. And parts, once more, are the reason why. Since you see
the top curve and left curve with opposite choices of figure and ground,
you carve them differently into parts. So they look different to you,
although geometrically they are the same. The bottom curve and left
curve are geometrically different, but you carve them into the same set
of parts. Two of the parts have different positions, it is true, and each
part is mirror-reversed. But having the same parts is the overriding factor for you. So the bottom curve looks most similar.

In short, similarity is your construction. You construct every line,
curve, and 3D shape that you see. You then describe these constructions
using, among other things, a language of parts. And you judge two of
your constructions to be similar if you have given them similar descriptions. Were you to use a different language of description, say one that
used different parts or dispensed with parts altogether, you would make

different judgments of similarity. Similarity, like beauty, is in the eye of the beholder.

Another test of the minima rule is drawings in which, as in the face-goblet, we see two interpretations of a single contour but in which, unlike in the face-goblet, we see no reversal of figure and ground. Two famous examples are the rabbit-duck and hawk-goose:

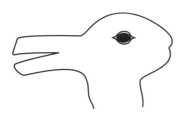 

The drawing on the left you can see either as a rabbit or a duck; the drawing on the right either as a hawk or a goose. Notice that when you switch interpretations, say from rabbit to duck, you do not switch figure and ground. Therefore when you switch interpretations you don't move the negative minima of curvature. The minima rule predicts, then, that you'll see the same part boundaries in both interpretations. This prediction is easily confirmed. What is an ear of the rabbit, for instance, is an upper bill of the duck.

The physicist Ernst Mach (1838–1916) made important contributions to optics, mechanics, wave dynamics, and vision. When we speak today of a jet flying at Mach 2, we use a measure of speed that he developed. In 1885, Mach noted that observers are more sensitive to symmetry than to repetition within a visual pattern. You can check this for yourself in this figure:

The object on the right is symmetric: it's left and right bounding contours are mirror images of each other. You can see this quickly and without effort. The object on the left is bounded on both sides by the same contour: the bounding contour on its right side is just a repetition of the bounding contour on its left side. You can see this, but it takes a little checking to be sure.

This figure supports Mach's observation, and so have careful experiments. Symmetry, in figures like this, is easier to detect than repetition. But it might seem puzzling. Repetition, after all, is just translation, whereas symmetry is translation *and* reflection. So why should symmetry be easier to detect?

If we detect repetition and symmetry by comparing curves point to point, then repetition should be easier to find because corresponding points are always exactly the same distance apart. But if instead we compare the curves part to part, then the minima rule predicts that symmetry should be easier. For as you can see in the figure, the symmetric curves have matching parts, whereas the repeated curves do not.

So on the assumption that we match parts, not just points, the minima rule explains Mach's observation. This was first noted and confirmed in experiments by the psychologists Gordon Baylis and Jon Driver. They also noticed another prediction of the minima rule: If we alter figure and ground so that repeated contours, but not symmetric contours, have matching parts, then repetition should be easier to detect than symmetry. Baylis and Driver confirmed this prediction in an experiment with figures like these:

The two objects on the right have a repeated contour. You can see this quickly and without effort. The two objects on the left have symmetric contours. You can see this, but it takes a little checking to be sure.

This is just the reverse of Mach's effect. Now repetition is easier to detect than symmetry. And the minima rule explains why. The repeated contours have matching parts, but the symmetric contours do not.

Another interesting result falls out of the experiments by Baylis and Driver. They find not only that you create parts according to the minima rule, but that you do so "preattentively": you create parts quickly and in parallel all over the visual field, and you can't stop yourself. Evidently parts are important to you. You devote substantial resources to creating them.

One reason may be that they are critical to your success at object recognition. And this suggests yet another test of the minima rule. Suppose that we take a picture of an object and delete some of it in such a way that you can't find the correct part boundaries. This should disrupt your ability to recognize the object far more than if you delete the same amount but preserve the part boundaries. An experiment by psychologists Irv Biederman and Tom Blickle tested this prediction with stimuli like these:

In the middle are the original drawings. On the right a lot of contour is deleted, but in such a way that you can still create the correct boundaries and parts. On the left the same amount of contour is deleted, but in such a way that you can't create the correct boundaries and parts. The minima rule therefore predicts that you should more easily recognize the objects on the right than on the left, a prediction you can check for your-

self. Subjects in Biederman and Blickle's experiment confirmed this prediction.

If you use parts defined by the minima rule to recognize objects,
then you should remember these parts more easily than randomly chosen "parts." After all, if you explicitly create minima parts but not other
"parts," then you can explicitly store minima parts, but not other
"parts," in your memory. An experiment by psychologists Mike Braunstein and Asad Saidpour tested this prediction. Using computer-
animated displays, they showed each subject a sequence of unfamiliar
3D objects. After showing each object they presented the subject with
four smaller pieces, and asked the subject to choose which one was really a part of the object just seen. Of the four choices, one was a part
defined by the minima rule, one a part defined by positive maxima of
curvature, and two weren't parts of the object at all. Subjects were twice
as likely to remember minima parts as maxima parts, once again sup-
porting the minima rule.

All negative minima of curvature are not created equal. All are
part boundaries, but some are stronger boundaries than others:

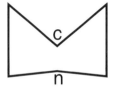 

The bow tie on the left has two concave cusps, labeled *c* and *n*. Both are
part boundaries, but *c* is more salient than *n*. What is the difference? The
angle at *c* is sharper than that at *n*. Similarly, the bow tie on the right
has two negative minima of curvature. Both are part boundaries, but the
one on top is more salient. What is the difference? The magnitude of
curvature at the top boundary is greater than that at the bottom.

What seems to be key in both cases is this. Remember what underlies your choice of part boundaries? Transversal intersections. These provide you a firm foundation for defining part boundaries, because they
almost always occur when generic shapes intersect in generic ways. So
you're looking for evidence of transversal intersections when you look for
part boundaries. The clearer the evidence, the stronger the boundary.

For the bow tie on the left, the lines meeting at *c* are a clear case of transversal intersection. But the two lines meeting at n are not. For the bow tie on the right, c has been slightly smoothed to form a clear negative minimum of curvature. But n, which was not clear to begin with, has been smoothed so much that it's hardly recognizable.

These ideas motivate your use of the following rules for boundary salience.

> **Rule 17.** The salience of a cusp boundary increases with increasing sharpness of the angle at the cusp.

> **Rule 18.** The salience of a smooth boundary increases with the magnitude of (normalized) curvature at the boundary.

The curvature in Rule 18 must be normalized because curvature changes as you shrink or expand a shape. A small circle has higher curvature at each point than a large one. This is a technical issue that we needn't worry about here since the intuitions behind the rule are clear.

These rules suggest an interesting variation on the face-goblet illusion:

On the right I made all part boundaries for the faces more salient, by increasing their curvature, and all part boundaries for the goblet less salient, by decreasing their curvature. I did the opposite on the left. Notice that it's easier to see the faces on the right and the goblet on the left. This was confirmed in an experiment by the psychologist Manish Singh. He found that subjects were three times more likely to see faces on the right, and three times more likely to see a goblet on the left.

This same effect works in numerous other figures. And it tells us something interesting about how you choose figure and ground.

Remember the problem you face: Once you've constructed a curve you must decide if that curve outlines an object. If it does, you must decide which side of the curve is the object. But how can you decide that until you know what the object is? Sounds like a real catch-22.

You get out of it by having rules for choosing figure and ground that don't depend on knowing what the object is. The Gestalt psychologists, especially Edgar Rubin, studied such rules in detail. Experiments by the psychologist Mary Peterson suggest that you check both choices of figure and ground and see if one leads to a recognizable object. If so, you take it. That normally helps, but not with the face-goblet example, since both choices lead to a recognizable object.

The rule you seem to use instead is this:

> **Rule 19.** *Salient boundaries:* Choose figure and ground so that figure has the more salient part boundaries.

The faces have more salient boundaries on the left, so you prefer to see them as figure. The goblet has more salient boundaries on the right, so you prefer to see it as figure.

If you use this rule, then you have to use it quickly. You can't mess around too long trying to decide figure and ground; your survival depends on doing it fast. We know that you create parts quickly and in parallel all over your visual field. Perhaps you quickly assess the salience of their boundaries as well to help you decide figure and ground. If so, then we should expect that boundary salience affects your choice of figure and ground even in very brief flashes of a drawing. Singh tested this prediction with these "modified staircases":

Both are versions of the Schröder staircase, modified so that boundaries of steps for one choice of figure are stronger than those for the other choice. According to the rule of salient boundaries, you should prefer to see the two dots as lying on separate steps. You can check that you do. Then try turning the drawings upside down, and notice that you still see the dots on separate steps, indicating that you keep the same choice of figure for all orientations of the drawings. This shows how powerful the rule of salient boundaries can be. If, by contrast, you rotate Schröder's standard staircase, you find that it easily flips figure and ground, since both choices of boundaries have equal salience.

Singh showed subjects the standard and modified staircases one by one and, to avoid afterimages that might extend the effective viewing time, followed each one with a "mask," an image of random dots. Subjects had to say whether the two dots were on the same step or on different steps. In half of the trials the dots straddled a weak boundary, and in half a strong boundary. From each response Singh could tell which choice of figure and ground was seen. He found that with the modified staircases, subjects choose figure to have the stronger boundaries by a factor of two to one, even if they see each staircase for just fifty milliseconds—one-twentieth of a second. This shows that you require less than fifty milliseconds to assess boundary salience and to use it in choosing figure and ground.

Boundary salience is not, of course, the only factor in your choice of figure and ground. You use symmetry, relative size, relative contrast, convexity, and, as we have mentioned, recognizability. When these work together, your choice is firm:

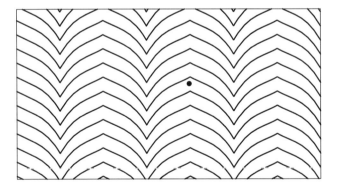

Where is the dot in this drawing, on top of a hill or in a valley? I see it on top of a hill, and so does everyone I've shown it. And it doesn't matter which way I turn the drawing. The choice of figure and ground almost never changes.

At least three factors work together here. There is boundary salience, which is stronger for the hills you see than for those you don't. Relative size and convexity are also larger for the hills you see. Together these factors make one set of hills far more salient to you than the other, even though they don't differ in their intrinsic recognizability. This difference in part salience drives your choice of figure and ground. The rule you seem to use here is this:

> **Rule 20.** *Salient parts:* Choose figure and ground so that figure has the more salient parts.

Boundary strength is just one factor in part salience, so this rule generalizes Rule 19—that you choose figure to have the stronger boundaries.

And the minima rule is just one factor in part creation. It's the most critical factor, but not the only one. It can't be, since in many cases it doesn't define a unique set of parts. Here's one example:

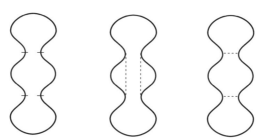

On the left is a silhouette with the negative minima marked by dashes. You could join them to form part cuts in at least two ways, as illustrated in the middle and at the right. Of the two, the parts on the right seem most natural. Why?

Symmetry, although it plays a role more generally, isn't the answer here; this silhouette is symmetric both vertically and horizontally. Trying to connect successive minima, which isn't the answer anytime, isn't the answer here; both partitions connect successive minima.

Minimizing the length of part cuts is a factor here. Experiments by psychologists Greg Seyranian and Manish Singh show that you strongly prefer short cuts to long ones. Indeed, for the shapes they tested, minimizing cut length is the strongest factor next to the minima rule. The parts on the right have shorter cuts than the parts in the middle.

But the main factor here is this. Notice that one of the parts in the middle drawing is shaped like a dog bone. Considered by itself, the dog bone has internal part boundaries. So it has parts itself, and they aren't just tiny ones. If you cut the dog bone into its three natural parts, then the middle drawing now has five parts. This is more than the number of parts on the right, and you prefer fewer parts.

This example might convince you that there's interesting work ahead in exploring how you create parts. You prefer fewer parts, shorter part cuts, convex parts, parts with more salient boundaries, and the list most surely goes on. How you orchestrate all these factors as you create your parts is a fascinating direction for further research. And so are the neurophysiological implications: points of highest curvature are critical to the creation of parts. Since you create parts in parallel all over your visual field, we can expect that you devote substantial cortical resources, perhaps in V1 or the adjacent area V2, to finding and analyzing points of highest curvature.

But for now the key point is that you create parts. The visual world doesn't come prepackaged into objects and parts. You create your visual world and you create its objects and parts. Because of the care you take in creating your parts, they serve you well as you try to navigate through your visual world and recognize its objects. You have countless ways you could in principle create parts. Most would be useless. But the way your visual intelligence creates parts has, as we have seen, the right magic.

This magic can get out of hand, as it does for schizophrenics with "paraprosopia." When these schizophrenics look at a face, or a photograph of a face, they see it at first as normal. Then, within seconds, the face transforms before their eyes into a fiendish monster, vampire, werewolf, or devil. The transformation is not a simple distortion of the whole face, such as a stretching or twisting. Instead it is a set of distinct, part-by-part distortions; different parts distort in different ways. The teeth grow into fangs, hair stands up on end, eyebrows become bushy, and the eyes grow large and theatening. This is a sophisticated, and horrifying, recreating of the parts of the face.

One paraprosopic, Daniel Paul Schreber (1842–1911), presided over the Dresden Court of Appeal, and wrote extensively about his own psychotic experiences, including this passage:

> They [the other patients] appeared absolutely silent when
> they entered the salon, one after the other. They also left the
> salon quietly, one after the other, apparently not taking
> notice of each other. I have repeatedly seen that individual
> patients exchanged heads while in the salon, i.e. without
> leaving the room, and suddenly walked around with another
> head during the period of my own observations . . .

This again is a transformation of parts. One part of the body, namely a
head, switches with another part, namely someone else's head. Our ability to create parts serves us well most of the time. But when it operates
without normal restraints, as in these schizophrenics, the creations can
be bizarre.

To construct objects we must construct parts. But we must also, as
mentioned earlier, assemble these parts in coherent spatial relationships.
It's a big step from a jumble of parts to the coherent organization of an
object, a step that most of us make with apparent ease.

But for many persons with "Williams syndrome" this step
becomes insuperable. Williams syndrome results from a genetic defect
in chromosome 7 that strikes about one person in twenty thousand, giving those afflicted a characteristic "elfin" facial appearance, mental retardation, high levels of calcium, heart and kidney defects, and malforma-
tions of the skeletal muscles and endocrine system. They are exception-
ally friendly and sociable and, despite their mental retardation, have
remarkable vocabularies and language skills. Many are musically talented, and can remember hundreds of songs and play them from memory.

But if you ask them to copy, or to draw from memory, a picture of
an object like an elephant, they're usually stumped. They'll draw a head,
trunk, ears, legs, and mouth, but put them in the wrong places. They
have the right parts but not the right spatial relationships between the
parts. This is not due to a lack of hand-eye coordination, for they can
trace objects with accuracy. Nor is it simply due to their mental retardation, for patients with Downs syndrome (mongolism) who are equally retarded, as measured by IQ, can produce drawings with parts in the
proper places. Rather it seems to be a specific inability to assemble parts
properly.

It will be interesting to see if a specific link can be made between
a particular genetic error and this inability to assemble parts. But the
Williams and paraprosopic cases underscore the sophistication and the
fragility of our visual intelligence. Normally it constructs parts and
assembles them into objects with every glance we take, a feat that can't

yet be duplicated by the world's fastest supercomputers. But a small genetic error in the case of Williams syndrome, or a small imbalance in neurotransmitters in the case of paraprosopics, can bring this sophisticated process to a grinding halt or launch it on bizarre tangents. Our visual intelligence walks a fine line.

FIVE

THE DAY COLOR
DRAINED AWAY

Imagine your surprise if one day you awoke to find that you no longer saw color, only a few dirty shades of gray. Roses weren't red, violets weren't blue, and even tomatoes were drained of their hue. The rainbow was stripped of its glory, and night followed day, not with the bang of a sunset but a whimper of gray. Surely the stuff of fairy tales and evil spells.

Now imagine your greater surprise if you awoke to see *half* the world in color, say the left half, and the other half in dirty grays. Your view of a shelf of Chintz china looked something like this:

That would be a curious experience, fitting for a trip in Wonderland. But neither case is fiction; for a few unfortunates, one case or the other is the world they entered one day.

Such was the fate of Jonathan I, an artist who worked with Georgia O'Keeffe in New Mexico and later enjoyed a successful career as an art director and commercial artist. Color was his livelihood until one day, at age sixty-five, he suffered a concussion in a minor car accident. Two days later he realized that he saw no colors, only dirty shades of gray. Tomatoes looked black, skin "rat-colored," and flowers an unappealing assortment of grays. Even his power to imagine colors, which before had been vivid, was gone. It never returned.

Mr. I was diagnosed by neurologist Oliver Sacks to have cerebral achromatopsia, a loss of color sensation throughout the entire visual field caused by damage to cerebral cortex. It is rare, but several such cases have been reported over the last three centuries. The typical cause, first discovered by Swiss ophthalmologist Louis Verrey (1854–1916) in 1888, is damage to the most inferior part of the occipital lobe, in the lingual and fusiform gyri:

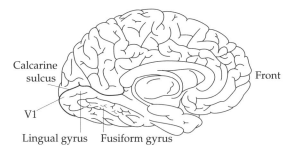

This figure shows the middle surface of the left hemisphere of the human brain. The lingual and fusiform gyri are, as you can see, toward the back of the brain and near the primary visual area V1. Based on his clinical and postmortem observations, Verrey concluded: "The centre for the chromatic sense will be found in the most inferior part of the occipital lobe, probably in the posterior part of the lingual and fusiform gyri." His idea was revolutionary—a portion of the brain devoted primarily to the construction of color. For most of his contemporaries it was too revolutionary, so his proposal was hotly contested and then largely ignored.

Until 1973, when the neurophysiologist Semir Zeki studied the analogous region of macaque monkey cortex, area V4, and discovered that the activity of many neurons there correlates best with perceived color. Subsequent studies have shown that cells of V4 process shape as well as color. This has led to a revival of interest in Verrey's proposal. In one recent test, researchers found that if they stimulate the lingual and fusiform gyri in human subjects by means of magnetic fields, the subjects report seeing chromatophenes—colored rings and halos. You don't need light or even eyes to see color; just stimulation of the lingual and fusiform gyri.

You might be wondering about the hemiachromatopsics. Why do they see color in half the visual field, but only grays in the other half? The answer is that they have damage to the lingual and fusiform gyri of only one cerebral hemisphere. Your brain has two hemispheres, wired up so that the left hemisphere constructs the right visual field, and the right hemisphere constructs the left visual field:

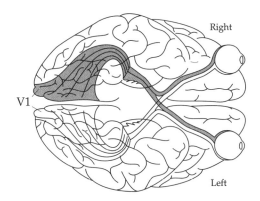

Here you see a bottom view of the brain showing the pathways from the eyes to V1. Notice that the pathway shaded gray originates from the right half of each eye. Because the optics of each eye reverse left and right (as well as up and down), the right half of each eye views the left half of the visual field. The gray pathway continues to V1 of the right hemisphere, so that the right hemisphere constructs what you see in the left visual field. A common mistake, but one which you will henceforth never commit, is to think that the right eye connects to the left hemisphere and the left eye to the right hemisphere. You can see in the diagram that this is not so. Both eyes connect to both hemispheres. It's the right visual field that connects to the left hemisphere and the left visual field to the right hemisphere.

So if you damage the lingual and fusiform gyri of just the left hemisphere, you can no longer construct color in the right visual field; you can only construct grays. Similarly, if you damage these gyri of just the right hemisphere, you can no longer construct color in the left visual field. The result in each case is the strange half-colored and half-gray world of hemiachromatopsia.

We can turn this around. Suppose that we use magnetic fields to stimulate, in normal subjects, just the lingual and fusiform gyri of the left hemisphere. Then we predict that they should see unusual colors in the right visual field. Similarly, we predict that stimulation in just the right hemisphere should lead to seeing unusual colors in the left visual field. This has been done, and both predictions are correct.

Suppose instead that we use magnetic fields to inhibit, in normal subjects, the lingual and fusiform gyri of just the left hemisphere. Then we predict that they should experience hemiachromatopsia, with a loss of color in the right visual field. Similarly, inhibiting the right hemisphere should lead to loss of color in the left visual field. Again both predictions are correct.

Fortunately, strokes and high-tech equipment aren't the only means to show that you construct color. We can catch you in the act with a few simple drawings. Perhaps the most compelling are drawings of neon color spreading, described in 1935 by the psychologist Hans Wallach. Consider, for instance, the neon worm:

On the left is a sequence of short blue lines. On the right is the same sequence, with black lines added as well. Of course, as we discussed in Chapter 3, you construct all the lines you see. But notice that on the right you construct something more: a glowing blue worm with clear subjective boundaries. Not only are the lines blue, so is the space between them. It's almost like looking at a neon sign. When I continue to view this figure, the effect becomes more striking: I see the lines as black even behind the blue transparent film.

If you measure the color between lines with a photometer, you won't find any blue. The blue you see between lines, and indeed the whole worm, is your construction. A photometer just can't create what you can.

Another engaging example was devised in 1981 by psychologists Christoph Redies and Lothar Spillmann:

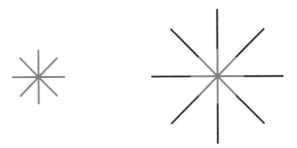

On the left are some red lines. On the right are the same lines, but with black lines attached. On the right you see, in addition to the lines, a red disk with a clear border. You can draw this on a napkin with a red pen and black pen of the same tip size. Just draw the red lines first, then start adding the black ones, being careful to join them smoothly. As you add black lines you'll see the red disk start to glow. Great way to amaze your friends. It's also easy to do the neon worm.

Suppose now that we use a photometer to study the light coming from the two points indicated by arrows:

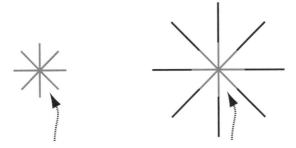

The photometer would indicate that their light is identical. But you see red at the point on the right, and not at the point on the left. Therefore the color you see at a point does not, in general, depend just on the light at that point. Instead, when you construct color you use a wider area of your visual field to determine the color at each point.

Another example of this is the color shuffle, devised by Jan Koenderink:

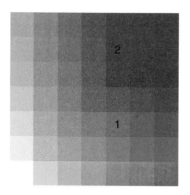 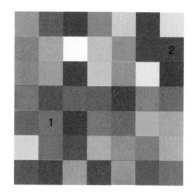

On the left is an array of forty-nine squares, each with a different mixture of ink, arranged so that you see a smooth transition of colors. On the right the same number of squares, with the same inks, are randomly shuffled. Notice that you see different colors on the right than on the left. The right has, for instance, some browns and grays that don't appear on the left. The differences are so large that it's hard to find corresponding squares between the left and right. So I've marked two of them. The two squares marked with a 1 both have identical ink, as do the two squares marked with a 2. Notice how different the corresponding squares look, even though their inks are identical. This again shows that the color you construct at a point depends not just on the light at that point, but on a wider area of the visual field.

Conversely, different inks can look the same color. This can happen even if the two inks are under precisely the same illumination. However, in this case it's usually possible to find another illumination under which the two inks look different. Restorers of buildings and paintings know this well: what looked like a good color match to the original paint under one light can look like a terrible match under another.

Thus the color you see at a point does not, in general, depend just on the ink or pigment at that point. You use a broader context to construct your colors. You can check this for yourself with paintings and photographs. Pick a point on the painting and pay close attention to the color you see at that point. Then take a long narrow tube, shaded a middle gray, and look again through the tube at that same point. You'll see that it's color has changed.

So it's not simply light at a point or pigment at a point that governs the color you construct. This has not always been evident to color theorists. The modern study of color begins with Sir Isaac Newton

(1643–1727) and his brilliant experiments with prisms. He studied the well-known effect that white light, if passed through a prism, emerges spread out into a spectrum of colors such as you see in a rainbow. As a result of his experiments he concluded:

> For the [light] Rays to speak properly are not coloured. In them there is nothing else than a certain Power and Disposition to stir up a Sensation of this or that Colour. . . . Colours in the Object are nothing but a Disposition to reflect this or that sort of Rays more copiously than the rest; in the Rays they are nothing but their Dispositions to propagate this or that Motion into the Sensorium, and in the Sensorium they are Sensations of those Motions under the Forms of Colours.

Newton and many of his successors thought that individual rays of light have the "Power and Disposition to stir up a Sensation of this or that Colour." The picture they developed is this. Light can be thought of as like a wave on a pond. And just as different waves can wiggle at different rates, some long and slow and others short and fast, so too different rays of light can wiggle at different rates, called frequencies. The frequency of a ray determines the color sensation you see. Blue results from rays with higher frequencies, yellow from intermediate frequencies, and red from lower frequencies.

It is a nice picture but, as we have seen with the color shuffle, much too simple to capture the subtleties of the way you construct color.

Similarly, Newton and many of his successors thought that "Colours in the Object are nothing but a Disposition to reflect this or that sort of Rays more copiously than the rest." Their idea is simple. Light is composed of different rays, which we now describe as having different frequencies. A given surface reflects certain rays and absorbs others. If it reflects low frequencies and absorbs high, then it is red. If it reflects high frequencies and absorbs low, then it is blue. The pattern of reflectance is the color of the surface.

But the color shuffle shows that this is too simple. Two squares with identical inks, and therefore identical reflectances, can look quite different in color. Thus you use more than just local reflectance to construct color.

Indeed this whole approach is too simple. When you construct color you do not construct just color. Instead you construct several visual properties at once, and try to make them all mutually consistent: you organize your visual world into objects, you endow those objects with three-dimensional shapes, place light sources that illuminate those objects, and assign color to both the light sources and the objects. As always, images are infinitely ambiguous. There are countless ways that you could interpret an image in terms of objects, their shapes, their colors, and their illuminants. You could trade off surface color for illuminant color, or surface shape for surface color. The possibilities are endless. But, again, you have rules, quite sophisticated rules that researchers have just begun to uncover, by which you select one interpretation from the countless possibilities.

You can see your own handiwork each time you go to a movie. When you settle into your seat and watch the movie, one way you could interpret your visual field is this: There's one large, white, flat object (the screen) and it's illuminated with lights of different colors at different places, and these lights keep changing. This is certainly a legitimate interpretation; a movie is, after all, changing patterns of colored light projected onto a white screen. But I doubt you would pay good money to go to the theater if that were the only interpretation you saw. Instead you pay good money because, when you watch the movie, you create a 3D world with colored objects that move and interact, and with colored lights that shine on those objects. It's this world that entertains you, not the screen and projected lights. They just provide you a suitable environment to create your own visual worlds and to be entertained by your own creations.

Of course, not just any projected lights will do. If I haphazardly project different lights on a screen, you won't create a beautifully crafted 3D world of objects and illuminants; you'll see a mess. It's not that sometimes you try to create visual worlds and sometimes you don't. You try to create them every time you open your eyes. It's just that you can't do something with nothing; put garbage in, and all that your visual intelligence can do is put garbage out. It takes a lot of work not to put garbage in; that's why the credits at the end of a movie go on so long. And that's why we so appreciate a well-filmed and well-edited movie. At some level the filmmaker understands the rules we use to create visual worlds, and gives us just what we need to make great creations. We love someone who helps us look good.

The color shuffle isn't quite up to the standards of modern film, but if you take a peek back at it you can see a simple example of your creative powers with color. Notice that on the left you see not only colored squares, but also colored lights illuminating those squares. A yellow light shines from one corner, red from another, blue and green from the remaining. But on the right, where the same squares have simply been rearranged, you no longer see different-colored illuminants. Instead you see a single uncolored illuminant shining uniformly over all the squares. Both figures have the same set of inks, but their different arrangements induce you to create different interpretations of surfaces and light sources.

Why? At least two rules are at work here.

Rule 21. Interpret gradual changes of hue, saturation, and brightness in an image as changes in illumination.

Rule 22. Interpret abrupt changes of hue, saturation, and brightness in an image as changes in surfaces.

Changes in surfaces include corners, object boundaries, and color changes (such as grain in wood or ink on paper). These two rules in fact understate your sophistication at interpreting changes in images.

The rules apply as follows to the color shuffle. On the left the squares are arranged so that changes in ink from one square to the next are as gradual as possible. These gradual transitions you interpret as illumination changes. You see a yellow light source shining from the lower left corner and a blue light from the upper right corner. The gradual transition between these corners you interpret as a change in balance of these two lights. There are also abrupt changes at the edges between squares. These you interpret as changes in surface color. Were there no edges, just a smooth transition, you would see no changes in surface color, just lights shining on a homogeneous surface.

On the right there are no smooth transitions of colors that cross several squares. Therefore you attribute none of the image changes to illumination changes: you see a single uniform illumination. Instead you attribute all of the image changes to changes in surface color.

This different parcelling of image changes between surface colors and illuminants is why squares of the same inks can look so different on the left and right sides of the color shuffle.

Returning once more to the movies, these rules also explain why, when you watch a western at your local theater, you don't see it as a flat white screen with complex and dancing lights. The filmmaker knows that your visual intelligence consistently interprets slow changes in images as due to lights, and abrupt changes as due to objects and surfaces. So the filmmaker has contrived, by means of a movie projector, to shine onto the movie screen a most unusual kind of light, one that has abrupt changes. This light from the projector tricks your visual intelligence, which interprets the abrupt changes in light as, instead, changes in objects and surfaces. Of course, as a veteran moviegoer, you know that you are viewing a flat white screen that doesn't change, and that only the light shining on the screen is changing. You know, when watching a western, that there aren't literally guns and horses and cowboys traipsing across the screen. But this knowledge never gets through to your visual intelligence, which continues to interpret images inside theaters by the same rules it interprets images outside of theaters. This is a clear limitation of your visual intelligence: it is impervious to contextual information you have, such as that you are in a theater, which might be useful for interpreting images. However, this limitation has its positive side. You can continue to enjoy movies, even while knowing how you are being tricked.

The psychologist Alan Gilchrist pointed out another example to me over dinner. We had a few white sheets of paper on the table. A small spotlight, shining from behind a potted plant, happened to cast a sharp, but low-contrast, shadow of the plant onto one of the sheets. At first glance we thought someone had spilled coffee on the sheet. This impression didn't go away until we jiggled the sheet and the "coffee stain" didn't jiggle with it. Then we saw the stains as shadows. But as soon as we stopped jiggling it, we saw the shadows once more as stains. We saw the luminance change as a change in surface color, because the change was abrupt. This is striking because the light within a shadow is just a scaled-down copy of the light outside the shadow, and one could in principle use such scalings to classify image changes as shadows. But here the shadow boundary was so abrupt that we saw it instead as a stain.

Of course, as I mentioned before, these rules are far from the whole story. You use many more, and more sophisticated, rules to construct objects, surfaces, and lights. Our best scientific theories of your prowess involve some nasty math. And even these theories, as powerful as they are, don't tell the whole story.

But there are still some interesting parts we can tell. I'll start first with grays and then move to color more generally. Consider, for instance, the "muffin pan":

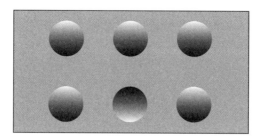

You probably see five bumps and one dent, each a homogeneous gray, and all lit by a single source that shines from the top of the page. Of course, there are countless ways you could, in principle, choose to interpret this image. You could, for example, choose to interpret it as simply one flat surface with changing patterns of pigment.

Turn the page upside down. Now you create a different scene. You probably see five dents and one bump, each a homogeneous gray, and all lit by a source from the top. This phenomenon was noted in 1786 by David Rittenhouse (1732–1796), astronomer and builder of the first telescope in these United States.

If you turn the page right side up and then upside down several times, you'll see each time that you flip between these same two interpretations. You are consistent and confident. This suggests that you're relying on powerful rules. Here are two:

Rule 23. Construct as few light sources as possible.

Rule 24. Put light sources overhead.

You see this figure as lit by one source, but you could in principle see it lit by more. For instance, you could construct six bumps, five lit from one direction and the bottom middle one lit from the opposite direction. However, you prefer to construct as few light sources as possible, so you make just one, place it overhead, and, to be consistent, make five bumps and one dent.

But if you're going to make one light source, why not place it below so that you see five dents and one bump? Because your rule is, where possible, to place your lights overhead. You do so every day with the sun, and you're not about to change your habits for this little figure.

Notice that I said you prefer to place light sources *overhead*, not *above*. The two are different, and make different predictions about what you'll see. So let's check it out with a critical experiment. Stand the figure upright on a table, so that you see five bumps and one dent. Now stand on your head, or just turn your head upside down, but don't move the figure. Notice what this does. Overhead is now below the figure, not above it. So if your rule is to put light sources overhead, you should now see five dents and one bump. But if your rule is to put light sources above, you should still see five bumps and one dent. The answer? You see five dents and one bump, so overhead wins and above loses.

Now consider this figure:

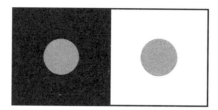

Here each image change is abrupt, and you see each as a surface change, all lit by just one source. You see a black square, a white square, and two gray disks. The disk on the right looks a bit darker than the one on the left. But if you measured each disk with a photometer, it would indicate they have precisely the same luminance. Once again, you are not a photometer. You construct grays in a more sophisticated manner than a photometer can.

This is due in part, as we discussed earlier, to simultaneous contrast. The disk on the right is surrounded by white, so it looks darker by contrast, whereas the disk on the left is surrounded by black, so it looks lighter by contrast. The idea is that you use local contrasts in luminance to assign grays, something a photometer does not do.

But you do something more as well. Check out this figure devised by the psychologist Michael White:

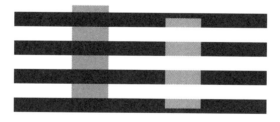

Here you see horizontal black bars separated by white bars, and you see two sets of gray bars, one set on the left and one set on the right. The set on the right looks much lighter than the set on the left. But a photometer would report no difference between them. This might be hard to believe, since the difference you see is so striking. But you can check it, if you don't have a photometer handy, by covering up all but one of the gray bars on the left and one of the gray bars on the right; then they look the same gray.

White's figure is a problem for the contrast theory. The gray bars on the left are surrounded mostly by black, and the gray bars on the right mostly by white. So, according to the contrast theory, the gray bars on the left should look lighter than those on the right. But the opposite is true.

What rules, then, are you using here? I think it's fair to say we don't know, and that this is an interesting open problem waiting for a bright mind to solve it. One idea that researchers are exploring is that you use sophisticated rules for grouping portions of the image together, and that you use the relative luminances of regions both within and between groups to create the grays you see. So, for instance, perhaps you group all the black bars of White's figure together and use these as the background comparison for the gray bars on the right. By this contrast, these gray bars would look relatively lighter. Moreover you compare the gray bars on the left against the white background of the page. By this contrast, these gray bars look relatively darker.

But we don't yet know if this explanation is on the right track. And if it is, we don't yet know what rules you use for grouping. Of course, in some sense you certainly do know the rules; after all, you're using them to see White's figure as you do. The trick, however, is to get that knowledge out of your visual system and onto the printed page.

Another example of your prowess at constructing grays is a checkerboard similar to one devised by the neurophysiologists Russ and Karen De Valois:

The checkerboard has two gray squares. The one on the left looks a darker gray than the one on the right. But—you guessed it—a photometer would measure the same luminance. So once again you construct the grays you see in a manner more sophisticated, by far, than a photometer measures them. We don't yet know the rules you use, but one guess is that you group the gray square on the right with the black diagonals passing through it. In contrast with that group, the gray square looks lighter. You group the gray square on the left with the white diagonals passing through it, and by contrast it looks darker.

You get a hint of how sophisticated your rules are in this next figure devised by the psychologist Ted Adelson and called the "corrugated Mondrian":

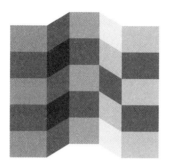

Here you see a variety of grays. Compare the grays of the two rectangles on the left which correspond to the rectangles labeled by A and B on the right. On the left, A looks much lighter than B, but they measure precisely the same luminance on a photometer. You also see this figure in three dimensions. It's possible, suggests psychologist Alan Gilchrist, that you group each surface with those that lie in the same 3D plane with it. Thus each vertical column would be a group. If so, then rectangle B would be darkest in its group, and A the lightest in its group, explaining why A looks lighter than B.

This account predicts that if we reduce the angles between planes, then this will reduce the strength of the vertical groupings, and hence reduce the difference in lightness between A and B. To test this, we can reduce the differences in angle to zero, but keep all luminances the same as above:

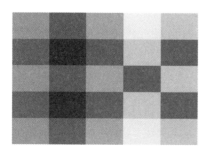

You can see for yourself that the difference in lightness between A and B in the flattened figure is much less than in the corrugated figure. This effect has been confirmed in experiments using several different angles between the planes.

This highlights again that you do not construct surface colors, or grays, in isolation. You construct them in the context of constructing 3D shapes and light sources, and you endeavor, as simply as possible, to make them all consistent with each other. A simple way to understand this is by means of a workshop metaphor introduced by psychologists Ted Adelson and Sandy Pentland. The metaphor is lengthy, but it illustrates that there are many different solutions to the problem of constructing visual scenes, and each different solution can be thought of as having different "costs" associated with it. Your visual intelligence tries to find a lowest-cost solution.

Suppose you're the director of a Broadway play, and you realize that Adelson's corrugated Mondrian is the perfect backdrop for a scene in your play. Not likely, I'll admit, but suppose. You take a picture of the corrugated Mondrian to the theater workshop, show it to the crew, and tell them to build a set that looks just like it. Budgets are limited, so you want them to do it as cheaply, but accurately, as possible.

The crew has three specialists: a painter, a lighting designer, and a sheet-metal worker. Their fees are as follows:

Painter:
Paint a rectangle:	$5 each
Paint a general polygon:	$5 per side

Sheet-metal worker:
Right-angle cut:	$2 each
Odd-angle cut:	$5 each
Right-angle bend:	$2 each
Odd-angle bend:	$5 each

Lighting designer:
Floodlight:	$5 each
Custom spotlight:	$30 each

Supervisor:
Consultation:	$30 per job

The crew could build the set in many ways. For instance, the painter could do most of the work, painting the corrugated Mondrian onto a flat sheet of metal and having the lighting designer put a single floodlight on it. Or the lighting designer could do most of the work, using masks to create custom spotlights to shine on a flat white sheet. Or the sheet-metal worker could do most of the work, bending metal sheets and having the lighting designer put a single flood light on them. Or the three specialists could all work together, coordinated by the supervisor, with the painter painting gray patches onto a flat metal sheet, the metal worker bending the sheet into a 3D zigzag, and the lighting specialist illuminating it with a single floodlight. This last solution seems the most natural.

We can figure the cost of each solution.

Painter's solution:

Paint 10 general polygons:		$200
Paint 15 rectangles:		$75
Set 1 flood light:	$5	
Cut 1 rectangle:	$8	
Total:	$288	

Sheet-metal worker's solution:

Cut 40 odd angles:	$200
Bend 10 odd angles:	$50
Set 1 floodlight:	$5
Total:	$255

Lighting designer's solution:

Set 25 custom spots:	$750
Cut 1 rectangle:	$8
Total:	$758

Supervisor's solution:

Supervisor's fee:	$30
Cut 1 rectangle:	$8
Paint 6 rectangles:	$30
Bend 4 right angles:	$8
Set 1 floodlight:	$5
Total:	$81

As you can see, the solutions vary in complexity and cost. The least complex and least expensive is the supervisor's.

Like most metaphors, this one has strengths and weaknesses. A strength is that the task of the set crew is like the task of vision: both, given an image, construct shapes, surface colors, and lights that together produce the image. And in both cases there are countless ways to do the job. Some are more complex and costly than others. So in both cases the goal is to find a best solution.

A weakness is that we aren't told how the supervisor found a good solution. In the metaphor it just appeared, magically, in final form. That's not good enough for our exploration of vision. We want to know how you construct visual worlds of shapes, colors, and lights. Why do you choose one solution rather than another, and how do you find a solution in the first place?

The metaphor also leaves out something else. Not only do you construct surface shapes, surface colors, and lights, but also, in coordination with all these, you construct transparent filters. The argyle, devised by Ted Adelson, nicely illustrates this:

Two of the diamonds have white dots. The diamond on the left looks darker than that on the right. But a photometer would measure no difference.

Notice that you also see light and dark strips overlying the pattern of diamonds. They look like light and dark filters through which you see the underlying pattern. The diamonds under the dark filters look lighter than those under the light filters.

The psychologist Fabio Metelli discovered that you have elegant rules, which we'll discuss shortly, for deciding when to construct transparent filters. The diamonds with four gray regions inside satisfy these rules, prompting your visual intelligence to construct the filters.

At the same time you also construct surface colors for the diamonds. All of the gray diamonds have the same luminance, so since you've decided that you see some through a dark filter, you give these diamonds a lighter surface color. Similarly, those that you see through a light filter you give a darker surface color. In so doing you construct a consistent world of colored surfaces and filters, a world that would produce the given image.

Suppose now that we alter the figure so that you don't construct transparent filters. Then, by the account just given, you should no longer assign different grays to the diamonds. This was checked by Adelson in these figures:

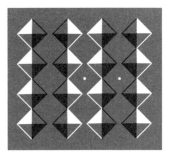

On the left we change the argyle by cutting the multigray diamonds. It no longer satisfies your rules for deciding to construct filters. So you don't. And notice that, as predicted, the two diamonds with dots now look the same gray.

On the right we change the argyle by pulling apart the uniform gray diamonds. It still satisfies your rules for deciding to construct filters. So you do. And notice that, as predicted, the two diamonds with dots again look to be different grays.

Everything turns, in this case, on whether you decide to create transparent filters. And since I said you have elegant rules for making this decision, you're probably wondering what they are. I'll mention two of them:

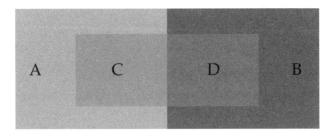

Here is a typical figure for which you construct a transparent filter. It has four regions, each with a different lightness. Regions C and D together look like a filter above regions A and B.

Your first rule is that filters don't invert lightness. Notice that B is darker than A. You require then that D be darker than C; if it's not, then you refuse to construct a filter.

Rule 25. Filters don't invert lightness.

Your second rule is that filters decrease lightness differences. Notice the difference in lightness between B and A. You require that the difference between D and C be smaller; if it's not, then again you refuse to construct a filter.

Rule 26. Filters decrease lightness differences.

There is, of course, more to the story, but these rules are the heart of the matter as far as lightness is concerned. But there's more to transparency than just lightness relations. Spatial relations are important as well. Consider, for instance, this figure:

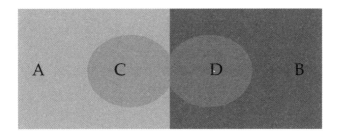

Regions A, B, C, and D all have the same lightnesses as before, but now, as Kanizsa observed in similar figures, you no longer create transparency.

What? Because, as Manish Singh has noted, it would violate genericity. Suppose C and D are two parts of a single transparent filter. As you can see in the figure, C and D meet at two concave cusps which, as we discovered in the last chapter, define a part boundary between them, according to the minima rule. This part boundary between C and D is a vertical line which coincides with the lightness boundary between A and B. This alignment is nongeneric: if C and D really were a transparent filter in front of A and B, then any small change in viewpoint would separate the part boundary between A and B from the lightness boundary between C and D.

If this account is right, then if we separate the part boundary and lightness boundary, you should again create transparency. As you can see here, that is indeed the case:

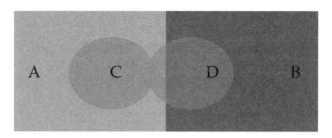

Thus the minima rule and part boundaries critically affect our construction of transparency.

So far I've made two main points about how you construct grays. First, to construct gray at one point you don't just use the luminance of the image at that point. And you don't, in general, just use nearby luminances either. Instead you use large portions of the image and sophisticated rules of grouping that we have yet to work out. Second, you don't just construct grays, or colors more generally, in isolation. Instead you construct them as part of a coordinated construction of surface shapes, surface colors, light sources, and transparent filters.

One principle you use to coordinate all these constructions is one we've seen at work many times before: the principle of generic views and generic positions. As Bill Freeman discovered, you do so in a clever way. Consider this image:

You probably see a glossy metallic bar, of uniform gray, shaped like a cylinder, and lit by one source from above. (For an even more compelling effect, view the figure through a long and narrow viewing tube, such as the cardboard center of a paper-towel roll.) But you could, of course, construct other solutions. Think again of the stage-crew metaphor. You could construct the painter's solution: a flat surface, painted in shades of gray, and lit with one floodlight. Or you could construct the lighting specialist's solution: a flat surface, painted a uniform white, and lit with a complex set of custom lights. Or you could construct a different 3D solution: a bar that is not glossy, is more sharply curved than a cylinder, and is lit by one source from above. All of these solutions, and countless more, would give the same image if photographed. How shall you choose among them?

We can forget solutions with complex lights, since you prefer one light source. But even with just one source you have the freedom, in principle, to put that source in countless different places. For each possible place, you could find a surface shape and glossiness that, together, give this image. Since you don't in fact see these possibilities, you must use some other rule to narrow your choices.

That rule is the rule of generic views, and you use it in a different way than we've seen before. The new idea is this: Choose the most stable combination of shape, color, and source.

Here's what I mean. Pick any combination of shape, color, and source that gives our target image. Call it a *fair pick*. Now randomly perturb the combination, ever so slightly; move the light source a tad, change the shape a tad, change the surface gray and gloss a tad. This changes, of course, the image you'd get if you took a photo. Now do this to every fair pick you can find, and each time check how much the image changes away from the target image. Some will change a lot, some very little. The fair picks with small changes are *stable*; the others are *unstable*. You opt for the fair pick that's most stable. This is the one for which perturbations of shape, color, and source lead to the smallest changes in the resulting image.

In this manner you construct that visual world for which the current image is the most generic view.

Rule 27. Choose the fair pick that's most stable.

This rule is powerful, since it cuts countless possibilities down to one and, in many cases, it accurately predicts the visual worlds you construct for shaded images.

This is all well and good. But you might wonder about a more basic question. If you construct grays from image luminance, how do you decide what is white, or what is black, and what the total range of grays will be? Suppose, for instance, that your image has a ten-to-one range of luminances. You could construct many different ranges of perceived grays. Here are two examples:

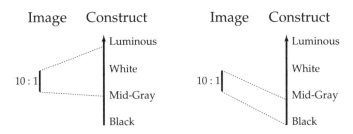

As shown on the left, you could interpret the lowest luminance as a middle gray, and the highest as self-luminous, using a large range of grays. Or, as shown on the right, you could interpret the lowest luminance as black, and the highest as a middle gray, using a smaller range of grays. You can, as Alan Gilchrist puts it, anchor luminance to perceived gray in many different ways. The question is, what anchoring rules do you use?

The answer is, again, we don't know. Some promising candidates have been tried and found wanting. For instance, it's been proposed that you choose to see the average luminance as a middle gray. And it's been proposed, instead, that you see the highest luminance as white. Neither captures what you do. Once again, you are more sophisticated. Take an image with just two regions—one small and brighter, one large and darker. The gray you assign to the large region depends on its size. The bigger it looks, the lighter gray you assign it. In this case, and in general, you use relative area as well as relative luminance to assign grays.

One rule that holds, but only because it's sufficiently general, is this:

> **Rule 28.** Interpret the highest luminance in the visual field as white, fluorent, or self-luminous.

Fluorence is white that is whiter than white, a super white that almost glows.

This rule captures one aspect of the way you construct grays. You might not, for some images, construct black, but you always construct at least white. You could, of course, have anchored low, interpreting the lowest luminance as black. Instead you anchor high, preferentially constructing whites and lights. How exactly you do this is simply not known; here is an interesting and open topic for research.

After this foray into gray, let's return again to color more generally.

It is the nature of science first to simplify, then to complexify. The study of color is no exception. The bulk of psychological experiments measure the colors you see in the simplest of situations: a small colored disk against a neutral surround. In these "aperture color" experiments, the colors you construct have an unusual quality. Unlike the colors you see normally, aperture colors don't appear to belong to a surface or an illuminant. There simply isn't enough structure in aperture displays for you to construct a visual world of surface shapes, surface colors, and lights. This is both an advantage and disadvantage for the study of color. The advantage is that simple displays lead you to simple behavior, and simple behavior is easy to understand. The disadvantage is that simple displays are artificial—that your behavior, though simple, might mislead us about how you construct color more generally. As the psychologist Larry Arend put it, if someone cuts off my arms and legs, then my behavior will indeed be simpler, but it won't be a good guide to my normal behavior.

With this caveat in mind, let's look at the colors you construct in aperture displays. They have a beautiful structure and a fascinating relation to the measurements made by a spectral photometer.

According to the photometer, one aperture display can differ from another in an infinite number of ways. But according to you, they can differ in only three: hue, saturation, and brightness. These are nicely illustrated in the color solid:

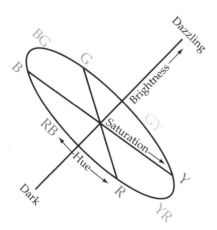

Hue refers to how much red, yellow, green, blue, and so forth are in a color. Saturation refers to the purity of a hue, and varies from neutral grays to highly pure hues; pink, for instance, is a less saturated red. Brightness varies from the barely visible to the dazzling.

So aperture displays, for you, differ in three dimensions, whereas for a photometer they differ in many more. As a result, two displays, or even thousands of displays, that to you are identical in color can to a photometer differ greatly. Such displays are called *metamers*. To you metamers look the same, but to the photometer they're different.

We've seen, of course, time and again that you aren't a photometer, so in one sense it's no surprise that you and the photometer differ here as well. But in most cases discussed so far, you see something that the photometer doesn't—an edge, a change in brightness, a change in color. Here it's reversed. The photometer reports differences that you don't.

What does the photometer report? Roughly, the energy of light at each of many frequencies. This deserves a little explanation.

Light is a mystery. Sometimes it's best described as a wave, sometimes as a particle, and sometimes, in recent experiments, as both wave and particle at the same time. When it's best described as a particle, we speak of light quanta. If this all sounds a tad confusing don't worry, you're in good company. It also confused Albert Einstein. In 1951, in a letter to his old friend Michelangelo Besso, he wrote:

> All these fifty years of conscious brooding have brought me no nearer to the answer to the question "what are light quanta?" Nowadays every Tom, Dick, and Harry thinks he knows it, but he is mistaken.

Since light itself is a mystery, what exactly a photometer does with light is also not quite clear. An oversimplified account goes like this. Light comes in discrete particles called quanta. Each quantum of light has a specific frequency. What the photometer does is to count up how many quanta of light there are at each specific frequency. Since there are many possible frequencies, the light coming from an aperture display can vary in many dimensions, one dimension for each possible frequency of light.

This account is too simple because, strictly speaking, light has no quanta and no specific frequencies until these properties are measured. Only in the act of measurement can one assert that light has specific frequencies. It isn't true that the photometer simply reports properties of light that were unambiguously there prior to being measured. Rather, it's consistent with our best theories of light to say instead that the photometer constructs the properties of light that it reports. The description that the photometer constructs is more detailed than what you construct. But it's no less a construction. Now is not the time to dwell on this. We'll return to it later. For now our focus is on your constructions, not the photometer's.

The story of how you construct the three color dimensions of hue, saturation, and brightness begins at the retina. There, as we discussed before, you have photoreceptors of two types: rods and cones. Rods mediate your vision in low light, cones in bright light. You have three different types of cones, each of which responds differently to light:

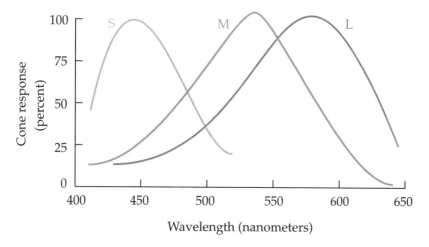

One type, labeled S, responds preferentially to high frequencies; another, labeled M, to intermediate frequencies; and the third, labeled L, to low frequencies. Often their responses are described not in terms of light frequencies but, as shown in this diagram, in terms of light wavelengths. It doesn't matter, since each frequency corresponds to one wavelength, and vice versa. The only trick is that high frequencies correspond to short wavelengths and low frequencies to long wavelengths.

Think of this diagram as showing the relation between reports of your cones and reports of a photometer. Cone reports are on the vertical axis, photometer reports on the horizontal. So, for instance, the diagram shows that if a photometer reports a quantum of light with wavelength 450, then the chance is about 100 percent that an S cone in a similar situation would report a quantum of light. The chance is about 25 percent for an M cone and 10 percent for an L cone. If instead the photometer reports a quantum with wavelength 575, then an L cone is most likely to report a quantum, followed by an M cone and then an S cone.

This part of the story, that there are three types of cones, was first guessed by Thomas Young (1773–1829) and announced in his Bakerian Lecture to the Royal Society in 1802:

> As it is almost impossible to conceive each sensitive point of the retina to contain an infinite number of particles, each capable of vibrating in perfect unison with every possible undulation, it becomes necessary to suppose the number limited, for instance to the three principal colours, red, yellow, and blue.

This brilliant insight was then largely forgotten until Helmholtz resurrected it much later in that century. As a result, this part of the story is called the Young-Helmholtz Trichromatic Theory of color vision.

We have since learned that the cones differ because they have different pigment molecules that respond differently to light. Each pigment molecule has two parts: a large protein called *opsin* and a derivative of vitamin A called *retinal*. The particular sequence of amino acids in the opsin determines the response of the pigment to light. Specific genes code for these opsin molecules, and their nucleotide sequences have been found.

If one of these genes is missing or defective, then you will lack the corresponding visual pigment. This in turn restricts the range of hues that you can construct, causing color blindness. If you lack the L pigment, a condition known as *protanopia*, then you can't construct differences between red and green. If you lack the M pigment, a condition known as *deuteranopia*, you again can't construct differences between red and green. And if you lack the S pigment, a condition known as *tritanopia*, then you can't construct differences between blue and yellow.

The genes for the L and M pigments both lie on the X chromosome. Men get only one X, whereas women get two. Therefore women are more likely than men to get a healthy copy of these genes, and men are more likely to get stuck with defective copies. This is why more men than women are red-green color-blind.

It has recently been found that the gene for the L pigment is polymorphous, which means that it comes in two different varieties in the normal population. These two varieties lead to two versions of the L pigment, which differ in position 180 of the amino acid sequence of the opsin. One version has alanine at position 180, and a peak sensitivity to light at 552.4 nanometers. The other version has serine at position 180, and a peak sensitivity to light at 556.7 nanometers. About 62 percent of males with normal color vision have the serine version and 38 percent have the alanine version. The two groups differ slightly in the colors they construct. For instance, they need slightly different mixtures of red and green to match a yellow.

This is interesting for two reasons. First it underlines again that you construct the colors you experience. And second, it is the first case where we have traced a difference in visual constructions to a difference at a single site of a gene. As John Mollon puts it:

> The significance of these discoveries for psychologists cannot be exaggerated. Here is a case where a difference of a single nucleotide places people in distinct phenomenal worlds and where we know almost all the steps in the causal chain from gene to molecule to neural signals; only the final steps from cortical activity to sensation elude us. It is the first such case in psychology. It cannot be the last.

The final steps from cortical activity to sensation are rather big ones. In fact, as we'll discuss later, the steps probably can't be taken in that direction. But the point about construction remains: a change in a single nucleotide can change in part how you construct your visual world.

The three cones and their relative responses are one part of the story on how you make color. Another was first guessed in 1878 by Ewald Hering (1834–1918). He noticed that certain hues never coexist in our perceptions of colors. For instance, we never see a hue that appears to be both reddish and greenish; nor do we see one that appears to be both bluish and yellowish. Pairs of hues that do not coexist in this sense, namely red/green and blue/yellow, are called *opponent colors*. Other pairs of hues can coexist. For instance, we can see both reddish and yellowish hues in orange, and we can see both bluish and greenish hues in cyan.

Opponent colors are something a photometer doesn't report. You do because you construct them. But the photometer doesn't: it makes no special distinction between reds and greens, nor between blues and yellows.

Here is a simple model of how you construct opponent colors:

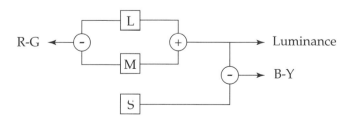

The boxes labeled L, M, and S represent cone responses. On the left, a difference between L and M cone responses creates red-green opponency, labeled R-G. On the right, a sum of L and M cone responses creates a dimension of luminance. A difference between this luminance and the S cone response creates blue-yellow opponency, labeled B-Y. Neurophysiological studies, both in nonhuman primates and in other animals, support this model.

Why you create color opponency is not known. The best guess so far is that since cone responses are highly correlated, color opponency is a good way to decorrelate them and thereby maximize the information available for your later visual constructions.

A remarkable aspect of your color construction can be seen with a pair of sunglasses. Take the glasses and hold them at arm's length. Notice that the objects you see through the lenses appear to be tinted the same color as the lenses. I have brown sunglasses, and holding them at arm's length in front of a white wall, I see the bit of wall behind the lenses as tinted brown. Now put on your glasses and look again. After a second or two of adjustment, the tint almost disappears. Looking at the white wall with my brown glasses on, I don't see the wall as brown but as white. And I see all other objects as having pretty much the same colors as when I take the glasses off.

You can do the same with illumination. Light a room with a tinted light and, after a short time, you see pretty much the same colors as when the room is lit with a white light. All day, in fact, the illumination outdoors changes as the sun rises and sets and dodges between clouds. But you don't see objects changing colors. They stay pretty much the same.

I say "pretty much" because the colors do shift a bit. Which is why we sometimes take that shirt or dress, which looks good by store light, and hold it by a window to check that it also looks good out of doors.

Your talent for creating roughly the same colors despite changes in illumination is called *approximate color constancy*.

Many researchers have studied this talent, but they haven't yet figured it out. None of the stories so far can explain, for instance, how you interpret the color shuffle, shown earlier in this chapter, in terms of lights and surface colors. The most promising stories to date are called *linear models*. They assume that there are only a handful of truly distinct illuminants, and that all other illuminants are really simple combinations of this basic handful. Similarly, they assume that there are only a handful of truly distinct ways a surface can reflect light, and that all surface reflectances are really simple combinations of this basic handful. Under these assumptions it's often possible to construct surface reflectances that vary little with changes in illumination. This is an encouraging start, but not yet enough to explain the color shuffle. Here again is an open area of research waiting for innovative thinkers.

Earlier in this chapter we saw that you construct surface grays, surface shapes, illuminants, and transparencies not one at a time and in isolation but all together and in mutual consistency. What is true when you construct surface grays is also true when you construct colors more generally. Here's an example:

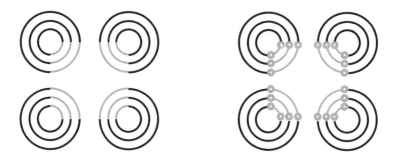

On the left you see a transparent blue square in front of black circles. The edges of the square are clear, except perhaps at the corners, and a desaturated blue fills the square right up to its edges. A photometer, however, wouldn't report a square at all; the only blue ink in the drawing is on arcs of circles. You construct the square, you create its edges, and you fill it with a ghostly blue. You create a consistent visual interpretation. As always, there are countless other interpretations you could create. For instance, you could decide that only the arcs of circles are blue, and forgo making a square.

In fact, that's what you do on the right. The square is gone, the ghostly blue is gone, and there are no edges. The only difference between the two drawings is that the one on the right has some little blue circles. This might strike you as strange. The drawing on the right has more blue contours, and yet you see less blue. Why?

It is, once more, the principle of generic views at work. Suppose that you create a transparent blue filter on the right. This interpretation requires a special view: the edges of the filter must be in front of and precisely align with the T-junctions where black arcs meet the small blue circles:

T-junction

On the left, one of these T-junctions is indicated. Notice that the cap of the T is blue, the stem is black, and the color changes precisely where the cap and stem meet. Now if there were a blue filter whose edge just happened to be aligned with this T-junction, and that was responsible for the color change from black to blue, then if you moved your view just a little to the left the result would be as shown on the right of this figure: the color change would no longer align with the T-junction. Since creating a transparent filter entails, in this manner, adopting an unstable view, you forgo the filter.

Is it really the rule of generic views at work, or is it just that you don't make filters when there are little circles hanging around? Let's check:

Here again you see transparent filters. In each drawing there are the same number of small circles as before. The only difference is that now these circles are scattered at random, so that the switch from black to blue, or from black to red, does not precisely align with T-junctions. So the trouble before was not the small circles, but the nongeneric view.

We have seen repeatedly how much you rely on the rule of generic views for your visual constructions. You might wonder if you use analogous rules in your other senses, such as hearing or touch. The answer is yes. In hearing, for instance, you construct subjective sounds, both simple and complex, just as in vision you construct subjective surfaces. Suppose I play a tone like middle C, then briefly turn off the tone and at the same time turn on a hissing noise (such as you hear when your television is between channels), then turn off the hissing noise and at the same time turn on the tone again. What you hear is different. You hear the tone all the time—even during the hissing noise, when in fact I wasn't playing it. You hear a subjective tone that you construct, even if you know that I'm not playing the tone. However, if there is a tiny delay between the end of the tone and the start of the hiss, then you don't construct a subjective tone. Why? The psychologist Rainer Mausfeld has suggested that just as you use a rule of generic position in space for vision, so also you use a rule of generic placement in time for sound. If I stop the tone at the precise moment that I start the hiss, you continue to construct the tone because it's not generic for one sound to stop precisely when another starts. In fact, I need careful work with the right audio equipment to make that happen. The rule of generic views, then, does have analogues in other sensory modalities.

So far I've shown you displays for which you create colored surfaces that are flat. But you can also create colored surfaces that curve in three dimensions. Here is an example, similar to ones created by Ilpo Kojo and his colleagues:

This is a stereo display. Cross your eyes slightly, so that the four disks on the left slide on top of the four disks in the middle. It may help to put a finger in front and look at it, while paying attention to the disks behind. When you get them fused you see, on the left, a ghostly red sheet of paper that curls in front of black disks. The sheet has clearly defined edges and vivid curvature in depth.

On the right you also see a red sheet of paper that curls. But now the red sheet is not in front of the black disks, it's behind. The disks look like holes through which you see the red sheet. And notice that the sheet is a different kind of red. It's not ghostly and transparent as on the left. Instead it's highly saturated and opaque. And notice also that the sheet curls away from you, rather than toward you as on the left.

What's different between the two cases that prompts you to make such different creations? Not much. The only difference is that what your right eye sees in one case is what your left eye sees in the other, and vice versa. You see the same images in both cases, but in opposite eyes.

Psychologists call this a switch in stereo disparity. What's striking here, as Ken Nakayama and Shinsuke Shimojo have pointed out, is that a mere switch in stereo disparity is enough to trigger you to construct very different surface colors, shapes, and depths.

These stereo displays are too much fun to show you just one example. So here's a couple more:

In each half of this drawing you create a surface that is flat, ghostly blue, and has clear boundaries. When you fuse them in stereo you again see a ghostly blue surface with clear boundaries, but now you make it curve well in front of the black circles.

Now I'll switch the two halves of the drawing, which switches the stereo disparity:

When you fuse this stereo display, you create an opaque blue surface, you make it curve like a cylinder, you put it behind the white page, and you make the black circles to be holes through which you see the blue cylinder.

An impressive construction. Admit it, you're good.

SIX

WHEN THE WORLD
STOPPED MOVING

n October 1978 a forty-three-year-old woman, whom we shall call L.M., was admitted to a hospital in a stupor. She had suffered for three days with severe headaches and vomiting. Several tests, run then and later, suggested that a stroke had damaged both sides of her brain at the lateral border between the temporal and occipital lobes, indicated here by a dark spot:

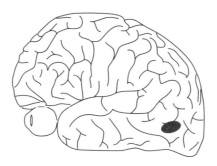

Nineteen months later, in May 1980, she was examined by neurologist Josef Zihl, and in most respects was found to be normal. She had trouble remembering names, but tests showed that her memory was in the range considered low normal. She could read, write, and calculate. She had no trouble moving her body. But, as Zihl reported in 1983, she had an unusual complaint:

The visual disorder complained of by the patient was a loss of movement vision in all three dimensions. She had difficulty, for example, in pouring tea or coffee into a cup because the fluid appeared to be frozen, like a glacier. In addition, she could not stop pouring at the right time since she was unable to perceive the movement in the cup (or a pot) when the fluid rose. Furthermore the patient complained of difficulties in following a dialogue because she could not see the movements of the face and, especially, the mouth of the speaker. In a room where more than two other people were walking she felt very insecure and unwell, and usually left the room immediately, because "people were suddenly here or there but I have not seen them moving." The patient experienced the same problem but to an even more marked extent in crowded streets or places, which she therefore avoided as much as possible. She could not cross the street because of her inability to judge the speed of a car, but she could identify the car itself without difficulty. "When I'm looking at the car first, it seems far away. But then, when I want to cross the road, suddenly the car is very near." She gradually learned to "estimate" the distance of moving vehicles by means of the sound becoming louder.

L.M. complained, and experiments confirmed, that she often did not see motion. By contrast, she had good acuity, could see depth from stereovision, had normal color perception, and could easily recognize objects. Her motion deficit was limited to vision; she easily perceived the motions of sounds and of objects on her skin.

An exam ten years after her stroke showed, unfortunately, no improvement in her perception of visual motion. She had found many ways to cope with day-to-day life despite her impairment, but crossing busy streets remained a problem.

The case of L.M. has drawn much attention, and rightfully so. It is striking that she could easily see an object, describe its shape in three dimensions, correctly report its colors, pick it up, and yet be unable to see it move. This defies common sense. How could you possibly see an object but not its motion? The two seem inseparable, not only to common sense but also to many careful thinkers as well. The philosopher John Locke (1632–1704), for instance:

Qualities thus considered in Bodies are, First such as are utterly inseparable from the Body, in what estate soever it be. . . . These I call *original* or *primary Qualities* of Body, which I think we may observe to produce simple ideas in us, *viz.* Solidity, Extension, Figure, Motion, or Rest, and Number.

2dly, Such *Qualities,* which in truth are nothing in the Objects themselves, but Powers to produce various Sensations in us by their *primary qualities, i.e.* by the Bulk, Figure, Texture, and Motion of their insensible parts, as Colours, Sounds, Tastes, *etc.* These I call *secondary Qualities.*

Here Locke asserts that, to our minds, a body and its motion are inseparable; a body and its color, however, are separable: Locke would probably not be surprised at the achromatopsia of Jonathan I. Color is secondary, not primary, so in principle we can separate object and color. But he would surely be surprised at the akinetopsia of L.M. Motion, for him, is primary and inseparable from body.

The solution is to recognize that motion, like color, is constructed by your visual intelligence. Since you construct the motion you see, if your constructive processes are impaired then you don't see motion.

In L.M.'s case the impairment, and loss of motion, appears to be permanent. But a technique called transcranial magnetic stimulation (TMS) allows anyone to experience, for a brief while, this same loss of motion. The trick is to use magnetic fields to impair normal electric function in V5, a small area of cortex about one centimeter in diameter, which was destroyed by stroke in L.M. In volunteer subjects, V5 can be temporarily impaired by TMS, so that the subject loses, for a moment, the normal power to construct motion. When TMS stops, the subject again sees motion as before.

The results with TMS on V5 are quite specific. Motion is impaired but not, for instance, color. And if TMS is applied to V5 on just the left side of the brain, then the subject loses motion on just the right half of the visual field. Conversely, if TMS is applied to V5 on just the right side of the brain, then the subject loses motion on just the left half of the visual field.

It may come as no surprise to you that you construct motion. After all, if, as we've discussed, you construct objects, their shapes in three dimensions, and their colors, then why not their motions as well? Indeed, it would seem a point of logic that if you construct objects then you must construct their motions. If what moves is your construction, then how it moves must be as well. The what and how of motion are, of necessity, intimately linked.

A clear demonstration of the link was found by Sigmund Exner, a student of Helmholtz, and reported in 1875. He flashed two sparks, one after the other. If the time and space between sparks is not too long and not too short, then observers see one spark, not two, and that one spark moves. It's easy to replicate Exner's effect on your home computer. Simply flash up one white dot against a black background, then remove the dot and flash up another one at a different position from the first. With the right timing between flashes, you see just one dot instead of two, and it moves. Let's use a circle to mark the position of the dot that flashes first and an X to mark the position of the one that flashes second. Then we can depict the motion display like this:

This indicates a display in which first one dot blinks on and off at the position marked by the circle, and then another dot blinks on and off at the position marked by the X. In the display itself, of course, no X and no circle appears, only two dots, one after another. (You can see the real display, and all other motion displays discussed in this chapter, on the internet. Just get the web address in the endnote for this page.)

It doesn't get much simpler than this: first one dot blinks on and off, and then so does a second. But even here you go to work constructing objects and motions. You have lots of options. For instance, you could construct two separate objects at two separate places, neither of which moves; one object appears and disappears on the left, then so does the other on the right. In fact that is what you construct if the time between the disappearance of the first dot and the appearance of the second dot, which is called the *interstimulus interval* or ISI, is greater than about half a second. But if the ISI is somewhere between about half a second and a tenth of a second, then you construct only one object and you have it move, at just the right speed, from left to right. (The precise range of ISIs here depends on the distance between dots.) And if the ISI is less than about a tenth of a second, then you construct two separate objects that don't move, but simply blink on and off separately.

What's interesting here is not simply that you construct objects and motions, but that you construct them interdependently. How you construct motion depends on how you construct objects, and vice versa.

If you decide to construct one object in Exner's display, then you make it move. If you construct two objects, then you make them blink but stay put.

This is the foundation of the motion picture industry. If you didn't make this construction, movies wouldn't work and Hollywood would go out of business. When you watch a movie at the theater, what the projector shows you is a bunch of still pictures, one after the other. Each second, the projector shows you twenty-four different still pictures, and it rapidly flashes each of these pictures on and off three times, for a total of seventy-two flashes per second. In between flashes the screen is dark. Indeed, much of your time in the theater, while watching a movie, is spent before a blank screen.

That's what you're given by the projector. But it's not what you see. What you see, of course, is what your visual intelligence constructs. Just as in Exner's simple display, where you construct one object that moves rather than two separate objects that stay put, so also in the movie theater you construct many objects that move rather than more objects that stay put. When that action hero punches a villain in the nose, what the projector shows you is a bunch of stills in which a fist is closer and closer to a nose. But you refuse to see this sequence as separate, unmoving fists. Instead you construct one fist, put it in motion, and make it hit that nose. The only motion in motion pictures is the motion that you construct. Brilliant explosions, graceful dancing, sinister morphing— these aren't put on the screen by the movie projector, they're put there by you. The projector gives you the raw materials, but you create the living, moving cinema. You are the genius behind special effects.

Your genius at making motion is hardly exhausted by Exner's simple display. Other displays reveal more of your talents. Let's look at a few of them.

In 1912, Max Wertheimer reported a clever variation on Exner's display. He made the first dot one color and the second dot a different color. The question is, what do you construct? One object or two? And if one, how is it colored? Suppose, for instance, that the first dot is green and the second red. Do you see a green dot that moves and then, at the last moment, turns red? Just when do you switch colors?

What you see, if the ISI is appropriate, is a single dot that moves from left to right. It's green for the first half of the motion and red for the rest.

Fair enough. You split the difference and give equal time to both colors. But something about this might bother you. If you see the moving dot turn from green to red at the half-way point, then it turns red *before* the red dot ever comes on. So how do you know to make it turn red? Do you have ESP, or can you look into the future?

In fact this is no more mysterious than your other constructions that we've discussed. Think of it this way. Suppose that we hook up a photometer to a clock, and measure the display with it. The description we get is something like this. At time 1 a light with most energy in middle wavelengths appears briefly at position 1. Then nothing. Then at time 2 a light with most energy in long wavelengths appears briefly at position 2.

The description you construct is different. A green dot appears at some time, moves to the right for a while, turns red as it continues to move, and later disappears.

What does this show? Simply, as we've found many times before, that you're not a photometer, nor a photometer with an attached clock. What you construct is typically more sophisticated than, and certainly different from, what a photometer and clock construct.

But still, you might feel, this is different. In this case time is involved, and we see something change color before it should.

But it's not different. You construct the 3D space you see, you construct the motions you see in that space, and therefore you construct the time sequence of events you see. Space and time are, in this sense, on equal footing: you construct both. If what you construct doesn't match the constructions of photometers, clocks, and rulers, that's no surprise. That's what you always do. And that's why you inhabit a much richer visual world, and have far more flexible and intelligent interactions with that world, than a photometer or clock. It's not that you've got it wrong because you disagree with the photometer and clock, it's that the photometer and clock aren't sophisticated enough to see what you do.

In Exner's display you construct motion in a straight line. But you can do more. In 1907, P. E. Linke found that you can construct motion over curved paths. Suppose, for instance, that you view the following display:

First we flash a dot at the position marked by the circle. Then we flash a curve, as shown. Then we flash a dot at the position marked by the X. With the appropriate timing of flashes, you construct a single dot and move it over the curve.

In 1916, Vittorio Benussi found that you also construct curved motions when no curve is flashed. In Exner's display, for instance, it's enough to place an obstruction in the way of straight-line motion:

The square remains on throughout the display. A dot flashes first at the spot marked by the circle, then at the spot marked by the X. With the right ISIs, you construct a single dot moving from left to right in a curved path above or below the square. Sometimes you make it move in front of or behind the obstructing square.

What you don't do is just as interesting. You don't construct paths with fancy loops and twists. And you don't construct lots of accelerations and decelerations of the object along the path. It's as though these paths and motions are too extravagant. You go instead for simple, or minimal, paths and motions. What exactly simple or minimal amounts to, no one has yet figured out, although there have been interesting proposals. You prefer a straight line and uniform velocity, but if this isn't open to you then you usually create a curved path with just one arc. Despite substantial work on this topic, we're still missing basic insights. With this disclaimer registered, we can state the following provisional rule:

Rule 29. Create the simplest possible motions.

Think of this rule, and each rule we've discussed, more as a topic for further research than as an ironclad truth.

Exner's display and its variants flash just one dot at a time. What happens if we flash two at a time? Josef Ternus checked it out in 1926 with this display:

First two dots flash at the spots marked by circles. Then two dots flash at the spots marked by X's. Notice that in the middle a dot flashes twice at the same spot.

You construct two different motions for this display. The first is *group motion*: two dots move together rigidly from left to right. The second is *element motion*: The dot in the middle stays put, and the dot on the left jumps around it from left to right.

Which motion you see depends on the timing of the flashes. If each flash lasts about a fifth of a second, and the ISI is a fiftieth of a second, then you see element motion. If the ISI is longer, say more than a tenth of a second, then you see group motion.

Why the ISI matters to you in this way is still a subject of some debate. Perhaps you have two different ways to construct motion: *short-range* and *long-range*. If the ISI is short, then your short-range motion maker takes precedence, and it says that the dot in the middle stays put. That forces you to make the dot on the left do a big jump from left to right around this unmoving center dot. So you see element motion. If instead the ISI is long, then your short-range motion maker shuts up. In particular, it doesn't say that the middle dot stays put. This frees up the long-range motion maker to make both dots move together in synchrony. So you see group motion.

Your constructions are typically multilayered: you use your own constructions as the raw materials for yet new levels of construction, and you repeat this to create many levels. Although you do this all the time, a particularly clear example is a Ternus display made with subjective dots:

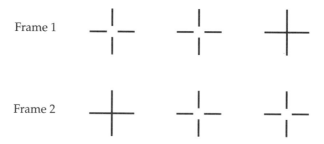

For Frame 1 you construct subjective dots on the left and middle, for Frame 2 on the middle and right. When we flash these frames, you construct motion for these subjective dots. As before, you make either group motion, in which the two dots translate together from left to right, or you make element motion, in which the dot in the middle stays put and the dot on the left jumps from left to right around it. Which motion you make depends again on the timing of the flashes. Here it's clear that you construct motion out of raw materials, namely the dots, that are themselves your construction. But what is clear here is also true nonetheless for the regular Ternus display. There too you construct the dots and then use them as raw materials to construct motion.

Showing you two dots at a time, as we've just seen, offers you more room for creative constructions than showing you just one. Paul von Schiller, in 1933, found another way that two dots offer you more creative freedom, in the following display:

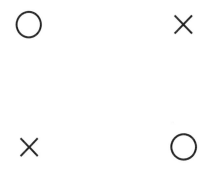

First we flash together two dots, one in the upper left corner and one in the lower right corner. Then we again flash two dots, this time one in the upper right corner and one in the lower left corner. For this display you construct two different motions. Either you move the dots up and down in straight lines, or you move them side to side in straight lines:

What you don't do is construct motions like these:

These motions make two dots merge into one, and leave one dot unmatched. You prefer to conserve objects as much as possible when you construct motion. You don't want to make two objects magically turn into one, and have another object magically appear, when instead you could just make two objects total, and conserve them over the two frames.

> **Rule 30.** When making motion, construct as few objects as possible, and conserve them as much as possible.

In 1985, Vilyanur Ramachandran and Stuart Anstis put together several of von Schiller's displays in synchrony:

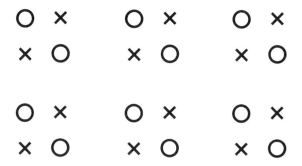

Here we have six of von Schiller's displays going at once to form one big display. If we show, repeatedly, the two frames of this big display, then you construct motion in each one of the six displays as before: motion up and down, or side to side. But here's the surprise: You make them all do the same motion. If one of the six goes up and down, then all of them go up and down. If, as you keep watching the display, one of them switches so that its motion is side to side, then all of them switch and go side to side. You prefer global coherence of motion.

Rule 31. Construct motion to be as uniform over space as possible.

So far we've considered displays where you construct translations. You're good at rotations as well. Max Wertheimer demonstrated this in 1912 with this display:

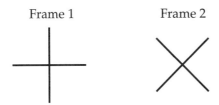

Frame 1   Frame 2

If you view these two frames repeatedly, 1–2–1–2–..., what you construct is a rotating windmill. Sometimes you make it turn clockwise. Then suddenly you switch and make it turn counterclockwise. You go back and forth between these two motions, making one for a few seconds and then the other, and showing no real preference between them.

Then in 1986 Stuart Anstis and Vilyanur Ramachandran tried this variant of Wertheimer's display:

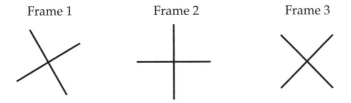

Frame 1   Frame 2   Frame 3

There is a new frame 1. Notice that counterclockwise motion, from frame 1 to frame 2, requires more rotation than clockwise motion: sixty degrees for counterclockwise and thirty degrees for clockwise. You prefer the smallest possible motion. So you create clockwise motion from frame 1 to frame 2. Now you get frame 3. Which motion should you make from frame 2 to frame 3—clockwise or counterclockwise? Both require a rotation of forty-five degrees, so your preference for smaller motion doesn't decide the issue. But here's what you do: You choose to continue the clockwise motion you started from frame 1 to frame 2. So you make this display rotate clockwise all the time. You never switch to counterclockwise. It's as though you invest your motions with inertia, so that once they start in a certain direction you tend to continue them that way.

This inertia decays with time. After all, in Wertheimer's display you do switch between clockwise and counterclockwise motions, holding one interpretation for just a few seconds before switching. The reason you never switch in Anstis and Ramachandran's display is that, as you repeatedly see the frames 1–2–3–1–2–3– . . . , you repeatedly construct clockwise motion between frames 1 and 2, and between frames 3 and 1, since this motion is smallest. This repeatedly renews the inertia for clockwise motion, and this inertia doesn't decay before it's renewed again by another repetition of frames 1 and 2, and of frames 3 and 1.

Have you ever noticed, while watching covered wagons rolling along in an old western, that the wagon wheels and their spokes sometimes spin the wrong direction? A wagon is moving, say, to the right, but its wheels spin as though the wagon should be moving left. A very strange effect, one that might make you wonder if the wagon was broken or if the movie got messed up somehow.

In fact the wagon and the movie are fine. You're the one who makes the spokes turn the wrong way. And the rules you use to do this are the ones we've just discussed. The movie projector shows you a bunch of still shots of the wagon. In one still the spokes are in some position. In the next still the spokes are in the slightly rotated position that they should be if the wagon is moving to the right. However, the part of your visual intelligence that handles this kind of motion "notices" that if it makes the spokes rotate the other way, as though the wagon were going left, then it can make a smoother and smaller motion of the spokes. As far as it's concerned, that settles the matter, and it constructs the backward motion. It doesn't notice that this construction conflicts with constructions, done elsewhere by other parts of your visual intelligence, which make the whole wagon move in the other direction. Sometimes the visual experts which compose your visual intelligence fail to communicate with each other. Wagon wheels that rotate the wrong way are one result.

Another example of your prowess with rotations was discovered in 1937 by J. Brown and A. Voth:

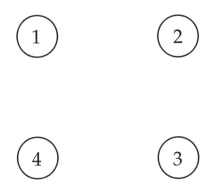

Four dots flash, one after another, at the four corners of an imaginary square. You construct two different motions. If the flashes and ISIs are longer, then you construct straight-line motions from 1 to 2, then 2 to 3, 3 to 4 , 4 to 1, and so on. But if the flashes and ISIs are shorter, then you construct one continuous smooth motion in a circle. These are quite different constructions. The first has straight paths and sharp changes in direction, the second has one curved path and no sharp changes in direction. Which you choose is, for reasons not yet known, entirely a matter of the timing.

How you construct rotations depends on the context. In 1929, Karl Duncker placed a light on the rim of an unseen wheel, and then rolled the wheel. You see the light not as rotating, but as bouncing something like a ball:

This motion is called a *cycloid*. Duncker then added a second light to the wheel, right at the hub, and rolled it again. Now you construct a completely different motion for the light on the rim. You make it rotate around the hub light, and you make the hub light travel in a straight line:

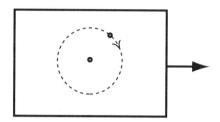

But, as the psychologists John Rubin and Whitman Richards found in 1988, this second light doesn't need to be right at the hub. You can put it almost anywhere, as long as it translates in a straight line at the right velocity; in each case, you still make the rim light rotate, but now around an imaginary hub.

In displays with two or more dots, like Duncker's, you often create two kinds of motion at the same time. The first is a global motion of all the dots together. The second is a motion of each dot relative to this global motion. In Duncker's display, for instance, the global motion is a uniform translation of the two dots together, indicated in the figure by a box with an arrow. The motion of the rim dot relative to this global motion is pure rotation, indicated by the circle with an arrow. The motion of the hub dot relative to the global motion is, in Duncker's display, zero.

It's not yet known what rules you use to divide motion into global and relative components. You probably use several. The psychologists James Cutting and Dennis Proffitt, for instance, suggested in 1982 that you divide motion so as to minimize both common and relative motions. This nicely predicts what you see in many displays, but not in the displays of Duncker and of Rubin and Richards: in these you minimize common motion, by making it uniform translation, but you don't minimize both common and relative motions together. If you did, you'd see both dots rotate about a point halfway between them. Here again is an interesting topic for research.

How and where we cut our hair changes all the time, and lately the trend has been away from the old-style barbershop. But there are still enough of them around that you've probably seen one sporting the traditional barber pole, with its rotating dark and white stripes. If so, you may have noticed, as did the psychologist J. P. Gilford in 1929, that its stripes move in a strange way:

As shown on the left, the barber pole turns in place about its long axis. But, as shown on the right, the stripes seem to move up. They don't turn with the pole. Why do you create such a paradoxical motion?

The answer to this lies in how you solve the so-called *aperture problem*, a problem first described in 1911 by the psychologist Pleikart Stumpf. We can pose the problem this way:

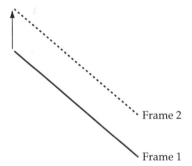
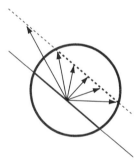

Suppose that you view a videotape of a line. Its positions at Frame 1 and Frame 2 are as shown on the left. In this case, the motion you construct between frames is depicted by the arrow. It looks natural enough. But now suppose that you can't see the line in its entirety; all you see is the part that lies in a circular aperture, as shown on the right. Now, since you can't see the endpoints of the line, you have countless motions you could create. A few are depicted by arrows. Which motion should you construct? That is one instance of the aperture problem.

In this instance you construct the smallest motion, the one depicted by the short arrow orthogonal to the line. So you see the line move without sliding at all along its length. This differs from what you construct on the left, where you see both orthogonal and sliding motion.

The aperture problem is not limited to straight lines. It can arise with curves as well:

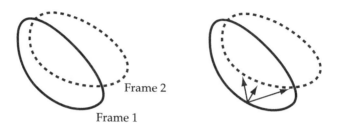

Frame 2

Frame 1

On the left are two frames of a curve. On the right are three possible motions you could construct for just one point of the curve. Clearly there are countless possible motions for this point, and for every other point on the curve. Which do you construct?

In 1982, Ellen Hildreth discovered an elegant rule of construction that you often use. Notice that you must construct a motion of the entire curve. As we've seen, we can represent the motion at each point on a curve by an arrow whose tail lies on the point, and whose direction and length indicate the motion of that point. So we can represent the complete motion you construct as a collection of arrows, one arrow for each point on the curve. This collection of arrows is called a *velocity field*. Here's one example:

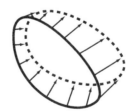

So to construct a motion for this curve means to construct a velocity field along the curve. And here's a rule you often use to do this:

Rule 32. Construct the smoothest velocity field.

"Smoothest" means the field in which arrows change least in direction and length as you go around the curve. Hildreth proved that there is always a unique smoothest velocity field, so long as the curve isn't perfectly straight. This is great, since it means that if you use this rule to construct velocity fields, you don't have to worry that it will give you more than one answer to choose from.

Hildreth also showed that this rule solves the puzzle of the barber pole. The smoothest velocity field has the stripes moving straight up, just as you see them move. To make the stripes go around the pole, rather than up the pole, would require a velocity field that is much less smooth. And that's against your rule. Hildreth showed that many other motions you construct, even though at first they seem paradoxical, like the barber pole, can easily be explained by this rule.

At the heart of this rule is this principle: The motion you construct at one point depends on the motion you construct at nearby points. It must, if you construct the smoothest velocity field. Smoothness is a relation; in this case, a relation between motions at different points.

Now it makes sense for you to construct motion this way if the points whose motions you smooth are on the same object. After all, you construct each object to be a coherent, and coherently moving, unit of your visual world. But what if the points are on different objects? Then it doesn't make sense to smooth their motions: you construct different objects, in part, so that the motions you give them can be independent.

So we see once again that constructing motion and constructing objects go hand in hand. Your decision about how to carve the visual world into objects interacts with your decision about which motions should together be smoothed.

Remember that scene in *Terminator 2* where Schwarzenegger says "Hasta la vista, baby," blows the frozen terminator into a million little pieces, and then watches in horror as the pieces slowly melt together and reform the terminator? The sophisticated special effects in that scene, called warping and morphing, exploit your visual penchant to construct smooth motions and coherent objects. To create a morphing effect, the animators choose an initial and final image. Then, using interpolation algorithms, they create a sequence of images which gradually, one small step at a time, transform the initial image into the final one. When you view the sequence, your visual intelligence then creates the smooth motion from one image to the next, with the result, in *Terminator 2*, that you see metal slowly transforming into a person. Your visual intelligence doesn't know that metal can't transform into people; it just knows that it can create smoothly changing objects from the sequence of images it's viewing—and so it does. And that's just great, for then we get to see and enjoy the impossible.

An interesting method to explore the interaction between the construction of objects and motions was designed in 1982 by Ted Adelson and Tony Movshon. First they created displays in which a series of lines, called a *grating*, slid under a circular aperture. Here are two examples:

The arrow by each grating indicates the motion that you always construct for that grating: a motion orthogonal to its lines (just as you do for a single line). Then they superposed these two gratings to create displays that look like plaids:

The question is, what motion do you construct? Do you see the two gratings slide past each other, as they each move independently in their own directions? This possibility is depicted on the left. Or do you integrate the two gratings into one coherently moving object? This possibility is depicted on the right.

The answer: You integrate, as on the right. You see the two gratings move together, in the direction of the arrow, as a single rigid object.

But this case is special, since the two gratings are identical except for orientation. What happens if the two gratings differ in size, contrast, depth, or color?

Adelson and Movshon found that if they differ a lot in size, then you don't integrate them into one object. Instead you see the gratings slide past each other, as shown here:

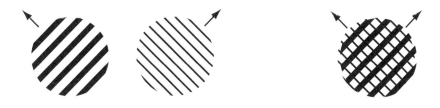

Similarly, Adelson and Movshon found that if the gratings differ a lot in contrast, then you don't integrate them:

And if, in stereo displays, the gratings appear at different depths, then again you don't integrate them. The same is true if they appear at different depths due to transparency:

On the left two gratings are superposed with no change in lightness where they intersect; you create one coherent motion. On the right two gratings are superposed with a change in lightness at intersections that you interpret as transparency, and therefore as differing depths. So you create two independent motions.

Finally, if the two gratings have the same hue (and are otherwise identical as well), then you integrate them and create one motion. If their hues differ, then the greater the difference the greater is your inclination to create independent motions.

All these studies with plaids show that you coordinate your creations of motions and objects, and that, in this process, you intelligently use size, contrast, depth, and color.

In some cases, you also use the powerful principle of *rigid motion*. This can be seen in many striking demonstrations:

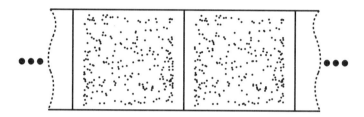

Here, for instance, are two frames from a movie in which dots appear at slightly different positions from one frame to the next. From these shifts in position you create motion in two dimensions. Nothing new there, of course; as we discussed, Exner knew that in 1875. Here's what's new: In this display you also create a 3D cylinder, place the dots on the surface of that cylinder, and make the cylinder and dots rotate rigidly about a vertical axis. An impressive act of creation, as impressive as any we've seen so far.

The medium of a book fails me here. It doesn't let me show you the display so you can witness your creativity firsthand. The closest you can get right now is to stereo fuse the two frames of the figure. You'll then create a 3D cylinder and place the dots on its surface. What you'll miss is the experience of rigid motion in three dimensions. Also, you'll miss the almost palpable surface of the cylinder. It's so vivid, I feel like I can reach out and touch it. You'll just have to check out the display on my web page.

You aren't, of course, limited to making cylinders. If I show you the appropriate displays of moving dots, you can create just about any shape—spheres, cubes, cars, faces, elephants, you name it. You are, however, very picky about the display. The dots have to move just right, or you refuse to create much of anything. When I made the cylinder display, for instance, I had to write a program that carefully put the dots in just the right places from frame to frame. Doing it by hand is out of the question.

Why are you so picky? And why do you create the shapes and motions that you do? As always, in principle you have countless options, but you narrow them down to one, or a few. What rules guide you?

An answer first proposed in 1953 by Hans Wallach and Donald O'Connell, and seconded by many psychologists since, is the rigidity principle. It can be stated as follows:

> **Rule 33.** If possible, and if other rules permit, interpret image
> motions as projections of rigid motions in three dimensions.

The idea of rigid motion is simple: Points in space move rigidly if all distances between them remain constant during the motion.

So the rule is this. As you go about the business of creating visual objects and motions, you check whether it's possible to create rigid objects and motions in three dimensions that are compatible with what you've constructed so far in two dimensions. It's only possible if the rigid motions in three dimensions project to what you have in two dimensions. If they do, this is such a special event that, most of the time, you decide to create the rigid object and motion.

This sounds nice in principle, but how can you do this in practice? How can you check whether a rigid construct is possible? An elegant answer, in the form of a theorem, was given in 1977 by the psychologist Shimon Ullman. He considered the case where you have a discrete sequence of images, such as the frames of a videotape.

> **Ullman's Rigidity Theorem.** Suppose you are given three
> frames, each containing at least four points. If the points are
> placed at random in each frame, then the probability is zero
> that they have a rigid interpretation in three dimensions. If
> the points do have a rigid interpretation, then they almost
> surely have exactly two interpretations (which are mirror-
> symmetric).

This means that you need little information, just three frames each having four points, to decide whether to construct a rigid 3D object and its motion, and to succeed if you so decide.

Many internet web pages now offer 3D virtual worlds for visitors to explore. One web site at UCLA, for instance, lets visitors tour through Rome as it was two thousand years ago, viewing its architecture and culture. Another site lets visitors tour the Los Angeles metropolitan area as it is today. These are unguided tours: visitors can go when and where they please throughout the virtual city. The educational advantages are obvious. What high school student wouldn't choose to explore the architecture of ancient Rome firsthand rather than read about it in a book? Immersion is more fun, and an effective method of instruction. These 3D virtual worlds are made possible by new computer languages such as VRML (Virtual Reality Modeling Language). But they are also made possible by your visual genius to construct 3D shapes from motion using rigidity and other similar rules. As you tour through virtual Rome using a mouse and computer screen, your visual intelligence interprets the sequence of changing images on the screen as your movements through a rigid 3D environment. It constructs that 3D environment using the rigidity rule, and constructs your motions through that rigid environment. The virtual Rome you explore and enjoy is a Rome of your own making. Of course, the researchers at UCLA deserve some credit as well. They provide carefully crafted images that trigger your visual constructions.

The rigidity rule and Ullman's theorem are now built into some computer vision systems, allowing them to "see" rigid objects and motions in three dimensions. In fact, many rules we have discussed are now built into computer vision systems. One way researchers test how well these rules model our visual intelligence is to implement them on computers and then compare the performance of the computers to human performance on similar images. The effort is instructive, allowing researchers to refine their understanding of human visual intelligence and to improve the performance of computer vision systems. One practical result of this effort is artificial vision systems of increasing sophistication for industry, home robots, and the visually impaired. At present, computer systems do well at constructing 3D shapes and motions. What they can't do well is recognize objects. Some systems can recognize various aircraft, others can recognize various tanks. But none can recognize the variety of objects that even a toddler can. Once this barrier is broken, watch for computer vision to be a multibillion-dollar industry that affects all aspects of our lives and culture.

The rigidity principle is powerful and widely applicable. But, like all rules, it has its limitations. A fascinating example of this is provided by so-called *biological motion*. In Prague, Czechoslovakia, a dance company called the Black Light Theater created an innovative form of dance in the 1960s. They dressed entirely in black. They attached to their heads and major joints small patches of material that glows under black lights. When the dancers stood still on stage, the audience saw nothing but a random assortment of glowing dots. But when the dancers moved, suddenly their forms and actions were easy to see, just from the motions of the dots.

Then in the 1970s the psychologist Gunnar Johansson developed a similar method. He placed small lights at the joints of actors, and filmed them in the dark so that only the lights were visible:

On the left is a typical frame from one of Johansson's movies. On the right is the proper connection of dots.

What's remarkable about these movies is that you create so much from so little. If the actor walks, jogs, dances, climbs stairs, or does push-ups, you can tell with no problem. You create all these activities just from the motions of a few dots.

This has, understandably, attracted much attention and research. Some of the more interesting findings are these. You need to see the movie only a fifth of a second to accurately discern the action of the actor. If the actor is someone you know, you can often recognize him or her just from the moving dots. If you don't know the actor, you can still usually determine the actor's gender. Even cats are pretty good with such movies made of other cats.

Here's the issue these displays raise for the rigidity principle. You have no trouble creating 3D objects and motions when you view Johansson's movies. But in these movies you can't have groups of four points that move together rigidly. The knee and ankle points, for instance, move rigidly, as do the knee and hip, but the hip and ankle do not. According to Ullman's theorem, if you are to use the rigidity principle you must be able to create groups of four rigid points. And you can't do that in Johansson's displays. But that doesn't stop you from constructing 3D objects and motions.

Shall we conclude from this that the rigidity principle is irrelevant to human vision? No. To do so would be a logical error. In fact, the most we can conclude is that if the rigidity principle is used by human vision to construct objects and motions in 3D (and I think it is), then it's not the only principle so used.

The question then arises, what other rules or principles might we use?

An interesting possibility is raised by looking at how our legs and arms move when we walk. Notice that individual links are rigid, like the upper leg or the lower leg, and that they tend to swing in a single plane for much of their motion. They are rigid because of our bones, and they swing in a single plane because of the nature of our joints and our tendency to minimize effort. This suggests the following "planarity" rule:

Rule 34. If possible, and if other rules permit, interpret image motions as projections of 3D motions that are rigid and planar.

Does this rule allow you to construct biological motion, where rigidity alone does not? Indeed it does. Although rigidity alone, as Ullman proved, requires four rigid points to construct a 3D object, rigidity and planarity together, it's easily proved, require only two. And pairs of points, rigidly linked, are exactly what we need to construct biological motion. This result, using rigidity and planarity together, has been implemented in computer vision systems, and effectively constructs biological motions from displays like Johansson's. Moreover, experiments with human subjects indicate that if displays like Johansson's are altered so that rigid/planar interpretations are not possible, then often you have trouble constructing anything at all.

But not always. There are displays for which neither rigidity alone nor rigidity with planarity will work, and yet you easily construct 3D objects and motions. So if you use rigidity, or rigidity with planarity, then you also use other rules as well: perhaps rules about smoothness of motion, or about motion having certain dynamical constraints. This is yet another area of interest to vision researchers.

It's also of great interest in the motion picture and computer gaming industries, where animated people, animals, and aliens pop up all the time. Movie viewers and game players expect compelling action from the aliens and animated heroes they watch. Give them boxy, jerky motions and watch ticket sales and game sales go nowhere. Give them believable animation and you might have a hit. The problem is that we don't know precisely how human vision constructs and judges biological motions, so that it's not yet easy to synthesize compelling displays. Most attempts end up looking boxy and jerky. So, many animators use the same trick as the Black Light Theater, only more high-tech. They place radio or infrared emitters on the main joints of an actor who performs the actions that are required of the animated creature. Then they use the recorded 3D motions of these emitters to animate the creatures. One of the big attractions of the 1997 Siggraph Convention at the Los Angeles Convention Center was a live demonstration of this technique. Two talented dancers performed live, onstage, with small emitters attached to their joints. At the same time, on large television screens, two Gumby-like animated creatures danced precisely the same moves as the live dancers, including overhead lifts. The dancing of the Gumby characters was realistic because it just was the dancing of the live dancers. Until we better understand our visual intelligence, this technique may be the best way to create compelling animations.

Displays composed entirely of dots, like Johansson's, are a useful tool to probe how you construct motion, primarily because they are simple and therefore easier to analyze. But to understand the full extent of your prowess, researchers must move beyond dots. With the advent of computers and graphics software, it's now possible to do so—to create displays that are complex and yet precisely controlled.

Dan Kersten and his collaborators have done just that. In an elegant series of experiments, they have studied how you construct, in coordinated fashion, shapes, motions, shadows, and light sources. They find, as usual, that you're in general quite clever. But they also find, and this is the surprise, that in some cases you're not clever at all.

First your cleverness:

In this display, you see a solid sphere start at position 1, move smoothly along a diagonal of the checkerboard to position 2, and continue back and forth between these two positions. You see the sphere's shadow move smoothly in step with the sphere. The sphere maintains a constant height over the checkerboard as it moves.

So far nothing new. Then Kersten made a small change in the display. The sphere still moved as before between positions 1 and 2, but the shadow moved smoothly to a different location, as shown here:

In this case you no longer make the sphere move back along a diagonal at constant height. Instead you make it move to the right, and you make it ascend higher above the checkerboard until it reaches position 2. Then you make it move left and descend until it reaches position 1, and so on.

If you trace the path of the sphere on the display screen, you find that it is identical in both cases. But the motion you construct in three dimensions is quite different, and depends not only on the sphere, but also on how you interpret the relation between it and its shadow.

Kersten followed this up with another variation:

The sphere moves in a straight line on the display as before, but the shadow moves along arcs, as shown by the dashed contour. Now you make the sphere move in three dimensions not in a straight line, but on a path that curves back and forth in depth as it ascends. You cleverly coordinate your construction of lights, shadows, and motions in space. And a key rule that you use is this:

Rule 35. Light sources move slowly.

After all, you could in principle interpret the motion of the shadow not as due to motion of the sphere, but as due to motion of the light source. Then you could see the sphere move in a straight path while the light source bounced around. But you don't like to create light sources that move quickly. You prefer to make objects move, not light sources.

Indeed, you are obstinate about this. So obstinate that you at times cease to be clever. Kersten took this same display and put some blocks on the checkerboard. He arranged that the shadows cast by these blocks shifted in synchrony with the motion of the sphere's shadow. This permits you in principle to construct a consistent interpretation of the display in which the sphere moves on a straight path, and the motion of all shadows is due to motion of a single light source. But you refuse to do this. Instead you construct an inconsistent interpretation: you see the moving shadows of the blocks as due to a moving light source (what else can you do, since the blocks don't move?), but you continue to see the sphere move on the same curving path as before, as though it's illuminated by an unmoving source.

Rules can be useful guides. But this time slavish adherence to one plunges you into inconsistency.

Kersten finds other lapses of cleverness. He finds, for instance, that he can change the shadow into a thin yellow square and, as long as it moves appropriately, you still use it to modify the motion of the sphere just as you do with a normal shadow. So you don't bother about the consistency of the shape or color of a shadow. You focus on its motion. If it moves properly, then for your constructions of motion in space it's a shadow, almost regardless of its color and shape. For other constructions, of course, you might take note of its color and shape.

Just how you coordinate color and motion has been a topic of interest at least since 1911, when Pleichardt Stumpf discovered that the motion of a colored object against a background is hard to see if the two have similar luminances. We've already seen that activity in cortical area V4 correlates well with your perception of color, and that activity in V5 correlates well with your perception of motion. These two areas appear to be parts of two different pathways of visual processing: the *magnocellular* pathway processes motion, luminance, depth, and coarse form; the *parvocellular* pathway processes color and fine form, but not much motion or depth. The anatomical segregation of the two pathways is clear, beginning at the retina, continuing through the lateral geniculate nucleus of the thalamus, through cortical areas V1 and V2, and at least up to areas V4 and V5. The functional segregation of the two pathways, especially after area V1, is a matter of much debate, with some researchers arguing that they interact little and others that they interact a lot.

Tom Albright and Karen Dobkins, among others, have argued for a higher degree of interaction. Their evidence is based in part on displays like this:

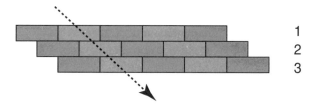

Here are three frames from a movie, labelled 1, 2, 3. Each frame has a band of red and green patches, all of the same luminance. From one frame to the next this band shifts horizontally by a precise amount: half the width of a patch. You view the display through an aperture so that you can't see the left and right ends of the band. The question is, which way will you make the band move, left or right? The answer is that you prefer to make it move to the right. By so doing you match green patches with green and red with red. In the process of making objects and motion, you prefer to make objects that don't change color. But this means that color affects your construction of motion, even if there are no luminance differences around. And this suggests that the parvocellular pathway, which "does" color, affects the magnocellular pathway, which "does" motion; or that the magnocellular pathway itself carries some color information.

That's one direction of interaction: color affects how you make motion. What about the other direction? Can motion affect how you create color?

Indeed it can. One way to show this is with *flicker colors*, discovered in 1826 by the French monk Bénédict Prevost, and rediscovered at least a dozen times since. The most famous rediscovery was in 1894 by C.E. Benham, who devised and sold a popular disk with this black-and-white pattern:

The "Benham's top," still available in some stores, is mounted on a spindle so you can spin it about its center. If you spin it counterclockwise at modest speed, you see an artificial spectrum: the outermost arcs form red rings, the next arcs form green rings, the next pale blue, and the innermost dark violet. If you spin it clockwise, the sequence of colors reverses, from red at the innermost to dark violet at the outermost.

A century later there is still no consensus on the nature of flicker colors. Are they, like the squeaky voice of one who has inhaled helium, just artifacts of abnormal input? Or do they reveal important aspects of your normal creation of color?

The topic has attracted much research. Among the interesting findings are that the honey bee also sees flicker colors, and that in humans both retinal and cortical processes are involved in their production. More research is of course required. But the phenomenon of flicker colors is one way that your creation of motion affects your creation of color.

I stumbled onto a second way in the summer of 1991. With classes over I had some time to think, and I wondered if motion could somehow trigger us to see neonlike colors. Over lunch I devised a method: Smoothly translate a few hundred small red dots together over a white screen; as any dot enters a virtual circle, about an inch in diameter, in the middle of the screen, change the dot from red to green; as it leaves the virtual circle, change it back from green to red. I predicted that I would see a neonlike green disk in the middle of the screen.

I was wrong. After lunch I hurried back to my office, made the display, and saw nothing. No neon disk, just dots changing color between red and green. I was disappointed and decided to get back to my other projects.

Then a variation occurred to me: Don't move the dots, move the virtual circle. So, as one last shot, I put a few hundred red dots on a white background, and didn't move the dots at all. Instead, from frame to frame, I moved the virtual circle within which the dots were painted green. Here are two frames from the movie:

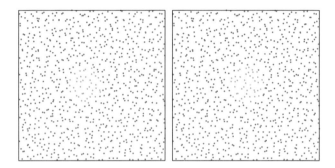

The frame on the left has nine hundred dots placed at random. The frame on the right has the same dots placed at exactly the same locations. So no dots move. The only difference between frames is in dot color: a different set of dots is colored green on the right than on the left.

This movie exceeded my expectations. In it I see a glowing green disk, much like a green spotlight, moving over the field of red dots. The green disk has an attractive ghostly glow, and a clear subjective border surrounding it. Too bad I can't show it to you here (but it's on the web!). You can get the idea by stereo-fusing the two frames shown above. You'll see a green disk floating above the field of red dots. The color and border, however, aren't as striking as in the movie.

This works with limitless combinations of colors and virtual shapes. Given the right displays you easily create, for instance, glowing red squares or glowing blue stripes. You can even create glowing shapes in three dimensions. My favorite is a display in which I see a glowing blue cigar rotating in space.

Sometimes you create a different interpretation of these displays. Instead of seeing the green disk (or other colored shape) in front, you see it behind:

As illustrated here, the computer screen is like an off-white sheet of paper, and all dots are like holes punched in the paper. Through the holes you see a red sheet of paper behind the white one. And sandwiched between these two sheets you see a moving green disk. Of course, the sheets don't look vertically and horizontally offset from each other as in the illustration. I've offset them just to show more clearly what you see.

This is an elaborate construction from just dots changing color. But there's more. When you see the disk in front, you make its surface glowing, transparent, and a desaturated green. But when you see it behind, you make its surface unglowing, opaque, and a saturated green. In this construction, your visual intelligence coordinates the qualities of the surface with the depths at which it's placed.

My collaborator, Carol Cicerone, and I call this effect *dynamic color spreading*. And what you do to create it is impressive. You create motion, even though all dots in the display stay put. You create an object and give it a shape, either in two dimensions or in three. You often, though not always, endow that object with a border, sometimes smooth and sometimes with sharp corners. You also endow that object with a surface of a definite quality, either opaque or transparent, either saturated or desaturated. You place that object in space, either in front of a white sheet or behind it. You move that object in space, either rotating it or translating it or both. And all this from a few dots that change color but never move. Your visual intelligence once again does so much from so little.

Have you ever stopped for a red light, with no other cars in sight, and fumed at the stupidity of traffic lights that waste your time and gas for nothing? Imagine if instead the traffic lights saw you coming, when you were still fifty yards away, and instantly gave you the green light.

This is not a distant dream. Computer vision systems are being developed that use rules from this chapter, and other rules, to track vehicles, detect jams and accidents, and control traffic lights. A system developed by the psychologist Scott Richman, for the California Department of Transportation, uses a video camera to capture digitized movies of traffic. Here's a typical digitized frame from such a movie:

Of course it's no problem for you, with the vast resources of your visual intelligence, to view a scene like this, find the cars, and determine how fast they're moving. It's another matter to put that intelligence into a computer. Several problems that Richman faced are evident from this picture: clutter, trees moving in the wind, shadows dancing on the road, cars in front hiding cars behind. A sophisticated analysis of motion, using several frames at once, allows Richman's system to distinguish the motion of cars from that of trees and shadows. Below we see the cars discovered by his system, together with small arrows indicating their velocities:

Richman's system can track cars through shadows, a feat that is trivial for our visual intelligence but, heretofore, quite difficult for computer vision systems. It's easy to underestimate our sophistication at constructing visual motion. That is, until we try to duplicate that sophistication on a computer. Then it seems impossible to overestimate it.

SEVEN

THE FEEL OF
A PHANTOM

n 1982, when he was thirty-one, F.A. had a serious accident. The beam of a sailboat fell on his right forearm, crushing it so severely that the arm could not be saved. It was amputated about eight centimeters below the elbow.

After the amputation, F.A. still experienced having a right hand, and still felt that he could move this phantom hand. This isn't uncommon in amputees. Many report experiencing a phantom limb after amputation, and many report that, at times, they feel pain in the phantom limb. The pain isn't ethereal or mystical; it can be so persistent and excruciating that it drives some to suicide. The treatment of phantom-limb pain is often difficult. A charley horse in a normal leg can be cured by walking it off, but what about a charley horse in a phantom leg?

For F.A. the phantom hand was vivid and, often, "telescoped": he experienced the hand as being attached directly to the stump of his right arm, with no forearm in between.

It has been known at least since the mid-1800s, and no doubt long before, that touching the stump of an amputated arm often causes two sensations: one is the normal sensation you expect from touching skin; the second is a referred sensation, a feeling that the phantom hand is also being touched.

F.A. was no exception. Ten years after the amputation, his experience of referred sensations was carefully tested by the psychologist Vilyanur S. Ramachandran and colleagues. They found, as expected, that touching certain points on F.A.'s stump made him feel a touch as well on his phantom hand. They also found something less expected. F.A. had, above his stump, two systematic maps of his phantom hand:

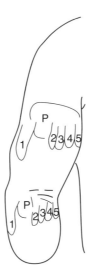

This figure shows the maps and their positions on his arm. The lower map was about six centimeters above the stump. The numbers on this map denote fingers of the phantom hand. If F.A. was touched anywhere in the region labeled 1, he felt a touch on the thumb of his phantom hand as well. If he was touched anywhere in region 5, he also felt a touch on the pinkie of his phantom hand. If he was touched in region P, he felt a touch as well on his palm.

The second map was about thirteen centimeters above his stump. As with the first map, if F.A. was touched in the region labeled 1, he also felt a touch on his phantom thumb, and so on. The two maps are, as you can see, similar. And they are separate. The skin of his arm between the maps had normal sensitivity. But if F.A. was touched anywhere in this area, he felt no sensation in his phantom hand.

As is common with amputees, F.A. could feel complex sensations in his phantom hand. Warm water, for instance, placed on one of his maps felt like warm water on his phantom hand. And it is common that vibration, pricking, heat, cold, and even breezes on a map are felt as the same sensations on the phantom limb.

Ramachandran measured F.A.'s maps every week for four weeks and found them remarkably stable over time. But he also found a simple way to make them change. F.A. reported that he normally felt his phantom hand in a position halfway between pronation (palm down) and supination (palm up), with its fingers slightly curled, as though grasping a vertical pole. Ramachandran immobilized F.A.'s right elbow with a clasp, and asked him to pronate (rotate palm down) his phantom hand. F.A. did so, and a remeasurement of his upper map showed that it had shifted systematically about one centimeter leftward, the same direction as the rotation. In a particularly vivid demonstration of this, a drop of water was placed on the pinkie region of the map; as F.A. pronated his phantom hand he felt the drop of water move from his phantom pinkie to his phantom ring finger. When F.A. then rotated his phantom hand back to its normal (pole-holding) position, the map shifted back to its original position.

There's more. The two maps we've discussed were not the only ones F.A. had. Like many other amputees, he had one more map of his phantom right hand, but this one was on his face, on the lower right side. It was similar to this map on the left side of the face of another amputee, V.Q.:

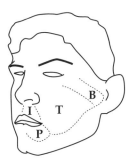

V.Q. was seventeen when his left arm was amputated six centimeters above the elbow. Four weeks later he was tested by Ramachandran and colleagues, who found a systematic map of his phantom hand on his left arm, about seven centimeters above the stump. They also found a map of the phantom hand on his face, on the lower left side, as shown in the drawing. If V.Q. was touched on his face in the area labeled T, he felt the normal sensation on his face, and he felt a touch on his phantom thumb. If touched in the area labeled I, he felt a touch on his phantom index finger; in area B, a touch on the base of his phantom thumb; in area P, a touch on his phantom pinky.

Interesting stuff, you might be thinking, but what's it doing in a book on visual intelligence? This is touch, not vision.

Indeed it is. But my purpose is this. I've argued now at modest length that everything you see you construct. From your barest sensation of color to your fullest perception of a visual scene, you are the creative genius who constructs them all. I've argued for this with examples, and by stating dozens of rules that you use in the constructive process.

But of course I'm after more. I don't want to claim only that you construct what you see. I want to claim that, at a minimum, you also construct all that you hear, smell, taste, and feel. In short, I want to claim that all your sensations and perceptions are your constructions.

And the biggest impediment to buying that claim comes, I think, from touch. Most of us believe that touch gives us direct contact with unconstructed reality. The eyes may fool us, and vision may be construction, but touch grants us a more firm foundation. You look at a table and admit, perhaps, that what you see is your construction. But then, to dispel all doubt, you simply pound on the table. And you believe that settles it, for in that pounding you have direct, not constructed, contact.

But you don't. Touch is every bit the creative process that vision is. When you run your hand over marble and feel its cool hard smoothness, you construct that feel. When you put your hand in your pocket or purse, fumble for your keys, and finally find them, you carve your world of touch into distinct tangible objects, such as keys, through a process no less active than when you carve your visual field into distinct visible objects. And when you, with eyes closed, simply hold out your hand, feel its position and orientation in space, feel the motion and temperature of the ambient air, and feel the tension of your arm muscles holding it out, you create every aspect of this entire complex of "feels."

One evidence of this: You continue to create all these feels even if your arm is amputated. The cases of F.A. and V.Q., and many others, show this quite clearly. And, as we shall see, there is other evidence as well.

And that, in short, is the reason for this brief foray into touch. Most of us have strong prejudices about the direct nature of touch. Strong prejudices need strong counterevidence, and we're now looking at that evidence. So let's get back to it.

Both V.Q. and F.A. had a map of their phantom hand on their face and on their arm above the stump. Touching something warm or cold to these maps led them to feel something warm or cold on the corresponding part of their phantom hand. It's only natural to ask: What happens if you touch something warm to, say, the pinkie of the face map and, at the same time, something cold to the pinkie of the arm map? What will the phantom pinkie feel, warm or cold? When Ramachandran tried this, several patients reported an alternation of sensations: the phantom pinkie felt a wave of cold followed by a wave of warm, and so on. This is analogous to alternating between two different interpretations of the Necker cube. When you construct two equally good interpretations, you alternate between them.

You don't just construct the simple feels, like warm and cold and simple touch. You construct all the complex ones as well. In several patients, Ramachandran found that if a drop of warm water trickled down their face, they also felt it trickle down the length of their phantom arm. In some cases the patient could, with his good hand, point to the trickle as it wandered down the phantom arm. The patient was, of course, pointing into empty space. But he clearly felt a trickle of warm water in that empty space.

What accounts for these maps of the phantom limb that appear after amputation? The explanation, in part, has to do with *somatosensory cortex*, a portion of your brain devoted primarily to processing touch and related sensations:

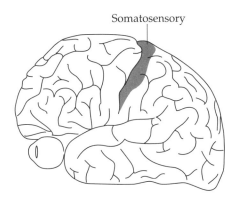

Somatosensory

In the 1930s, Wilder Penfield and his colleagues found that if, using small electric shocks, they stimulated somatosensory cortex in awake patients, these patients reported sensations of touch in parts of their body:

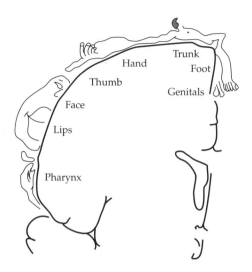

Here's a slice through somatosensory cortex in one hemisphere of the brain, with a map of the touch sensations that Penfield found. Over each bit of cortex is drawn that part of the body which feels touched when the bit of cortex is stimulated. As you can see, stimulating nearby bits of cortex usually makes one feel touched in nearby parts of the body. There is, in fact, a systematic map of the body on the somatosensory cortex. The genitals and feet are modestly hidden deep in the middlemost region. As one moves laterally over the cortex one moves systematically up the body. Some regions of the body get a lot of cortex devoted to them, some just a little; that's why the hand, for instance, is drawn so much bigger than the torso. Regions of the body with larger representation in cortex have better sensitivity and discrimination for touch.

Notice that the cortex devoted to the hand is, on one side, next to cortex devoted to the face and, on the other side, next to cortex devoted to the arm. This suggests an interesting idea. If the hand is amputated, then it can't send neural signals to its bit of cortex. Does this bit then go silent? Or does it instead get signals that go to nearby bits of cortex, namely from the face and arm? If it does, this would explain the maps of the phantom hand on the face and arm. The face and arm regions of cortex "invade" the cortex that normally processes the hand.

This idea was tested in 1994 by Tony T. Yang and colleagues using a technique called *magnetic source imaging*, which allowed them, without opening the skull, to measure brain activity with fine spatial precision. In both amputees that they studied, they found that the face and arm regions had indeed invaded the region that served the amputated hand.

This is of interest in part because it reveals a degree of cortical plasticity in adults that was heretofore unknown. It's also of interest here because it, together with the discoveries of Penfield, indicates that you construct the feeling of touch in each part of your body, and that you can do so for each body part even if that part is amputated.

The argument so far is this. I claim that you construct all you feel. If that claim is true, then you should be able to construct feeling in any body part, even if that part is amputated. And the evidence now strongly indicates that you can.

How about the converse prediction? If a body part is intact but your constructive processes are not, then you should have trouble with touch. This too is a clear prediction of the claim.

And one that has been confirmed. A revealing case is E.C. In December of 1989, when she was sixty-two, E.C. had a stroke that damaged a small bit of parietal cortex in her left hemisphere; the technical name for this bit is area 39 and 40 of Brodmann. After this stroke, she complained that her right hand felt numb, and that she couldn't recognize objects in her purse using this hand.

Nine months later she had a second stroke, this time damaging temporal and occipital cortex of her right hemisphere, and leaving her partly blind in the left half of her visual field.

Clinical tests, conducted in April 1991, showed that E.C. had normal intellect, language, and motor skills. She had trouble remembering visual objects, probably because of her right-hemisphere stroke. And her right hand had tactile agnosia, an inability to recognize objects by touch, probably because of her left-hemisphere stroke.

Her tactile agnosia was confined only to her right hand; her left hand had no trouble recognizing objects. And the problem with the right hand was not that it had no feeling. In fact it was just as good as the left hand in every test of basic touch sensation. Experiments by Catherine Reed and her colleagues showed that it could tell, just as well as the left hand, whether it was being poked by two points or by one point. It could detect vibrations just as well as the left hand. It could discriminate sandpapers, judge weights of objects, judge relative lengths of sticks, judge relative areas of flat objects, judge orientations and relative positions of simple shapes, just as well as the left hand. In short, it had normal sensation.

What it could not do well was recognize objects. All the basic ingredients were there, all the basic touch sensations. But E.C.'s stroke impaired her ability to put it all together, to construct recognizable objects of touch.

We don't normally think of ourselves as constructing objects of touch. We think instead that we feel those keys, that lipstick, that wallet, not by construction but just as they are. But we're fooled again by our constructive prowess. It's only because we're so fast and so effective at constructing objects of touch that it feels to us that we don't construct them at all. It's only when these constructive processes are slowed or badly impaired, as with E.C., that we realize they've been there all along.

So far I've used pathologies to argue my case. But what about those of us with no pathology? Is there clear evidence that we, as well, construct what we feel?

Not nearly as much as there is for vision. But that's simply because touch has, to this point, been studied much less than vision. Fortunately, however, there is an engaging example to tell.

It's the case of the cutaneous rabbit, discovered by accident in the early 1970s by Frank Geldard and Carl Sherrick. They hooked up the forearm of a normal subject to three small vibrators:

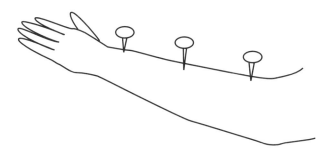

Normally the vibrators each delivered a gentle buzz to the forearm. But one day a technical error changed the experiment. Instead of a gentle buzz, each vibrator delivered a few distinct taps, first the vibrator near the wrist, then the one in the middle of the forearm, and finally the one by the elbow. The subject was surprised, of course, not to feel the usual three buzzes, but even more surprised to feel a series of taps go up his forearm, not just where each vibrator touched his skin, but also on the skin between them. He felt as though a little creature, like a rabbit, were hopping up his arm:

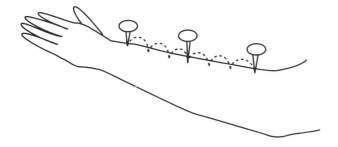

Instead of fixing the technical error, the researchers studied the new effect. They found that they could elicit the rabbit not just on the arm, but just about anywhere on the body. In each case you feel distinct taps on your skin in places where there are no vibrators; so distinct, in fact, that you can point to the places on your skin where these invisible taps occur. Three vibrators aren't required to create the rabbit, only two. If the first vibrator gives two taps, and then the other gives one, you feel the second tap of the first vibrator hit your skin somewhere between the two vibrators. Just where depends on the timing of the taps.

You can create two rabbits at once. Just arrange three vibrators on the skin to form a triangle. Have one of the vibrators give a couple taps, then have the other two vibrators each give a tap. Two rabbits start from the first vibrator; each hops to one of the other two vibrators.

This confirms what we've already found with the phantom limbs: you create what you feel and where in space you feel it. An amputee creates the feel of the phantom hand and places it at a distinct location in empty space. You create the hop of the rabbit and place it at a distinct location on your skin where there's no visible stimulator.

The rabbit shows, moreover, that you create not just the what and where of feels, but also the when. Can you know which way to make the rabbit hop before the second vibrator does its tap? Of course not. This tap tells you which direction to send the rabbit, so you must create the rabbit afterward. But do you feel this tap before you feel the rabbit? No, you feel it afterward. So you create the rabbit after you get this tap, but you experience the rabbit before you experience this tap. You create the timing of the taps that you feel.

Technology is about to usher us into an era of virtual touch. Your power to create what you feel is the foundation for many high-tech products now entering the market, from arcade games that place you not only in virtual visual worlds but also in virtual tactile worlds, to surgi-

cal simulators in which surgeons not only see but also feel the tissues of
the virtual body on which they practice their techniques. Some high-
tech companies now stake their financial futures on your prowess at creating what you feel.

Right now our knowledge of the rules you use to create "feels" lags
far behind our knowledge of such rules for vision. But this gap will soon
shrink as the power and possibilities of virtual touch become common-
place. Already there are harbingers of what is to come. Several companies, for instance, now manufacture joysticks with "force feedback" for
video games at arcades and on home computers. These joysticks actively push and vibrate the hand of the player, inducing the player to create
a tactile reality that, if the software works properly, is in consonance
with the visual reality the player sees. The combination of the two, virtual vision and virtual touch, leads to a much more compelling sense of
immersion into the virtual world. As Immersion Corporation puts it in
its web page:

> Imagine flying a space ship across the galaxy and feeling real-
> istic re-entry forces as you navigate into a planet's atmosphere.
> Imagine driving a race car off the road and feeling the jarring
> and bouncing jolts as you tackle rough terrain. Imagine feel-
> ing g-forces as you pull a tight turn on your simulated F-16
> aircraft. Imagine grabbing an icon in a Windows desktop and
> feeling its weight, or resizing a window and feeling its com-
> pliance. Imagine interacting with another user over the inter-
> net and feeling realistic physical forces as you tug on the same
> piece of cyber-material. The possibilities are endless.

Indeed they are. A library of possibilities, though, is now being
compiled for use in games. Already in the library are specifications for
driving a joystick so that you create the feeling of a revolver, shotgun,
laser pulse, machine gun, tank treads, rough roads, engine hum, air tur-
bulence, sandpaper, ice cubes in a bucket, and more. As virtual tactility
catches on, more and more developers are writing software to induce you
to create new feels as you play their games. And competition is fierce.
Market share will depend critically on the range and quality of feels that
products allow. The range is limited only by the imagination, and the
imagination of Diane Ackerman is quite good:

> After all, our palette of feelings through touch is more elabo-
> rate than just hot, cold, pain, and pressure. Many touch recep-

tors combine to produce what we call a twinge. Consider all the varieties of pain, irritation, abrasion; all the textures of lick, pat, wipe, fondle, knead; all the prickling, bruising, tingling, brushing, scratching, banging, fumbling, kissing, nudging. Chalking your hands before you climb onto uneven parallel bars. A plunge into an icy farm pond on a summer day when the air temperature and body temperature are the same. The feel of a sweat bee delicately licking moist beads from your ankle. Reaching blindfolded into a bowl of Jell-O as part of a club initiation. Pulling a foot out of the mud. The squish of wet sand between the toes. Pressing an angel food cake. The near-orgasmic caravan of pleasure, shiver, pain, and relief that we call a back scratch . . .

This is a challenging range of feels to create. But where there's a market, there's a way.

One convincing experience of virtual tactility will do more than all the arguments I can muster to convince you that you create what you feel. Even with the relatively primitive technology currently available, many report that the primordial sense that you'd better believe what you feel with your fingers, that touch gives you direct contact with unconstructed reality, gets shaken to the core. Howard Rheingold reported, after playing a virtual violin in Grenoble, France: "It twanged something inside me that the most vivid visual illusions alone had failed to reach." So if the brief arguments of this chapter don't convince you that you create what you feel, stop by your local video arcade.

Need surgery for an injured knee or an inflamed gallbladder? You'll be glad to know that there are endoscopic and laparoscopic surgical techniques that require only tiny incisions, and that greatly reduce the postoperative pain and recovery time. The surgeon inserts through the incision a long thin tube with tiny instruments at one end, and expertly manipulates those instruments from the other end. That's the good news. The bad news is that this surgery is difficult, and it takes surgeons lots of practice to perfect their skills. Some practice can be done with animals, but there's nothing like the real thing. So the only option is to let less experienced surgeons try their hand on real patients, like you. Now, we all understand that this must be done, but we'd all prefer, thank you, that the practice be done on someone else, and that only the real expert be allowed to cut on our knees and gallbladders.

Virtual reality to the rescue. There are projects underway at UC Berkeley and elsewhere to develop virtual-reality training stations for surgeons. MRI, CAT, and other types of images allow surgeons to see virtual human bodies in three dimensions. The surgeons wear special gloves that give them virtual force feedback, so that as they practice surgery on the virtual bodies they get appropriate feelings of pressure, resistance, and cutting. Practice with realistic 3D images and with realistic feelings of touch allows a surgeon to develop skills that transfer readily to the genuine operating room, and to your knee. So, because you construct what you feel, and surgeons construct what they feel, surgeons can get the feel of what it's like to cut on you without actually having to cut on you. That you construct what you feel is not just an abstract idea, in this case it's a concrete reality that benefits both your knee and the surgeon's nerves.

EIGHT

PEEKING BEHIND
THE ICONS

My wrist didn't hurt when I spiked it, and my opponents just laughed when it hit them in the head. I was playing virtual volleyball with a dozen players, and many spectators were waiting in line to get in the game. It was a popular attraction at the Virtual Reality Exhibit in the Los Angeles County Museum of Science and Industry.

By today's standards, that volleyball game was low-tech; the ball and players appeared only in silhouette. Virtual reality has long since progressed from a futuristic curiosity in museums to a present and powerful force in medicine, education, architecture, and entertainment. Billions of dollars are at stake as companies position themselves in this burgeoning market and as evolving technologies create increasingly realistic virtual worlds.

Of course, it's not technology per se that creates realistic virtual worlds. It's the customers, the ones paying their hard-earned cash, who are the real creators. Virtual reality is only possible because we, the customers, construct what we perceive. We are the source of the stock cars we pass in a virtual drag race, the prospective stadium we scrutinize in a virtual architectural walk-through, the molecules whose 3D shape we see and whose electric forces we feel in a virtual chemistry course, and the delicate, bleeding tissues we slice in a virtual open-heart surgery. The high-tech displays cleverly prompt us to construct these scenes, and the more clever the prompting the better scenes we can construct (and the more we're willing to pay). But the displays can only prompt, they can't construct the virtual realities for us. What makes one display more compelling than another is that it more fully engages the constructive processes of the customer.

But now let's use virtual reality for another purpose, as a metaphor to explore questions that have probably nagged you about the story on perceptual construction. Questions like these: If we each construct all we see, then why do we all see the same things? What is the relationship between "reality" and our constructions?

For concreteness, imagine that you've gone to your local arcade, and you're about to play the latest game of virtual volleyball with nine other players. Each of you gets a helmet that can immerse you in stereo sound and stereo images of high resolution. Each of you also gets a high-tech bodysuit that can incite sensations of pressure, light bumps, and other forms of force feedback. The helmets and bodysuits communicate, via radio signals, with a nearby supercomputer that hosts the software for virtual volleyball and numerous other virtual attractions. The arcade manager proudly tells you that the volleyball software occupies a hundred gigabytes of memory and represents hundreds of hacker-months of program development. Which is why, of course, this ten-minute game costs so much.

After you put on your helmet, you find yourself on a sandy beach with nine other players dressed not in the ugly high-tech bodysuits you saw just a moment ago, but in flattering bathing suits. You're surrounded by palm trees and blue skies, with light puffy clouds. You hear the soft screeching of gulls, and the gentle pounding of surf. You see an off-white volleyball lying before you on the sand, and a volleyball net already set up. Five players on the other side of the net, and four more on your side, are all anxious to play. You're first to serve, so you bend over and grab the volleyball.

This is no cheap plastic volleyball. It sports soft, high-quality leather that warms to the touch. You bounce it lightly on your wrist a couple times, and nod approvingly to the other players.

Then you serve and the fun begins. You and the others are soon completely absorbed as you dig, set, feint, and spike with abandon. This goes on for a few wonderful minutes.

Then, suddenly, you are plagued with philosophical worries about the game you're now playing. Between points, and in lulls in the action, question after question comes to mind. The first is this:

Are we all seeing and playing with the same volleyball?

It sure feels like you are. Just a moment ago you did a beautiful set, placing the ball in perfect position over the net, and then one of your teammates spiked that ball, that very same ball, to give your team a side out. So you must be seeing and playing with the same ball.

But you've been reading *Visual Intelligence*, and you remember that the phrase *what you see* has both a phenomenal and a relational sense. In the phenomenal sense, what you see means "the way things look to you," "the way they visually appear to you," "the way you visually experience them." But in the relational sense it means "what you interact with when you look."

So you decide to ask the question in the phenomenal sense.

Are we all, in the phenomenal sense, seeing and playing with the same volleyball?

And here the answer seems plainly no. You wear your own separate helmet with its own stereo display, as does each of the other players. Your display sprays a shower of photons onto your eyes. This shower engages the constructive genius of your visual system, which then constructs your volleyball experience. There is no volleyball experience in the shower of photons itself. That shower merely triggers you to construct your own volleyball experience. Similarly for each of the other players. So you each construct your own volleyball experience. Those experiences are not, as the philosophers would put it, "numerically identical," that is, one and the same. And therefore you and your teammates do not, in the phenomenal sense, see and play with the same volleyball.

You decide next to ask the question in the relational sense.

Do we all, in the relational sense, see and play with the same volleyball?

This one is more disturbing. What you interact with when you see that volleyball, or anything else right now, is a supercomputer with a hundred gigabytes of software running on it. And your teammates interact with that same supercomputer and software. So "what you interact with when you look" is the same thing as what your teammates interact with when they look, namely the computer and its software. That means that the answer is yes: in the relational sense you all see and play with the same volleyball.

What's disturbing about this conclusion, though, is that circuits and software don't in any way resemble volleyballs. You've looked inside your PC, and you've done a little programming in your time, and you know without a doubt that none of this looks remotely like volleyballs. It feels strange to conclude that you all see the same volleyball because you all interact with the same circuits and software. That's not at all what you had in mind when you first thought that you were setting the same volleyball that your teammate then spiked.

Apparently, when you look at a volleyball or anything else, what you see in the phenomenal sense and what you see in the relational sense can be as different in nature as you like, as different as a soft leather ball on the one hand and intangible software and cold hard circuits on the other. Maybe even more different. There need be no resemblance.

If there's no resemblance, is there no relation at all? That can't be right either. After all, the volleyball experiences that you construct prove a useful guide for playing the computer's game, a guide that is quicker and more effective than poring over computer printouts. Computerphobes, who've never programmed and know nothing about registers or software, can put on the helmet and suit and, just by hitting the volleyball that they experience, alter those computer registers as deftly as the most inveterate hacker. Ignorance can be bliss.

There is a relationship, then, in the normal case, between what you see in the phenomenal and relational senses. What you see in the phenomenal sense is a useful and simplified *interface* to what you see in the relational sense. It summarizes a myriad of complexities in a way that lets you interact with that complexity without tedium and distraction. What it provides you is indeed phenomenal—a phenomenal interface.

So the answer to your first question—*Are we all seeing and playing with the same volleyball?*—is both yes and no. No, you each have constructed your own volleyball experiences. And yes, you each are interacting with the same hidden world of circuits and software. There are as many phenomenal volleyballs as there are players. There is only one relational volleyball, and it doesn't resemble a volleyball at all.

That first question took you to unexpected places, so you try another.

Is the volleyball still there when I don't look?

Again the answer depends on the volleyball. Your phenomenal volleyball is your construction. When you don't look you don't construct it. So the phenomenal volleyball *isn't there* when you don't look. However, the relational volleyball doesn't depend on your constructive powers for its existence. The relational volleyball is just the circuits and software. So the relational volleyball *is there* when you don't look. It just doesn't resemble a volleyball.

Is the volleyball an off-white color when I don't look?

The phenomenal volleyball isn't there when you don't look, so it isn't off-white or any other color. Nor is it round or soft or leathery. The relational volleyball is circuits and software, and it isn't literally off-white either. There may be portions of the software whose intent is to spray photons on your eyes such that you will construct an off-white phenomenal volleyball. But this software isn't any color at all. And the color of the circuits is irrelevant to the color of the phenomenal volleyball. So the answer is no, for both the phenomenal and relational volleyballs. And this same answer holds for the shape, texture, motion, position in space, hardness or softness, and other such properties of the volleyball.

What causes me to see a volleyball?

Is it something that resembles a volleyball, something round and off-white and leathery? No. The only such thing here is the phenomenal volleyball, and it is the result, not the cause, of my perceptual constructions. So the only possible cause must be the relational volleyball, which doesn't resemble a volleyball at all.

Is the volleyball conscious? Does it have experiences?

The relational volleyball is just circuits and software. Although proponents of "strong" artificial intelligence (AI) grant that computers can be conscious, I see no need to grant consciousness here. This computer doesn't simulate consciousness, it plays volleyball. Even if strong AI is true, it doesn't follow that this computer, and therefore this relational volleyball, is conscious.

The phenomenal volleyball is my construction. But from the fact that I am conscious, and that I construct the phenomenal volleyball, it doesn't follow that the phenomenal volleyball is itself conscious. I would need further, currently lacking, evidence to reach that conclusion. So I can't conclude that the phenomenal volleyball is conscious.

Are my teammates conscious?

The phenomenal teammates are, like the phenomenal volleyball, my constructions. If the phenomenal volleyball needn't be conscious, then why should my phenomenal teammates be conscious? What differentiates the two? For now, nothing of importance, so I can't conclude that my phenomenal teammates are conscious.

My relational teammates, like the relational volleyball, are circuits and software. But these circuits and software receive radio signals from my "real" teammates, who are conscious, so that ultimately I interact with them. Thus the relational teammates are conscious, although my phenomenal ones are not.

Enough questions for the moment. The score is 14 to 13, and you're serving for the win, when time expires and your helmet goes blank. You return it and the body suit, and thank your teammates for a good game as you head for the exit.

The exit is teeming with volleyball accessories and memorabilia— sunglasses, tank tops, postcards—but the volleyballs catch your eye. They're the same off-white color as the virtual volleyball you just played with. You pick one up and bounce it. It's the same soft leather with the same texture as the virtual volleyball. In fact, phenomenally, they're identical. You gaze in admiration.

Then a question spoils the moment.

This phenomenal volleyball is identical to the one I just played with. What about the relational volleyballs? Are they identical?

The relational volleyball in the game was circuits and software. It seems unlikely, however, that the same is true for the volleyball you now have in hand. After all, volleyballs were around before computers and software. So the relational volleyball is not circuits and software. But then, what is it? Tough question. We'll come back to it.

The arcade has educational exhibits, and you try one called the Virtual Brain. You enter a small room crammed with high-tech equipment and put on a helmet and bodysuit, and a voice announces, "Welcome to the Virtual Brain. The brain you are about to see is your own. Through the miracles of modern technology, we can scan your brain and create images of its structure and activity. These images are, in every detail, what you would see if you removed your skull and looked at your own brain. If this prospect bothers you, you may leave now."

This prospect intrigues you, so you stay. The helmet display flashes on, and you see a brain floating before you. You look around and realize that you and the brain are in a large vat filled with fluid. Also inside this vat are a host of high-tech devices—magnetic stimulators, electrodes, microscopes, surgical tools, and others.

The headphones continue, "This is your brain. Feel free to hold it, rotate it, and look at it from any angle you wish."

You reach out, gently grasp the brain, and look it over. A handsome specimen indeed.

"Neuroscience has revealed that different parts of your brain have different functions. If you'll just pick up the electrode to your right, you can explore this for yourself."

You pick up the electrode, and an arrow appears pointing to the back of the brain. "This part of your brain does vision. If you stimulate it with your electrode, our new proprietary Noninvasive Magnetic Brain Stimulator, or NIMBS, will stimulate the corresponding part of your own brain, so that you can experience for yourself what it does. Go ahead."

You gingerly touch the electrode to the back of the brain on the right side and press a button labeled "Stimulate" on the handle of the electrode. Immediately you see a flash of light, up and to the left. As you move the electrode up the back of the brain, this flash of light moves systematically across your visual field. You let go of the Stimulate button, and the flash disappears.

Then you try this on the left side of the brain in an area that the headphones have told you is "somatosensory cortex." As you stimulate the brain, you feel a tingling sensation in your right knee. As you move the electrode down the side of the brain, the tingling sensation moves up your body.

As you stimulate other areas of the brain, you have different experiences. A buzzing sound, the smell of smoke. One area makes your leg twitch.

"Now put away the electrode, and try the magnetic inhibitor on your left. This inhibits the electrical activity in a small region of your brain, and gives you an idea of what it would be like to lose that bit of your brain to a stroke."

An arrow pops up, pointing to a spot on the lower left side of your brain. You put the inhibitor there and push the Inhibit button. To your amazement, the color drains away from the right half of your visual field, leaving you seeing only shades of gray. You let go of the Inhibit button and, to your relief, color flows back into the right visual field.

The arrow moves back a little. You try the inhibitor there, and suddenly all motion stops in the right visual field. You wave your virtual hand in front of you. You see it move just fine when it's in the left visual field, but it jumps as if you were viewing it with a strobe light when it's in your right visual field.

Such demonstrations go on for the next ten minutes, educating you about the activities of individual neurons, synapses, neurotransmitters, neural networks, distributed processing, synchronous oscillations, receptive fields, topographic maps—all demonstrated live on your own virtual brain.

When it's all over, the headphones conclude, "And so ends our tour of your brain. As you've seen for yourself, and as research in neuroscience has triumphantly confirmed, your brain creates all your conscious experiences. Your mind *is* what your brain does. Thank you and goodbye."

You slip off your helmet, in awe at the triumphs of neuroscience, and in awe at the complexity and creative power of your own brain. As you leave the Virtual Brain, its last pronouncements go around and around in your head: ". . . your brain creates all your conscious experiences. Your mind *is* what your brain does."

This sounds plausible enough, you think. But then those pesky questions start again.

Which brain creates all my conscious experiences? The phenomenal brain or the relational brain?

The brain you just experienced in the Virtual Brain was of course a phenomenal brain. Indeed, the Virtual Brain's headphones told you that this phenomenal brain was indistinguishable from the phenomenal brain you would find if you opened up your skull.

So is it this phenomenal brain that creates all your conscious experiences? No. The phenomenal brain, with all its phenomenal neurons and synapses and neural networks, is your constructed experience, just like the phenomenal volleyball. If you don't look, it's not there. And if it's not there, it can't do anything. But you have conscious experiences even when you don't see your phenomenal brain. In fact, until just a few minutes ago, you had probably never seen your phenomenal brain. So the phenomenal brain can't be what constructs your conscious experience.

That leaves your relational brain. If it's true that your brain creates all your conscious experiences, then it must be your relational brain, not your phenomenal brain, that is the creator.

But what is your relational brain? Does it resemble your phenomenal brain? There's no reason to suppose it does. In fact, as we saw with the volleyball, there's no reason to suppose that the nature of the phenomenal brain in any way constrains the nature of the relational brain. Your phenomenal brain is simply a graphical interface that allows you to interact with your relational brain, whatever that relational brain might be. And all that's required of a graphical interface is that it be systematically related to what it represents. The relation can be as arbitrary as you wish, as long as it's systematic. The trash can icon on your computer screen is a graphical interface to software that can erase files on your computer disk. The trash can icon is systematically related to that erasing software, but the relation is arbitrary: the trash can icon doesn't resemble the erasing software in any way. It could be any color or shape you wish and still successfully do the job of letting you interact with the erasing software. It could be a pig icon or a toilette icon instead of a trash can icon. All that matters is the systematic connection.

A fascinating illustration of the arbitrary but systematic nature of the connection between the phenomenal and relational realms is "synesthesia," a condition enjoyed by just ten people in a million, in which they experience by two separate senses what the rest of us experience by just one. One synesthete, a professor at the California Institute of Technology, told me that he heard distinct sounds for each shape he saw. Puffy clouds in the sky, for instance, sounded like "putt, putt, putt." Another synesthete, studied by the neurologist Richard Cytowic, felt what he tasted. A squirt of Angostura bitters on his tongue led him to describe what he felt as follows: "It has the springy consistency of a mushroom, almost round, but I feel bumps and can stick my fingers into little holes in the surface. There are leafy tendril-like things coming out of the holes, about six of them. . . ." Each different taste had, for him, a different feel. Mint, for instance, felt like smooth, cool columns of glass. A given taste always had the same feel. That is, there was a systematic but arbitrary association between feels and tastes. Such associations endure basically unchanged for the life of the synesthete, as has been demonstrated by tests forty-six years apart on one synesthete.

Why should mint feel like cool columns of glass, and puffy clouds sound like "putt, putt"? No good reason. Are columns of glass an intrinsically better representation of the true nature of mint than, say, sheets of ice? I would be hard pressed to justify one over the other. On what grounds would I make the judgment? Both are arbitrary. Columns of glass or sheets of ice would both work just fine, as long as the association was systematic and enduring.

But the same questions can be asked about the experiences the rest of us nonsynesthetes enjoy. Why should mint taste like mint and not, say, like vanilla? Our mint experience itself is just as arbitrary as a synesthete's experience of columns of glass. So are our experiences of colors, shapes, sounds, and smells. These experiences are systematically related to the relational world, but the relation is arbitrary. One can easily imagine that we would do just fine if our color experiences were inverted, so that reds looked green, blues looked yellow, and so on. If the inversion is systematic, we lose no information and therefore no abilities. One can also easily imagine such inversions in each of our other modes of experience. Indeed, designers of virtual reality systems may soon take us into new virtual worlds where we experience, and perhaps learn to adapt to, just such inversions. A small step in this direction was taken in 1896 by George M. Stratton, who had volunteers wear prisms that make the world appear upside-down. At first they find it hard to get along in the upside-down world. But after consistently wearing the inverting prisms for a few days, they find that everything once again looks "normal" and that they can carry on their daily activities just fine. When the prisms are then removed, everything again looks upside down and it takes them some time to readjust. When the psychologist Jan Koenderink repeated this experiment, he saw individual objects or object parts turn right side up while the rest of his visual world still looked upside down. Eventually his whole visual world turned right side up. It's possible, then, to alter the arbitrary but systematic relationship between our phenomenal and relational worlds, and for us to adjust quickly and successfully to the new relationship.

So, returning to our brain example, the phenomenal brain that you saw in the Virtual Brain and the phenomenal brains that neuroscientists study in their labs are wonderful graphical interfaces and eminently worthy of study, but they are not the relational brain and they alone cannot determine the true nature of that relational brain. The relationship between the phenomenal brain and the relational brain is systematic and arbitrary, as arbitrary as the relation between mint and columns of glass.

Back now to the virtual reality arcade, where you decide to check out the Virtual Supercomputer, an exhibit that promises to reveal "the real power behind virtual reality."

You don a helmet and bodysuit. The helmet display flickers on, and you see, slowly rotating before you, a sleek steel box with a dozen flashing lights, and the label "MPC-9000" written in a slanting script. The headphones begin, "Welcome to the Virtual Supercomputer. Here you will meet the real star of virtual reality, the key actor responsible for the success of Virtual Volleyball, Virtual Dogfighter, and our other popular attractions. That star is the MPC-9000, the latest and fastest Massively Parallel Computer, boasting nine thousand parallel central processing units, and delivering one hundred teraflops of computing power. The MPC-9000 will now give you a tour of its inner self. The images you are about to see are, in every detail, precisely what you would see if you looked inside its steel case."

Two arrows appear, pointing to two buttons on opposite sides of the steel case. The headphones continue, "Push the two buttons indicated by the arrows, and remove the top of the case. Then remove its sides as well." You do so, and see a bewildering complexity of glistening metal, wires, cables, cubes, and other paraphernalia. For the next fifteen minutes you explore this complexity to your heart's content, using virtual magnifying glasses and virtual microscopes for a closer look. You're free to pull out individual cubes and cables, and to probe them with virtual electrodes while the headphones describe their functions. You learn that the MPC-9000 is a sophisticated synthesis of gallium arsenide, optical, and even quantum computing, and that, unlike earlier MPCs whose circuits were fabricated in two dimensions, this one has circuits fabricated in three dimensions, giving it unprecedented speed and compactness. You also have a chance to look through virtual volumes of software printouts, one for Virtual Volleyball and one for each of the other arcade attractions.

When the fifteen minutes are up, the headphones announce, "This concludes our tour of the Virtual Supercomputer. The MPC-9000 is the reality behind virtual reality. The next time you fly a virtual fighter jet or spike a virtual volleyball, just remember, it's the circuits and software of the MPC-9000 that make it all possible. Thank you and goodbye."

You remove your helmet and bodysuit, duly impressed with the prowess of the MPC-9000, and with a better understanding of why the attractions cost so much. As you leave the Virtual Supercomputer, its final words of wisdom continue to echo in your thoughts: ". . . it's the circuits and software of the MPC-9000 that make it all possible."

You can't help yourself. You have to ask the question.

Which circuits and software make it all possible? The phenomenal or the relational?

By now this question is easy. It's not phenomenal circuits and software that make it possible, say, to spike a virtual volleyball. It couldn't be. There need be no phenomenal circuits and software, for you or anyone else, when you spike the volleyball, so therefore phenomenal circuits and software can't be what makes that spiking possible.

The answer must be that it's the relational circuits and software that make it possible to play virtual volleyball. But of course this raises another question.

What are relational circuits and software?

We know that they needn't in any way resemble the phenomenal circuits and software that we experience. But what more can we say about them?

This raises a general and important question. If the relational realm needn't resemble the phenomenal, then what can we safely say about the nature of the relational realm?

Not much. However, we can propose theories and see how they stack up against our experiences. This is an intriguing enterprise, and one that has attracted lots of attention. There are now many theories of the relational realm that are compatible with all the evidence we have from the phenomenal realm.

These theories come in three basic kinds: *physicalism*, *idealism*, and *dualism*.

Physicalism proposes that the relational realm is mindless. There are many versions of this proposal. The one most influential, at present, proposes that the basic building blocks of the relational realm are the particles, fields, and other entities within the province of microphysics. The behavior of these entities is mindless, governed entirely by probabilistic laws.

Idealism proposes that the relational realm is made of minds. It may be one mind, as in Berkeley's proposal that it's the mind of God, or it may be many distinct and finite minds in interaction. In the latter case, the behavior of these minds has also been described by probabilistic laws.

Dualism proposes that the relational realm is made both of minds and mindless entities. There are probabilistic laws governing the minds, the mindless entities, and the interactions between the two.

These three theories disagree primarily on whether the relational realm is mindless. Physicalism says it is, idealism says it's not, and dualism says it's both. None of the three has, to date, been ruled out by what we know of the phenomenal realm through the investigations of science. All three are compatible with the probabilistic laws of nature discovered by physicists. Probability can, with equal facility, describe the behavior of minds or the mindless. It can describe the mindless roll of dice or the conscious choices of a shopper.

Because all three theories are compatible with everything science has discovered about vision and visual experience, I've been careful to say that human vision "constructs" the objects and properties we experience, rather than that it "recovers" or "reconstructs" them. The neutral term "constructs" lets us discuss the phenomenal realm of vision without tacit claims about the relational realm. Saying that human vision recovers the 3D shapes of objects might suggest a version of physicalism in which there are 3D objects whose shapes are, in the normal case, dutifully recovered by human vision. This might be true or not. But we needn't decide the issue to profitably investigate your visual intelligence and how it constructs your visual experiences.

It might come as a surprise that all three theories are still compatible with all we know. Haven't the advances of physics by now settled the case in favor of physicalism? Not at all. The advances of physics have served to sharpen the issues and increase the debate, but not to settle it. And they've led to this interesting discovery: Construction is at the heart of quantum physics. A central feature of quantum theory that has puzzled theorists for decades is the critical role of observation. When an atom or electron is not observed it has no definite position, no momentum, nor any other dynamical properties. Instead it's in a "superposition" of perhaps countless possible positions or momenta. Only when the atom or electron is observed does it have a definite value of position or momentum. For many theorists the puzzle is that this behavior of quantum objects seems so different from the behavior of everyday objects, such as volleyballs. After all, they point out, a volleyball, unlike an electron, does have a position, a momentum, a 3D shape, a color, and other such properties, whether or not the volleyball is observed. Why should observation be critical to electrons but not to volleyballs?

The puzzle is due, however, not to the strangeness of electrons but to a misconception about volleyballs. A volleyball no more has a position or momentum when it's not observed than does an electron. Only in the act of observation do you construct a phenomenal volleyball with a position, motion, color, and shape. Similarly, only in the act of observation is an electron constructed with a position, or momentum, or other dynamical properties. All phenomena are constructed by observation, whether quantum phenomena or volleyball phenomena.

If physics hasn't settled the nature of the relational realm, what about biological evolution? Don't the probabilistic processes of random mutation and natural selection, the main engines of evolutionary theory, settle the case for physicalism? After all, they can account nicely for the unity and continuity within the diversity of biological organisms, and they drive a synthesis that in principle spans from the humble amoeba to the phenomenal brain of man.

That may be, but physicalist, idealist, and dualist accounts are all viable. There is, to date, no valid argument whose premises are the probabilistic rules of evolution and whose conclusion is the nature of the relational realm.

This last statement might seem mistaken. After all, according to natural selection those creatures whose perceptions are better adapted to the environment have a competitive advantage in the struggle for survival over those whose perceptions are less adapted. Over eons of time, creatures with less adapted perceptions have presumably disappeared, and those that remain have perceptions that are well adapted. We're among those that remain, and we see physical objects. So doesn't this settle the case for physicalism?

Not at all. Granting that our perceptions are well adapted, we must ask: Well adapted in what sense? In the sense that perceptual experiences now resemble the relational realm? But this is more than natural selection delivers. Experiences need not resemble the relational realm to be well adapted, they need only be a useful guide for behavior. The icons on your computer screen are a useful guide for behavior toward your computer, but those icons don't resemble the circuits and software that ultimately determine how well adapted your behaviors are. Indeed, the icons are a useful guide to behavior precisely because they don't resemble circuits and software. Circuits and software are extremely complex, and if your icons resembled them it would take you forever to get anything done on your computer. Your behavior would be less adapted, not more. Just try doing graphic design on your computer by setting registers and flipping switches, and you'll soon toss out your computer in favor of pen and paper. And that's why programmers put big effort into designing icon interfaces, and why consumers put big dollars into buying them: to provide a means of interacting with the computer that is useful precisely because it hides the complexity of the circuits and software they interact with.

If "well adapted" doesn't mean "resembles," then what does it mean? It means a systematic but arbitrary relation. Our perceptual experiences are well adapted to the relational realm because they provide a systematic but arbitrary guide to those aspects of the relational realm that are critical to our needs and our survival—just as the icon interface on your computer is well adapted because it provides a systematic but arbitrary guide to the computer's unseen circuits and software.

Something might still seem wrong here. Look, you say, when I see a snake slithering toward me in the grass, then I would be a fool not to think that there really is a snake, and I would be a fool not to get out of the way. Natural selection has seen to it that when I see snakes, there are snakes, and there is real danger.

Granted, when you see snakes there are snakes, and you must take them seriously. Similarly, when you see a trash can icon on your computer screen, there really is a trash can icon, and when you see a document icon representing that text file you've been editing for the last five hours, there really is a document icon. And you must take these icons seriously. If you drag that document icon into that trash can icon then you'll lose your last five hours of work. That's a serious consequence. To say that experiences provide a systematic but arbitrary guide to the relational realm is not to deny that experiences are real and must be taken seriously. Snake experiences are real experiences and must be taken seriously. But they don't entail that anything in the relational realm resembles a snake, just as a trash can icon doesn't entail that circuits and software resemble a trash can.

Neither biology nor quantum theory dictates the nature of the relational realm. Nor does any other science. Each studies certain phenomena, and describes these by precise theories. In no case do the phenomena or the theories dictate the nature of the relational realm. We might hope that the theories of science will converge to a true theory of the relational realm. This is the hope of scientific realism. But it's a hope as yet unrealized, and a hope that cannot be proved true.

So this is a small sample of what happens when we peek behind the icons, when we ask what else there might be in addition to our perceptual constructions. We find a myriad of fascinating questions. We find that we've entered the province of philosophy and religion. Because the phenomenal and relational realms need not resemble each other, because their relationship is arbitrary and systematic, the tools of science can help us guess at the nature of the relational realm, but might never dictate a final verdict.

EPILOGUE

W hen he was thirty, D.S. had a traffic accident that left
him in a coma for three weeks. He recovered quickly, so
that within a year his intelligence, speech, and general
mental abilities were back to normal—with one excep-
tion: He regarded his father and mother, and other people he knew, as
impostors. When the psychologists William Hirstein and V.S.
Ramachandran asked him why he thought his father was an impostor,
he replied, "He looks exactly like my father but he really isn't. He's a
nice guy, but he isn't my father, Doctor." When they asked him why
someone would do this, he replied, "That is what is so surprising,
Doctor—why should anyone want to pretend to be my father? Maybe
my father employed him to take care of me—paid him some money so
that he could pay my bills. . . ." Remarkably, D.S. would treat his parents as impostors only when he saw them. When he talked to them on
the phone, he regarded them as real.

D.S. suffered from a rare disorder known as Capgras syndrome.
The precise nature of this disorder is still debated. It is not a problem
in face recognition, or of vision more generally. Many Capgras patients,
including D.S., have normal vision and a normal ability to discriminate
and recognize faces. Instead Hirstein and Ramachandran suggest that
the problem is a disconnection between vision and emotion. When you
see your father, your visual intelligence goes to work constructing the
3D shape of his face, the color and texture of his skin, his expression,
and ultimately his identity. Then, in the normal case, the constructions
of your visual intelligence engage the resources of your emotional intel-

ligence, and you have feelings appropriate to your father, perhaps feelings of love and warmth. In Capgras patients, however, the connection between visual intelligence and emotional intelligence is cut, so that the Capgras patient doesn't have appropriate feelings when he sees his father. Since the man in front of him looks like his father but doesn't feel like his father, the Capgras patient concludes, perhaps naturally enough, that the man must be an impostor. He certainly feels like an impostor.

Experiments suggest that this explanation might be right. Using equipment similar to that in lie detector tests, Hirstein and Ramachandran found that D.S. did not have normal emotional responses when shown pictures of his mother. The constructions of his visual intelligence were apparently not getting to his emotional intelligence.

Visual intelligence occupies almost half of your brain's cortex. Normally it is intimately connected to your emotional intelligence and your rational intelligence. It constructs the elaborate visual realities in which you live and move and interact. It forwards these constructions to your emotional and rational intelligence, which use them as raw materials in further constructions. The emotional world you inhabit is, like your visual world, a product of your own constructive genius. This insight is not just of theoretical interest, it is the foundation of cognitive therapy, which has proved successful in treating depression, anxiety, phobias, and other psychological disorders. Just as impairments in the normal processes of visual construction can lead to debilitating visual syndromes, so also impairments in the normal processes of emotional construction can lead to debilitating emotional syndromes. Fortunately, psychologists have identified many of the common impairments of emotional construction and can help patients trade in faulty emotional constructions for more healthy ones. Changing one's constructions is more difficult in vision, where the constructive processes seem to be more "hardwired" than those of emotion, and therefore less susceptible to change by conscious effort.

We are complex beings with many facets, including the visual, the emotional, and the rational. Understanding each of these facets and how it interacts with all the others is critical to understanding who we are as human beings and how we can improve ourselves and our environment. If percentage of cortex is any measure, then visual intelligence is a major facet of who we are as a species, and its understanding is a key to what we might become.

The progress we've made so far in understanding visual intelligence has already transformed our technological and cultural landscape, giving us movies, television, virtual reality, smart bombs, cameras on Mars, and computer vision systems that can drive cars down freeways. As powerful as these technologies are, they're but a hint of what's ahead as we further explore and discover the creative genius of our mind's eye.

NOTES

Preface

xi. The case of Mr. P: Pallis, 1955.

xiii. Some 3-D movies in addition to *Dial M for Murder* (1954): *Amityville 3-D* (1983); *Andy Warhol's Frankenstein* (1974); *The Charge at Feather River* (1953); *Comin' at Ya!* (1981); *Devil's Canyon* (1953); *Freddy's Dead: The Final Nightmare* (1991); *House of Wax* (1953); *Jaws 3-D* (1983); *Knickknack* (1989); *La Marca del Hombre Lobo* (1968); *Metalstorm: The Destruction of Jared-Syn* (1983); *Muppet*vision 3-D* (1991); *Pardon My Backfire* (1953); *Spooks* (1953). Source: The Internet Movie Database, http://uk.imdb.com.

xv. Galen: Translated by Margaret T. May. Ithaca, 1968. pp. 490–491.

1. A Creative Genius for Vision

2. Ripple: Hoffman, 1983; Hoffman & Richards, 1984.

3. Magic square: Albert & Hoffman, 1995.

4. Devil's triangle: Gregory, 1970; Kulpa, 1983; Penrose & Penrose, 1958; Reutersvärd, 1982.

5. Gregory's wooden construction of the devil's triangle: Gregory, 1970, p. 56.

6. Phenomenal and relational seeing: Dancy, 1988; Robinson, 1994; Schwartz, 1965.

7. Semivision: Horridge, 1991. Bee vision: Boacnin & Ventura, 1995; Horridge, Zhang, & O'Carroll, 1992; Neumeyer, 1980; 1981; Werner, Menzel, & Wehrhahn, 1988. Fly vision: Poggio & Reichardt, 1976; Reichardt & Poggio, 1976;

1979. Goldfish vision: Dörr & Neumeyer, 1996; Neumeyer, 1985; 1986; 1988; 1991; 1992. Praying mantis: Horridge, 1991; Rossel, 1986.

8. Mantis shrimp: Cronin, Marshall, & Land, 1994; Cronin & Marshall, 1989. Macaque vision: Siegel & Andersen, 1988. Goslings: Lorenz, 1965. Blackbird nestlings: Tinbergen & Kuenen, 1939.

9. Chickens and ducks: Tinbergen, 1951; see also Johnson & Morton, 1991. Frog and toad vision: Ewert, 1987.

10. Alhazen quote: Sabra, 1978, p. 176; Lindberg, 1976. Ptolemy, in the second century A.D., describes vision as a process of unconscious inference in his *Optics*. Malebranche quote: Atherton, 1990, p. 39; Malebranche, 1980, p. 733. Perception modeled as Bayesian inference: Bennett, Hoffman, & Prakash, 1989; Clark & Yuille, 1990; Geman & Geman, 1984; Hoffman & Richards, 1984, note 7; Knill & Richards, 1996; Szeliski, 1989; Witkin, 1981. One way to understand vision as Bayesian inference is as follows. One is given an image, or set of images, I, and one wishes to infer an interpretation, W, of the world. That is, one wishes to compute the conditional probability of W given I. By the Bayes theorem we have

$$P(W \mid I) = \frac{P(I \mid W)P(W)}{P(I)}$$

The factor $P(I \mid W)$ is a probabilistic model of the image formation process. $P(W)$ encodes the probabilistic prior assumptions of the observer about the nature of the world. $P(I)$ can be viewed simply as a normalization constant.

11. Helmholtz quote: Helmholtz, 1910; Warren & Warren, 1968, p. 174. See also Meyering, 1989. Marr quote: Marr, 1982, p. 31.

12. Gombrich on visual construction: Gombrich, 1977. Leonardo da Vinci quote: da Vinci, 1956, No. 76; quoted in Gombrich, 1977, p. 159. Kellman quote: Kellman, 1995. Kids blink at approaching objects: Yonas, 1981; Yonas & Granrud, 1985; Yonas, Pettersen, & Lockman, 1979. Kids use motion to construct object boundaries: Crayton & Yonas, 1988; 1990; Granrud et al., 1984; Kaufmann-Hayoz, Kaufmann, & Stucki, 1986. Kids use motion to construct 3D: Arterberry & Yonas, 1988; Kellman, 1984; Kellman & Short, 1987; Yonas, Arterberry, & Granrud, 1987. Kids use stereo to construct 3D: Atkinson & Braddick, 1981; Birch, Gwiazda, & Held, 1982; Fox, Aslin, Shea, & Dumais, 1980; Held, Birch, & Gwiazda, 1980; Petrig, Julesz, Kropfl, Baumgartner, & Anliker, 1981. Kids use shading to construct depth: Granrud, Yonas, & Opland, 1985. Kids use perspective to construct depth: Oross, Francis, Mauk, & Fox, 1987; Yonas, Cleaves, & Pettersen, 1978. Kids use interposition to construct depth: Granrud & Yonas, 1984. Kids use prior familiarity to construct depth: Granrud, Haake, & Yonas, 1985; Yonas, Pettersen, & Granrud, 1982.

13. Kids learn a word every ninety minutes: Carey, 1978; Lorge & Chall, 1963; Miller, 1991; Pinker, 1994. Molyneux quote: Pastore, 1971, p. 68. Berkeley quote: Berkeley 1709/1963, p. 19.

14. Gibson on vision: Gibson, 1950; 1966; 1979. Chomsky quote: Chomsky, 1975, p. 11.

15. Pinker quote: Pinker, 1994, p. 32.

2. Inflating an Artist's Sketch

17. Cheselden quote: Cheselden, 1728, pp. 448–449; reprinted in Pastore, 1971, pp. 413–416.

18. Locke quote: Locke, 1694, p. 187; reprinted in Pastore, 1971, p. 66.

19. Berkeley on Cheselden case: Berkeley, 1733, *Theory of vision or visual language: vindicated and explained* (see Turbayne, 1963). For more cases of the blind restored to sight: Gregory, 1974; Sacks, 1991; von Senden, 1960; Valvo, 1971. Necker cube: Necker, 1832.

22. Kopfermann cubes: Kopfermann, 1930.

25. Generic view: Biederman, 1987; Binford, 1981; Freeman, 1994, 1996; Hoffman & Richards, 1984; Huffman, 1971; Koenderink, 1990; Koenderink & van Doorn, 1979; Lowe, 1985; Lowe & Binford, 1981; Ullman, 1979; Witkin, 1981; Witkin & Tenenbaum, 1983.

28. Gestalt psychology: Ellis, 1937; Koffka, 1935; Köhler, 1929/1947; Petermann, 1932. Kanizsa's irregular solids: Kanizsa, 1974; Kanizsa, 1979, p. 106.

29. Devil's triangle: see note 4. Rock on the devil's triangle: Rock, 1983, p. 319.

30. Trading towers: Albert & Hoffman, 1995. Attached box: Jepson & Richards, 1993.

31. Necker cube with bubbles: Albert, 1995; Albert & Hoffman, 1995.

34. Alberti on painter's perspective: Alberti, 1435. Leonardo on perspective: little survives of his writing on perspective except for some pages in his *Notebooks;* da Vinci, 1958. Euclid's *Optics*: Euclid, 300 B.C.; Burton, 1945. Natural and linear perspective: Pirenne, 1970.

35. "The Whipping Punishment": 1410, *Middle Rhein Altarpiece*, in the Museum Catharijneconvent, Utrecht, Netherlands; see their edukatieve dienst #9.

36. Surface normals: Described in any text on differential geometry, such as Do

Carmo, 1974. Greek painters discover foreshortening: Beazley & Ashmole, 1966; Gombrich, 1977, p. 99.

37. Dürer's woodcut, *Man Drawing a lute*: Dürer, 1525.

39. Whitney's theorem about projections of smooth surfaces and their singularities: Whitney, 1955; Koenderink & van Doorn, 1976. Marr's puzzlement with Picasso's *Rites of Spring*: Marr, 1982, pp. 217, 218.

40. Koenderink's key to seeing 3D curvature in 2D silhouettes: Koenderink, 1984; 1990. Principal curvatures and directions: Do Carmo, 1974.

41. Alberti quote: Alberti, 1435/1956.

42. Badt quote: Badt, 1963; translated into English by Koenderink & van Doorn, 1982, p. 130. Koenderink's rules: Koenderink, 1984.

44. Shepard's table tops: Shepard, 1981, p. 298; 1990, p. 48.

3. The Invisible Surface That Glows

47. Visual form agnosia of Mr. S: Benson & Greenberg, 1969; Campion, 1987, pp. 222–223; Efron, 1968; Farah, 1990, pp. 8–9; Grüsser and Landis, 1991, p. 202ff; Zeki, 1993, p. 314.

48. Kanizsa's triangles: Kanizsa, 1955; 1974; 1979, p. 193–194.

49. Ehrenstein's disks: Ehrenstein, 1941; 1954. Devices that construct subjective contours: Grossberg, 1994; Grossberg & Mingolla, 1985a; 1987; Heitger & von der Heydt, 1993; Peterhans, von der Heydt, & Baumgartner, 1986; Skrzypek & Ringer, 1992.

50. Parks' subjective disk: Parks, 1980. Kanizsa's subjective wiggle: Kanizsa, 1976. Prazdny's subjective square: Prazdny, 1983; 1985. Kennedy's brightness figure: Kennedy, 1979; 1987; 1988. Schumann's first scientific paper on subjective figures: Schumann, 1900, 1904. Koryusai's woodcut *Crow and Heron in the Snow*: Riccar Art Museum, Japan; reproduced in Neuer, Liberston, & Yoshida, 1981, p. 150.

51. Medieval and Renaissance woodcuts with subjective surfaces: Jacobi, 1951. Dürer's *The Satyr Family*: Hapgood, 1992, pp. 12–14. Wallpapers with subjective surfaces: The Victoria and Albert Colour Books, 1986, *Ornate Wallpapers,* New York: Harry N. Abrams, Inc., especially plate 8. Many coins also have subjective contours and surfaces: a sun, created in the manner of Ehrenstein's disks, shines in a 2-ducat gold coin minted near Austria in 1682 (Krause & Mishler, 1986, p. 55); another such sun shines on the American $20 Liberty gold piece (Krause & Mishler, 1986, p. 603). Lion with subjec-

tive contours in Chinese cave temple: Wilson, 1994, p. 90; Whitfield & Farrer, 1990. Mesopotamian cylinder seal of lion with subjective contour: Wilson, 1994, p. 59; Collon, 1987, no. 158. Ukrainian bracelet, made of mammoth ivory, with subjective contours: Golomshtok, 1938, p. 350, plates 59-2 and 59-3; Rudinsky, 1931; Wilson, 1994, p. 28. Paleolithic cave drawing of bison with subjective contours: Leroi-Gourhan, 1967, plate 91; see also plates 89 and 92.

52. Kanizsa proposes symmetry as cause for subjective figures: Kanizsa, 1955. Kanizsa rejects symmetry as cause for subjective figures: Kanizsa, 1974; 1976; 1979.

53. Albert's curved crosses figure: adapted from Albert, 1993, figure 3a.

54. Simultaneous brightness contrast: Gilchrist, 1994. Simultaneous brightness contrast as a theory for subjective figures: Brigner & Gallagher, 1974; Day & Jory, 1978; Frisby & Clatworthy, 1975; Jory & Day, 1979; Kennedy, 1979. Varin and Kanizsa figures: Kanizsa, 1979, p. 202, 203, 216; Varin, 1971. Other principles proposed to explain subjective figures: Familiarity: Rock, 1983; 1987. High-level cognitive inferences about gaps: Gregory, 1972; 1987. Depth cues: Coren 1972; Gregory, 1972. Low-pass filtering of images: Becker & Knopp, 1978; Ginsburg, 1975; 1987.

55. Shipley and Kellman quote: Shipley & Kellman, 1990, p. 259; see also Kellman & Shipley, 1991.

56. Subjects can see subjective borders in displays with no cusps: Albert, 1995; Albert & Hoffman, 1995; 1996; Shipley & Kellman, 1990. A cusp-free display of subjective borders: Albert & Hoffman, 1995, p. 107. On the distinction between subjective borders that occlude and those that do not: Albert & Hoffman, 1995; 1996; Bonaiuto, Giannini, & Bonaiuto, 1991; Kennedy, 1978; 1988; Purghe, 1991; Purghe & Katsaras, 1991.

58. Illusory ellipses by Albert: Albert, 1993, Figure 7. Evidence that support ratio affects clarity of subjective borders: Shipley & Kellman, 1992; 1993. Evidence against the support ratio in abutting gratings: Soriano, Spillmann, & Bach, 1996.

59. Principle of nonaccidental relations: Witkin & Tenenbaum, 1983; Lowe, 1985. Morinaga's figures that show we group parallel curves into objects: Morinaga, 1941, figures 27–29; Metzger, 1975, figures 43 and 44; Rock, 1983, figure 6-6; Albert, 1993, figure 2.

61. Albert's illusory ellipses: Albert, 1993, Figure 7.

63. Kanizsa's triangle blocked by line segments: Kanizsa, 1974; 1979, Figure 12.26b; Rock, 1987.

64. The structure of the eye: A good photomicrograph is in Dowling, 1987, p. 8.

65. Galen and his predecessors on the anatomy of the eye: Galen, *On the usefulness of the parts of the body*; Lindberg, 1976, pp. 11, 219; Saint-Pierre, 1972. Kepler's theory of the retinal image: Kepler, 1604/1939; Lindberg, 1976, p. 185ff. The Greek atomists on vision: Bailey, 1928/1964; Lee, 1978; Lindberg, 1976; von Fritz, 1953. Epicurus quote on intromission theory of vision: Epicurus, "Letters to Herodotus," in Diogenes Laertius *Lives of Eminent Philosophers*, 10, 48–49, translated by R.D. Hicks, 2: 577–579; quoted in Lindberg, 1976, p. 2. Plato quote on extramission theory of vision: Cornford, 1937, pp. 152–153; Lindberg, 1976, p. 5.

66. Extramission theory of Euclid: Euclid, 300 B.C.; Burton, 1945; Lejeune, 1948. Lindberg, 1976, pp. 12–14. Extramission theory of Ptolemy: Lindberg, 1976, pp. 15–17; Lejeune, 1948. Extramission theory of Leonardo da Vinci: Leonardo da Vinci, 1491 (MacCurdy, 1939, p. 234); Lindberg, 1976, pp. 154–168. Leonardo's rejection of the extramission theory: Leonardo da Vinci, 1492 (Richter, 1970, volume 1, pp. 139–140); Lindberg, 1976, p. 160. Photomicrograph of the retina: Curcio, Millican, Allen, & Kalina, 1993, p. 3291, Figure 10a. Other images of photoreceptors: Dowling, 1987; Hirsch & Curcio, 1989; Miller, Williams, Morris, & Liang, 1996.

67. Ten photons on one cone is enough to see light: Williams, 1992, p. 17.

68. Computational work on edge detection and line finding: Canny, 1986; Deng & Lyengar, 1996; Marr & Hildreth, 1980; Law, Itoh, & Seki, 1996; Park, Nam, & Park, 1995. Alan Cowey on the problems of inferring neural function from neural physiology: Cowey, 1994, pp. 14–15.

69. On-center and off-center retina ganglion cells: In cats: Enroth-Cugell & Robson, 1966; Kuffler, 1953; In frogs: Gaze & Jacobson, 1963; In ground squirrels: Michael, 1968; In monkeys: de Monasterio, 1978. Receptive fields in LGN: Evarts, 1966; Hubel & Wiesel, 1961; Schiller, 1986; Sperling, Crawford, & Espinoza, 1978.

70. Hubel and Wiesel discover line-detecting edges in primary visual cortex: Hubel & Wiesel, 1959; 1962; 1968; 1977. Cells in macaque V1 detect subjective borders: Grosof, Shapley, & Hawken, 1993; see also Lamme, van Dijk, & Spekreijse, 1993.

71. Cells in V2 detect subjective borders: von der Heydt, Peterhans, & Baumgartner, 1984; Peterhans & von der Heydt, 1989; 1991. Neural network models of the construction of subjective borders: Finkel & Edelman, 1989; Grossberg & Mingolla, 1985a; 1985b; Heitger & von der Heydt, 1993; Kellman & Shipley, 1991; Lesher, 1995; Peterhans, von der Heydt, & Baumgartner, 1986; Ullman, 1976. Cells in areas 17 and 18 of cat detect subjective borders: Redies, Crook, & Creutzfeldt, 1986. Scanning electron micro-

graph of Purkinje cell in rat cerebellum, magnification of 4030: Shepherd, 1983, cover.

72. Subjective borders and surfaces that curve in 3D: Carman & Welch, 1992; Gregory & Harris, 1974; Gregory, 1987; Ramachandran, 1987.

73. Kanizsa's triangle poked by lines: Kanizsa, 1979, p. 219, Figure 12.29c.

75. Heywood Petry's subjective Necker cube: Bradley, 1987, p. 207, Figure 22.8; Bradley, Dumais, & Petry, 1976; Bradley & Petry, 1977.

76. Charles Bonnet syndrome: Bonnet, 1760; Damas-Mora et al., 1982; Morsier, 1936. The case of Mrs. B: Halligan et al., 1994.

4. Spontaneous Morphing

79. Tyler's patient with dorsal simultanagnosia: Farah, 1990, pp. 16–25; Tyler, 1968. Other cases of dorsal simultanagnosia: Girotti, Milanese, Casazza, Allegranza, Corridori, & Avanzini, 1982; Godwin-Austen, 1965; Hecaen & Ajuriaguerra, 1956; Holmes, 1918; Holmes & Horrax, 1919; Kase, Troncoso, Court, Tapia, & Mohr, 1977; Luria, 1959; Luria, Pravdina-Vinarskaya, & Yarbuss, 1963; Williams, 1970. See also Farah, 1990, pp. 16–25; Grüsser & Landis, 1991, pp. 215–217.

82. You recognize line drawings as quickly as color photographs: Biederman & Ju, 1988.

83. Part theories using basic shapes: Polyhedra: Roberts, 1965; Waltz, 1975; Winston, 1975; Generalized cones and cylinders: Binford, 1971; Brooks, 1981; Marr & Nishihara, 1978; Marr, 1982; Geons: Biederman, 1987; Superquadrics: Pentland, 1986.

84. Transversal intersections in differential topology: Guillemin & Pollack, 1974. Rule of concave creases: Bennett & Hoffman, 1987; Hoffman, 1983a; 1983b; Hoffman & Richards, 1984. Schröder staircase: Schröder, 1858.

86. The Möbius band, a surface with only one side, was discovered by Augustus Möbius and Johann Listing, both students of the famous mathematician Gauss. You can make a Möbius band by taking a strip of paper, giving it a single half-twist, and then gluing the two free ends to form a loop. See, e.g., Devlin, 1994, p. 179.

89. Minima rule: Bennett & Hoffman, 1987; Beusmans, Hoffman, & Bennett, 1987; Hoffman, 1983a; 1983b; Hoffman & Richards, 1982; 1984. Human vision is sensitive to changes in curvature: 2D curves: Triesman & Gormican, 1988, Wilson & Richards, 1985; 1989; Wolfe, Yee, & Friedman-Hill, 1992; 3D surfaces in structure from motion or motion parallax: Cornilleau-Peres &

Droulez, 1989; Koenderink & van Doorn, 1986; Norman & Lappin, 1992; Norman & Todd, 1993; Rogers & Graham, 1983; Saidpour & Braunstein, 1994; Todd, 1984; Todd & Norman, 1991; 3D surfaces in stereo or motion parallax: Rogers, 1986; Rogers & Cagenello, 1989; Rogers & Collett, 1989; Rogers & Graham, 1983.

90. Attneave's disk: Attneave, 1974.

92. The *Weeping Willow* picture puzzle: Pastore, 1971, p. 6. Turton's frontispiece: Turton, 1819. Edgar Rubin's study of the face-goblet illusion: Rubin, 1915/1958.

94. Half-moons experiment: Hoffman, 1983a; 1983b; Hoffman & Richards, 1984.

96. Experimental confirmations of Mach's observation on symmetry and repetition: Baylis & Driver, 1994; 1995; Bruce & Morgan, 1975; Corballis & Roldan, 1974.

97. Confirmation of the minima rule with contour-deletion experiments: Biederman, 1987; Biederman & Blickle, 1985; Biederman & Cooper, 1991. A failure to replicate this finding is reported by Cave and Kosslyn, 1994, but their study suffers from a fatal flaw: Stimuli in their critical "Unnatural-disconnected" case permit easy recovery of the natural parts. This makes these stimuli as easy to identify as those in the "Natural-disconnected" case.

98. Confirmation of the minima rule with memory experiments: Braunstein, Hoffman, & Saidpour, 1989. Advantages of "good" parts: They are better retrieval cues for recalling shapes: Bower & Glass, 1976; They are themselves better recalled: Palmer, 1977; They are more easily identified in mental images: Reed, 1974. See also Schyns & Murphy, 1994, on the interaction of the minima rule with category formation.

99. For technical discussion of curvature normalization: Hoffman & Singh, 1997. Experiment with modified face-goblet illusion: Hoffman & Singh, 1997.

100. Object recognition processes operate simultaneously on both sides of edges before figure-ground relationships are determined: Peterson & Gibson, 1993; 1994. Factors that determine figure and ground: Symmetry: Bahnsen, 1928; Hochberg, 1964; Size and contrast: Rubin, 1915/1958; Koffka, 1935; Convexity: Kanizsa & Gerbino, 1976; Stevens & Brookes, 1988. Experiment with modified Schröder staircases: Hoffman & Singh, 1997.

102. You prefer shorter part cuts: Singh, Seyranian, & Hoffman, 1997.

103. "Magic" might best describe what you can do with the right choice of parts, as the mathematicians Stefan Banach (1892–1945) and Alfred Tarski

(1902–1983) discovered. According to the Banach-Tarski theorem, you can take a solid sphere, break it into five parts, and, if you picked the right parts, reassemble two of the parts into a solid sphere of the same size as the original, and you can reassemble the remaining three parts into another solid sphere of the same size. So you start with one filled sphere and, by breaking it into the right parts, you end up with two filled spheres, each the same size as the original and each as solidly packed as the original. You can repeat this on each of the two new spheres to create four, and so on for as long as you wish. From one sphere you can create millions of identical copies, if you just use the right parts. Spheres aren't special, either; you can do this kind of magic with any solid shape. And there are hints that this magic with parts might go on with subatomic particles like protons. The Banach-Tarski theorems: Banach & Tarski, 1924; Dekker & de Groot, 1956; Mycielski, 1955; von Neumann, 1929; Robinson, 1947; Wagon, 1985. Strong interaction phenomena of elementary particles can be modeled with the Banach-Tarski theorem: Augenstein, 1984; 1994. Paraprosopia in schizophrenics: Dewdney, 1973; Grüsser & Landis, 1991, p. 289.

104. Quote on Daniel Paul Schreber's paraprosopic experiences: Grüsser & Landis, 1991, p. 290; Schreber, 1903/1973, p. 75. Williams syndrome: Bellugi et al., 1988, 1994; Bertrand et al., 1997.

5. The Day Color Drained Away

107. Chintz China image: Gery Souza Design, modified with permission.

108. The case of Jonathan I: Sacks, 1995; Sacks & Wasserman, 1987. Cerebral achromatopsia: Collins, 1925; Cowey & Heywood, 1997; Critchley, 1965; Damasio et al., 1980; Green & Lesell, 1977; Heywood, Cowey, & Newcombe, 1994; Heywood, Gaffan, & Cowey, 1995; MacKay & Dunlop, 1899; Meadows, 1974; Mollon et al., 1980; Rizzo et al., 1993; Sacks, 1995; Setala & Vesti, 1994; Zeki, 1990; 1993. Hemiachromatopsia: Freedman & Costa, 1992; Gowers, 1887; 1888; Paulson et al., 1994; Silverman & Galetta, 1995; Verrey, 1888; Zeki, 1990; 1993. V4 and color: Desimone et al., 1985; Desimone & Schein, 1987; Dufort & Lumsden, 1991; Heywood et al., 1992; Lueck et al., 1989; de Monasterio & Schein, 1982; Motter, 1994; Schein et al., 1982; Yoshioka & Dow, 1996; Yoshioka et al., 1996; Zeki, 1973; 1980; 1983a; 1983b; 1985; Zeki et al., 1991. Chromatophenes: Sacks, 1995, p. 28; Zeki, 1993, p. 279.

109. Chromatophenes confined to one hemifield: Zeki, 1993, p. 279.

110. Magnetic inhibition of lingual and fusiform gyri leads to temporary achromatopsia: Sacks, 1995, p. 34. Neon color spreading: Bressan, 1993a; 1993b; 1995; Bressan & Vallortigara, 1991; Day, 1983; Grossberg & Mingolla, 1985a; Kaihara et al., 1994; Nakayama et al., 1990, Prinzmetal & Keysar, 1989; Redies & Spillmann, 1981; Takeichi et al, 1992; van Tuijl, 1975; van Tuijl &

de Weert, 1979; van Tuijl & Leeuwenberg, 1979; Varin, 1971; Wallach, 1935; Watanabe & Sato, 1989; Yoshimichi et al., 1984.

111. The Redies-Spillmann figure: Redies & Spillmann, 1981.

112. The color shuffle: I learned this trick in a talk given on November 23, 1995, by Jan Koenderink at the Zentrum für interdisziplinäre Forschung (ZiF) der Universität Bielefeld.

113. Newton quote: Newton, 1730/1950, pp. 124–125.

114. You create color in the context of creating objects, shapes, and illuminations: Adelson & Pentland, 1990; Bergström, 1977; 1982; 1994a; 1994b. The movie example: Larry Maloney suggested this in discussions at the ZiF early in 1996.

115. Rules for interpreting abrupt and gradual image changes: These are part of many theories of color and lightness, especially the retinex theory of Land: Land, 1959; 1977; 1983; 1986a; 1986b; Land & McCann, 1971. Problems with these rules, and interesting fixes, are discussed in Rubin & Richards, 1982; 1987; Witkin, 1982. Possible neural instantiation of Land's lightness detectors: Schein & Desimone, 1990. Theories of color and color constancy: Retinex theory of Land: (referenced above); The linear models theory: Cohen, 1964; D'Zmura, 1992; D'Zmura & Iverson, 1993a; 1993b; Iverson & D'Zmura, 1994; Judd et al., 1964; Knoblauch & Maloney, 1996; Maloney, 1985; 1986; Maloney & Wandell, 1986; Marimont & Wandell, 1992; Wandell, 1995, chapter 9.

117. Inverting bumps and dents: Knill & Kersten, 1991; Ramachandran, 1986; Rittenhouse, 1786. Seeing the light source above or overhead: Bergström et al., 1984, experiment 2; von Fieandt, 1938; von Fieandt & Moustgaard, 1977; Herschberger, 1970; Hess, 1950; 1961; Howard et al., 1990 (first to distinguish overhead from above); Kleffner & Ramachandran, 1992; Oppel, 1856; Rittenhouse, 1786; Schröder, 1858.

118. Simultaneous contrast: This is described in any standard treatise on vision. See, e.g., Fiorentini et al., 1990. White's figure: White, 1981. Perceived gray is a function of grouping principles: Gilchrist et al., 1996. Transparency may also play a role in the perception of White's figure: the gray bar on the right often appears transparent, whereas the gray bar on the left appears opaque. But this can't be the whole story, since it's possible to see the gray bar on the right as lying *behind* the horizontal white bars (which appear to bend); in this interpretation the gray bar on the right no longer appears transparent, but it still looks much lighter than the gray bar on the left.

119. The De Valois checkerboard: De Valois & De Valois, 1988, p. 229.

120. Corrugated Mondrian figure: Adelson, 1993. Gilchrist's explanation of the cor-

rugated Mondrian: Gilchrist et al., 1996. The lightness difference in the corrugated Mondrian varies as a function of the perceived angles between planes: Wishart et al., 1995.

121. Workshop metaphor: Adelson & Pentland, 1990; 1996.

123. The argyle figure: Adelson, 1993.

125. Your rules for deciding to construct transparent filters: Beck et al., 1984; Bressan, 1993a; Metelli, 1970; 1975a; 1975b; 1976; 1985; Metelli et al., 1985. Kanizsa on the importance of spatial relations in the perception of transparency: Kanizsa, 1979, pp. 151–162. Singh on generic views applied to transparency: Personal communication, 19 August 1996.

126. Generic-view principle for assigning lights, shapes, and surface colors: Blake, 1994; Brainard & Freeman, 1994; Freeman, 1994; 1996.

128. The anchoring problem: Gilchrist et al., 1996. The average luminance rule: Helson, 1943; Hurlbert, 1986. The highest luminance rule: Land & McCann, 1971; McCann, 1987; Horn, 1977; Wallach, 1948; 1963. Perceived gray depends on area relationships: Cataliotti & Gilchrist, 1995; Diamond, 1953; 1955; Heinemann, 1955; Helson, 1964; Helson & Joy, 1962; Helson & Rohles, 1959; Leibowitz et al., 1953; Stevens, 1967; Stewart, 1959; Torii & Uemura, 1965. Flourence: Bonato & Gilchrist, 1994; Evans, 1948.

129. The color solid: Burnham et al., 1963.

130. Light behaves as particle and wave at the same instant (violating complementarity principle of Bohr): Mizobuchi & Ohtake, 1992. Einstein quote: Gribbin, 1995, p. 120; Home & Gribbin, 1991. Measurement according to quantum theory: Albert, 1992; Gribbin, 1995; Wheeler & Zurek, 1983; Zurek, 1990.

131. Diagram of cone responses: adapted from MacNichol, 1964.

132. Quote of Thomas Young: Young, 1802. Nucleotide sequences found for visual pigments: Applebury & Hargrave, 1986; Nathans, 1987; 1989; Nathans et al., 1986a; 1986b. Color blindness: Hurvich, 1981; Mollon, 1990; Thompson, 1995. Two normal versions of L pigment: Merbs & Nathans, 1992. Two L pigments account for different Rayleigh matches: Neitz & Jacobs, 1986; Winderickx et al., 1992. L pigment with serine in about 62 percent of normal males: Winderickx et al., 1992.

133. Quote by John Mollon: Mollon, 1992, p. 378. Opponent colors: Hering, 1905; 1964; Jameson & Hurvich, 1955; 1959; Larimer et al., 1975. Diagram of simple model of color opponency: After Lennie, 1984.

134. Neurophysiological evidence for color opponency: Derrington et al., 1984; DeValois et al., 1958a; 1958b; DeValois, 1965a; 1965b; DeValois et al., 1966; Gouras, 1968; Lennie et al., 1990; Svaetichin, 1956; Wiesel & Hubel, 1966. For a sophisticated mathematical approach to opponent colors see Mausfeld & Niederée, 1993. Color constancy and the linear models approach: see Note 115.

135. The transparent blue square: de Weert & Kruysbergen, 1987. Using generic view assumption to make the blue square disappear: Albert & Hoffman, 1992; 1995.

136. You construct subjective sounds: Miller & Licklider, 1950; Warren, 1984.

137. You might use a genericity principle in constructing sounds: Rainer Mausfeld, personal communication, 20 June 1997. You can create colored surfaces in three dimensions: Kojo et al., 1995.

138. A switch in stereo disparity can switch interpretations of surface color between modal and amodal: Nakayama et al., 1990.

6. When the World Stopped Moving

139. The akinetopsia of L.M. and others: Baker et al., 1991; Hess et al., 1989; Rizzo et al., 1995; Vaina, 1994; 1996; Zeki, 1991; Zihl et al., 1983; 1991.

140. Zihl quote: Zihl et al., 1983, p. 315.

141. Locke quote: Locke, 1690/1975, Chapter VIII, Section 9–10. Transitory akinetopsia induced by transcranial magnetic stimulation: Beckers & Hömberg, 1992; Beckers & Zeki, 1995.

142. Exner's experiments on visual motion: Boring, 1942, p. 594; Exner, 1875; 1888. The web address for all motion displays in this chapter: http://aris.ss.uci.edu/cogsci/personnel/hoffman/vi6.html

143. Wertheimer's experiment with colored dots: Wertheimer, 1912.

144. Linke's curved path motion: Koffka, 1931, p. 1185; Linke, 1907; Shepard & Zare, 1983.

145. Benussi's curved path motion: Benussi, 1916; Boring, 1942, p. 597, 606; Koffka, 1931, p. 1185. Benussi's work was with tactual motion, but the application to vision was obvious. Proposals for how you create simple motions: Borjesson & Ahlstrom, 1993; Cutting & Proffitt, 1981; 1982; Johansson, 1950; 1973; Proffitt & Cutting, 1980; Restle, 1979; Shepard, 1984; Wallach, 1965; 1976.

146. The Ternus display: Pantle & Picciano, 1976; Petersik & Pantle, 1979; Ternus,

1926; Ternus credits J. Pikler, 1917, for the original display, but I have not found Pikler's paper. Braddick's short- and long-range motion processes: Anstis, 1980; Braddick, 1974; 1980. Evidence against Braddick's distinction and for a first-order versus second-order stimulus distinction: Cavanagh & Mather, 1989; Chubb & Sperling, 1988.

147. Von Schiller's display: von Schiller, 1933, p. 188.

148. Ramachandran and Anstis create synchronized von Schiller displays: Ramachandran & Anstis, 1985; Sekuler et al., 1990, p. 219.

149. Anstis and Ramachandran create variant of Wertheimer's windmill: Anstis & Ramachandran, 1986; Sekuler et al., 1990, p. 218.

151. Brown and Voth's display: Brown & Voth, 1937; Shepard, 1984, p. 428. Duncker's displays: Duncker, 1929/1937; early work on rotary motion was also done by Rubin, 1927.

152. Rubin and Richards' extension of Duncker's displays: Rubin & Richards, 1988. You divide motion into common and relative components: Borjesson & Ahlstrom, 1993; Cutting & Proffitt, 1981; Johansson, 1950; Proffitt & Cutting, 1980; Proffitt & Kaiser, 1995; Wallach, 1965; 1976.

153. First psychological paper on the barber pole illusion: Gilford, 1929. First psychological paper on the aperture problem: Stumpf, 1911; see especially his Figure 1 on page 322. See also Todorović, 1996. Other early studies of the aperture problem: Metzger, 1953/1975, p. 573 of 1975 edition; Scott & Noland, 1965; Wallach, 1935; Wertheimer, 1912.

155. Hildreth's rule of smoothest velocity fields: Hildreth, 1982; 1984. Related work on motion integration: Adelson & Movshon, 1982; Albright, 1984; Anandan & Weiss, 1985; Bülthoff, Little, & Poggio, 1989; Fennema & Thompson, 1979; Horn & Schunck, 1981; Marr & Ullman, 1981; Nagel & Enkelmann, 1986; M.E. Sereno, 1987; M.I. Sereno, 1989; Stoner & Albright, 1993; Wang, Mathur, & Koch, 1989; Yuille & Grzywacz, 1988. Warping and morphing special effects: Watkins et al., 1993.

156. The moving gratings and plaids of Adelson and Movshon: Adelson & Movshon, 1982; 1984.

157. Size and contrast affect motion integration: Adelson & Movshon, 1982; Vallortigara & Bressan, 1991. Stereo depth affects motion integration: Adelson & Movshon, 1984; Nakayama, Shimojo, & Silverman, 1989; Shimojo, Silverman, & Nakayama, 1988; 1989.

158. Transparency affects motion integration: Kersten, Bülthoff, Schwartz, & Kurtz,

1992; Stoner & Albright, 1992; 1993; Stoner, Albright, & Ramachandran, 1990; Trueswell & Hayhoe, 1993. Color affects motion integration: Albright, 1991; Dobkins, Stoner, & Albright, 1992; Kooi, DeValois, & Switkes, 1992; Krauskopf & Farrell, 1990; Stoner & Albright, 1993. The rigidity principle: Braunstein, 1976; Braunstein, Hoffman, & Pollick, 1990; Gibson & Gibson, 1957; Green, 1961; Hay, 1966; Hildreth et al., 1995; Hoffman, 1983b; Hoffman & Bennett, 1985, 1986; Huang & Lee, 1989; Johansson, 1975; Koenderink & van Doorn, 1991; Liter, Braunstein, & Hoffman, 1993; Longuet-Higgins & Prazdny, 1980; Todd, 1984; Todd & Bressan, 1990; Treue et al., 1995; Ullman, 1977; 1979; 1983; 1984; Wallach & O'Connell, 1953. The web address for all motion displays in this chapter: http://aris.ss.uci.edu/cogsci/personnel/hoffman/vi6.html

159. Ullman's rigidity theorem: Ullman, 1977; 1979. My statement of the theorem simplifies on two points: I omit that Ullman assumes orthographic projection and that the two solutions are orthographic reflections of each other about the image plane.

160. The virtual Rome web site at UCLA: http://www.aud.ucla.edu/~/dabernat/rome/index.html. The virtual Los Angeles web site at UCLA: http://www.gsaup.ucla.edu/bill/LA.html. For VRML (Virtual Reality Modeling Language): http://www.sdsc.edu/vrml/.

161. The Black Light Theater dancers: Proffitt & Kaiser, 1995, p. 234. Johansson's biological motion movies: Johansson, 1973; Mass et al., 1971. You discern actions in one fifth of a second: Johansson, 1973. You discern gender in Johansson's movies: Barclay, Cutting, & Kozlowski, 1978; Cutting & Kozlowski, 1977; Cutting, Proffitt, & Kozlowski, 1978; Kozlowski & Cutting, 1977. Cats perceive biological motion: Blake, 1993.

162. The rigidity plus planarity rule for constructing biological motion: Hoffman & Flinchbaugh, 1982. Johansson displays that violate the planarity rule are more difficult to interpret: Proffitt & Bertenthal, 1988. Other rules you might use to construct objects and motions in three dimensions: Rigid fixed-axis motion: Webb & Aggarwal, 1981; 1982; Hoffman & Bennett, 1986; Nonrigid fixed-axis motion: Bennett & Hoffman, 1985. Siggraph 97 at the Los Angeles Convention Center: http://www.siggraph.org/s97/.

163. The experiments of Kersten and his collaborators on the role of shadows in constructing motion: Kersten et al., 1994. See also Kersten's online movie at http://vision.psych.umn.edu/www/kersten-lab/images/ball-in-a-box.mov.

165. The discovery that motion of colored objects is hard to see at isoluminance: Stumpf, 1911; Todorović, 1996; see also the work of Liebmann, 1927, on the perception of colors at isoluminance. Later work on motion at isoluminance: Cavanagh, Tyler, & Favreau, 1984.

166. The magnocellular and parvocellular anatomical pathways: DeYoe and Van Essen, 1988; Lennie, 1980; Spillmann & Werner, 1990. Argument that magnocellular and parvocellular pathways are functionally distinct: Livingstone & Hubel, 1987; Ramachandran & Gregory, 1978. Argument that the pathways interact: Dobkins & Albright, 1993a; 1993b; Stoner & Albright, 1993.

167. The discovery of flicker colors: Prevost, 1826. The many rediscoveries of flicker colors: Cohen & Gordon, 1949. Benham's top: Abney, 1894; Benham, 1894; 1895. The honey bee sees flicker colors: Srinivasan, Lehrer, & Wehner, 1987. Flicker colors involve both retinal and cortical processing: von Campenhausen & Schramme, 1995.

169. Dynamic color spreading display on the Internet: http://www.socsci.uci. edu/cogsci/personnel/hoffman/dcs-demo.html. Dynamic color spreading: Cicerone & Hoffman, 1991; 1992; Cicerone et al., 1995; Cunningham, Shipley, & Kellman, 1996; Shipley & Kellman, 1994. Related effects in the achromatic case: Andersen & Cortese, 1989; Cortese & Andersen, 1991; Kellman & Shipley, 1992; Shipley & Kellman, 1993.

170. California Department of Transportation: http://www.dot.ca.gov/.

7. The Feel of a Phantom

173. The case of F.A.: Ramachandran, 1993a; 1994; Yang et al., 1994. Early literature on the experience of referred sensations in the phantom limbs of amputees: Cronholm, 1951; James, 1887; Mitchell, 1871. The earliest description of the phantom limb phenomenon in the medical or philosophical literature: Paré, 1551/1552. Other early descriptions of the phantom limb: Price & Twombly, 1978.

174. The maps on the arm of F.A.: adapted from Ramachandran, 1993a, Figure 3, p. 10416.

175. The case of V.Q.: Ramachandran, 1993a; 1993b; 1994; Ramachandran, Rogers-Ramachandran, & Stewart, 1992; Ramachandran, Stewart, & Rogers-Ramachandran, 1992.

178. Penfield's study of somatosensory cortex: Cholewiak & Collins, 1991; Penfield & Boldrey, 1937; Penfield & Rasmussen, 1950. Face and arm cortex invade region devoted to amputated hand: Yang et al., 1994.

179. The tactile agnosia of E.C.: Reed & Caselli, 1994; Reed, Caselli, & Farah, 1996.

180. The cutaneous rabbit: Geldard, 1975; 1977; Geldard & Sherrick, 1972; 1983; 1986.

182. Quote from Immersion Corporation web page: http://www.immerse.com.

For more information on joysticks with force feedback: http://www.cyber-net.com.

183. Quote from Diane Ackerman: Ackerman, 1990, pp. 80–81. Quote from Howard Rheingold: Rheingold, 1991, p. 328.

184. Virtual reality to train surgeons in endoscopic techniques: http://robotics.eecs.berkeley.edu/~mcenk/medical/. See also the MedWeb: http://www.gen.emory.edu/MEDWEB/keyword/virtual_reality_in_medicine.html.

8. Peeking Behind the Icons

188. Resemblance between phenomenal and relational realms: I argue that there need be no resemblance. But Berkeley has an ingenious argument that goes much further, and is probably valid. He argues that there *cannot* be a resemblance between them. The argument appears at the end of the first dialogue of his *Three Dialogues Between Hylas and Philonous*. The argument, in part, is this: "How can that which is sensible be *like* that which is insensible? Can a real thing, in itself *invisible*, be like a *colour*; or a real thing, which is not *audible*, be like a *sound*? In a word, can anything be like a sensation or idea, but another sensation or idea?" See, e.g., Berkeley, 1965, pp. 169–170. I neither need nor insist on the validity of Berkeley's argument, but find it fascinating nonetheless. Some might argue that it suffers from the "intensional fallacy" (see, e.g., Churchland, 1984, p. 32), but I think not. Some Kant scholars interpret him as saying that the relational realm, the thing-in-itself, is unknowable, so that the question of resemblance between the phenomenal and relational is moot. For interesting discussion, see, e.g., Allison, 1983.

192. The view that the brain is responsible for creating consciousness is popular among many in the cognitive sciences. For discussion pro and con see, e.g., Baars, 1988; Chalmers, 1996; P.M. Churchland, 1995; P.S. Churchland, 1986; Crick, 1994; Dennett, 1991; Dretske, 1995; Edelman, 1989; 1992; Harth, 1993; Herbert, 1992; Humphrey, 1992; Jackendoff, 1987; Kosslyn & Koenig, 1992; Marcel & Bisiach, 1988; Penrose, 1989; 1994; Popper & Eccles, 1985; Searle, 1984; 1992; Tye, 1995.

193. Synesthesia: Cytowic, 1989; 1993; Cytowic & Wood, 1982a; 1982b; Luria, 1968; Messiaen, 1956; Nabokov, 1966. Quote from Cytowic on the feel of Angostura bitters: Cytowic, 1993, pp. 64–65. Synesthetic perceptions endure a lifetime: Cytowic, 1993, p. 76.

194. Perceptual effects of inverting prisms: Kohler, 1962; Stratton, 1896; 1897a; 1897b. Jan Koenderink's inverted prisms experiment: Jan Koenderink, personal communication, 15 June 1997. On inferring properties of the mind from differential effects of brain damage: Goodman, 1984, p. 15.

196. Behavior of finite minds in interaction described by probabilistic rules: Bennett,

Hoffman, & Prakash, 1989. Probability entails no ontology: Let X be an arbitrary abstract space. A collection χ of subsets of X is called a σ-*algebra* if it contains X itself and is closed under the set operations of complementation and countable union. The pair (X, χ) is called a *measurable space* and any set A in χ is called an *event*. A *measure* on the measurable space (X, χ) is a map μ from χ to $\mathbf{R}\cup\{\infty\}$, such that the measure of a countable union of disjoint sets in χ is the sum of their individual measures. There is no deductively valid inference whose premises consist of these definitions and whose conclusion is an ontology, i.e., a statement about the nature of the relational realm. Similar remarks hold for the definition of a stochastic process, or of any other mathematical structure.

197. Theories of the relational realm taking into account quantum theory: von Neumann (1955), London & Bauer (1983), and others have proposed variants of idealism, giving conscious observers the central role in the construction of quantum phenomena. Chalmers (1996), Herbert (1993), Popper & Eccles (1985), Wigner (1961), and others have proposed variants of dualism. Bohm (1952), Cramer (1986), Penrose (1994), and others have proposed variants of physicalism. There are many interesting books on the puzzle of observation in quantum theory. In addition to those listed above, see d'Espagnat (1995), and especially his concept of "veiled reality." For a mathematically rigorous examination of the relationship between visual perception and quantum theory see Bennett, Hoffman, & Prakash, 1989, which is available online (free) at http://aris.ss.uci.edu/cogsci/personnel/hoffman/ompref.html. Popular accounts of evolution: Dawkins, 1987; Gould, 1991. A critical analysis of evolutionary theory: Johnson, 1993. A probabilistic formulation of the evolution of perception: Bennett, Hoffman, & Prakash, 1997.

Epilogue

201. The case of D.S.: Ramachandran, 1996; Hirstein & Ramachandran, 1997. Capgras syndrome: Capgras & Reboul-Lachaux, 1923; Ellis & Young, 1990.

202. Cognitive therapy and the constructive nature of emotions: Burns, 1989; Stuart et al., 1997.

REFERENCES

Abney, W. de E. 1894. The artificial spectrum top. *Nature, 51*, 292.

Ackerman, D. 1990. *A natural history of the senses.* New York: Random House.

Adelson, E.H. 1993. Perceptual organization and the judgment of brightness. *Science, 262,* 2042–2044.

Adelson, E.H., & Movshon, J.A. 1982. Phenomenal coherence of moving visual patterns. *Nature, 300,* 523–525.

Adelson, E.H., & Movshon, J.A. 1984. Binocular disparity and the computation of two-dimensional motion. *Journal of the Optical Society of America, A, 1,* 1266.

Adelson, E.H., & Pentland, A.P. 1990. The perception of shading and reflectance. *Vision and Modeling Technical Report 140,* MIT Media Laboratory.

Adelson, E.H., & Pentland, A.P. 1996. The perception of shading and reflectance. In Knill & Richards, 1996.

Albers, J. 1975. *Interaction of color.* New Haven, Conn. : Yale University Press.

Albert, D.Z. 1992. *Quantum mechanics and experience.* Cambridge, Mass.: Harvard University Press.

Albert, M.K. 1993. Parallelism and the perception of illusory contours. *Perception, 22,* 589–595.

Albert, M.K. 1995. Genericity and the perception of visual contours and surfaces. *Ph.D. Thesis,* UC Irvine.

Albert, M.K., & Hoffman, D.D. 1992. Topological factors in neon color spreading. *Advances in Color Vision Technical Digest, 1992* (Optical Society of America, Washington, D.C.), 4, 158–160.

Albert, M.K., & Hoffman, D.D. 1995. Genericity in spatial vision. In D. Luce, K. Romney, D. Hoffman, & M. D'Zmura (Eds.), *Geometric Representations of Perceptual Phenomena: Articles in Honor of Tarow Indow's 70th Birthday.* New York: Erlbaum.

Albert, M.K., & Hoffman, D.D. 1996. Generic views and illusory contours. Under review.

Alberti, L.B. 1435/1956. *On painting.* Translated by J.R. Spencer. London: Routledge and Kegan Paul.

Alberti, L.B. 1435/1991. *On painting.* Translated by C. Grayson. London: Penguin.

Albright, T.D. 1984. Direction and orientation selectivity of neurons in visual area MT of the macaque. *Journal of Neurophysiology, 52,* 1106–1130.

Albright, T.D. 1991. Color and the integration of motion signals. *Trends in Neurosciences, 14,* 266–269.

Allison, H.E. *Kant's transcendental idealism.* New Haven, Conn.: Yale University Press.

Anandan, P., & Weiss, R. 1985. Introducing a smoothness constraint in a matching approach for the computation of optical flow fields. *Proceedings of the IEEE Workshop on Computer Vision: Representation and Control*, Bellaire, MI, 186–194.

Andersen, G.J., & Cortese, J.M. 1989. 2-D contour perception resulting from kinetic occlusion. *Perception & Psychophysics, 46,* 49–55.

Anstis, S.M. 1980. The perception of apparent motion. *Philosophical Transactions of the Royal Society of London, B, 290,* 153–168.

Anstis, S.M., & Ramachandran, V.S. 1986. Visual inertia in apparent motion. *Vision Research, 26,* 755–764.

Applebury, M.L., & Hargrave, P.A. 1986. Molecular biology of visual pigments. *Vision Research,* 26, 1881–1895.

Armington, J.C., Krauskopf, J.E., & Wooten, B.R. (Eds.). 1978. *Visual psychophysics: Its physiological basis.* New York: Academic Press.

Arterberry, M.E., & Yonas, A. 1988. Infants' sensitivity to kinetic information for three-dimensional object shape. *Perception & Psychophysics, 44,* 1–6.

Atherton, M. 1990. *Berkeley's revolution in vision*. Ithaca: Cornell University Press.

Atkinson, J., & Braddick, O.J. 1981. Development of optokinetic nystagmus in young infants: An indicator of cortical binocularity? In D.F. Fisher, R.A. Monty, & J.W. Senders (Eds.), *Eye movements: Cognition and visual perception*. Hillsdale, N.J.: Lawrence Erlbaum.

Attneave, F. 1974. Multistability in perception. *Scientific American, 225*, 63–71.

Augenstein, B.W. 1984. Hadron physics and transfinite set theory. *International Journal of Theoretical Physics, 23*, 12.

Augenstein, B.W. 1994. Speculative model of some elementary particle phenomena. *Speculations in Science and Technology, 17*, 21–26.

Baars, B. 1988. *A cognitive theory of consciousness*. Cambridge: Cambridge University Press.

Badt, K. 1963. Wesen der Plastik. In *Raumphantasien und Raumillusionen*. Cologne: M. DuMont Schauberg.

Bahnsen, P. (1928). Eine untersuchung über symmetrie und asymmetrie bei visuellen wahrnehmungen. *Zeitschrift für Psychologie, 108*, 355–361.

Bailey, C. 1928/1964. *The Greek atomists and Epicurus*. Oxford: Oxford University Press.

Baker, C.L., Hess, R.F., & Zihl, J. 1991. Residual motion perception in a "motion-blind" patient, assessed with limited-lifetime random dot stimuli. *Journal of Neuroscience, 11*, 454–461.

Ballard, D., & Brown, C. 1982. *Computer Vision*. Englewood Cliffs, N.J.: Prentice-Hall.

Banach, S., & Tarski, A. 1924. Sur la decomposition des ensembles de points en parties respectivement congruentes. *Fundamenta Mathematica, 6*, 244–277.

Barclay, C.D., Cutting, J.E., & Kozlowski, L.T. 1978. Temporal and spatial factors in gait perception that influence gender recognition. *Perception & Psychophysics, 23*, 145–152.

Barlow, H., Blakemore, C., & Weston-Smith, M. (Eds.). 1990. *Images and understanding*. Cambridge: Cambridge University Press.

Barrow, H.G., & Tenenbaum, J.M. 1978. Recovering intrinsic scene characteristics from images. In Hanson & Riseman, 1978, pp. 3–26.

Baylis, G.C., & Driver, J. 1994. Parallel computation of symmetry but not repetition in single visual objects. *Visual Cognition, 1*, 377–400.

Baylis, G.C., & Driver, J. 1995. Obligatory edge assignment in vision: The role of figure and part segmentation in symmetry detection. *Journal of Experimental Psychology: Human Perception and Performance, 21*, 1323–1342.

Beazley, J.D., & Ashmole, B. 1966. *Greek sculpture and painting to the end of the Hellenistic period.* Cambridge: Cambridge University Press.

Beck, J. (Ed.) 1982. *Organization and representation in perception.* Hillsdale, N.J.: Lawrence Erlbaum.

Beck, J., Prazdny, K., & Ivry, R. 1984. The perception of transparency with achromatic colors. *Perception & Psychophysics, 35*, 407–422.

Becker, M.F., & Knopp, J. 1978. Processing of visual illusions in the frequency and spatial domains. *Perception & Psychophysics, 23*, 521–526.

Beckers, G., & Hömberg, V. 1992. Cerebral visual motion blindness: transitory akinetopsia induced by transcranial magnetic stimulation of human area V5. *Proceedings of the Royal Society of London, B, 249*, 173–178.

Beckers, G., & Zeki, S. 1995. The consequences of inactivating areas V1 and V5 on visual motion perception. *Brain, 118*, 49–60.

Bellugi, U., Sabo, H., & Vaid, J. 1988. Spatial deficits in children with Williams syndrome. In J. Stiles-Davis, M. Kritchevsky, & U. Bellugi (Eds.), *Spatial cognition: Brain bases and development.* Hillsdale, N.J.: Lawrence Erlbaum, pp. 273–298.

Bellugi, U., Wang, P.P., & Jernigan, T.L. 1994. Williams syndrome: An unusual neuropsychological profile. In S.H. Broman & J. Grafman (Eds.), *Atypical cognitive deficits in developmental disorders: Implications for brain function.* Hillsdale, N J · Lawrence Erlbaum, pp. 23–56.

Benham, C.E. 1894. The artificial spectrum top. *Nature, 51*, 200.

Benham, C.E. 1895. The artificial spectrum top. *Nature, 51*, 321.

Bennett, B.M., & Hoffman, D.D. 1985. The computation of structure from fixed-axis motion: nonrigid structures. *Biological Cybernetics, 51*, 293–300.

Bennett, B.M., & Hoffman, D.D. 1987. Shape decompositions for visual shape recognition: The role of transversality. In Richards & Ullman, 1987, pp. 215–256.

Bennett, B.M., Hoffman, D.D., & Prakash, C. 1989. *Observer mechanics: A formal theory of perception*. New York: Academic Press.

Bennett, B.M., Hoffman, D.D., & Prakash, C. 1997. Perception and evolution. *Institute for Mathematical Behavioral Sciences, Memo 97-10*, University of California, Irvine.

Benson, D.F., & Greenberg, J.P. 1969. Visual form agnosia: A specific defect in visual discrimination. *Archives of Neurology, 20,* 82–89.

Benussi, V. 1916. Versuche zur Analyse taktil erweckter Scheinbewegungen. *Arch. ges. Psychol., 36,* 59–135.

Bergström, S.S. 1977. Common and relative components of reflected light as information about the illumination, colour, and three-dimensional form of objects. *Scandinavian Journal of Psychology, 18,* 180–186.

Bergström, S.S. 1982. Illumination, color, and three-dimensional form. In Beck, 1982, pp. 365–378.

Bergström, S.S. 1994a. Color constancy: Arguments for a vector model for the perception of illumination, color, and depth. In Gilchrist, 1994, pp. 257–286.

Bergström, S.S. 1994b. Can the Johansson vector analysis be applied to the perception of illumination, color and depth? In Jansson et al., 1994, pp. 347–356.

Bergström, S.S., Gustafsson, K.-A., & Putaansuu, J. 1984. Information about three-dimensional shape and direction of illumination in a square-wave grating. *Perception, 13,* 129–140.

Berkeley, G. 1709/1963. *Works on vision*. C.M. Turbayne (Ed.). New York: Bobbs-Merrill.

Berkeley, G. 1965. *Berkeley's philosophical writings*. D. Armstrong (Ed.). New York: Macmillan.

Bertrand, J., Mervis, C.B., & Eisenberg, J.D. 1997. Drawing by children with Williams Syndrome: A developmental perspective. *Developmental Neuropsychology, 13,* 41–67.

Beusmans, J., Hoffman, D.D., & Bennett, B.M. 1987. Description of solid shape and its inference from occluding contours. *Journal of the Optical Society of America, A, 4,* 1155–1167.

Biederman, I. 1987. Recognition-by-components: A theory of human image understanding. *Psychological Review, 94,* 115–147.

Biederman, I., & Blickle, T. 1985. The perception of objects with deleted contours. Unpublished manuscript, State University of New York at Buffalo.

Biederman, I., & Cooper, E.E. 1991. Priming contour-deleted images: Evidence for intermediate representations in visual object recognition. *Cognitive Psychology, 23*, 393–419.

Biederman, I., & Ju, G. 1988. Surface vs. edge-based determinants of visual recognition. *Cognitive Psychology, 20*, 38–64.

Binford, T.O. (1971, December). Visual perception by computer. *IEEE Systems Science and Cybernetics Conference, Miami, FL.*

Binford, T.O. 1981. Inferring surfaces from images. *Artificial Intelligence, 17*, 205–244.

Birch, E.E., Gwiazda, J., & Held, R. 1982. Stereoacuity development for crossed and uncrossed disparities in human infants. *Vision Research, 22*, 507–513.

Blake, A. 1994. Improbable views. *Nature, 368*, 498–499.

Blake, A., & Bülthoff, H. 1991. Shape from specularities: Computation and psychophysics. *Philosophical Transactions of the Royal Society of London, Series B–Biological Sciences, 331*, 237–252.

Blake, R. 1993. Cats perceive biological motion. *Psychological Science, 4*, 54–57.

Blakemore, C. 1990. *Vision: Coding and efficiency.* Cambridge: Cambridge University Press.

Bloomer, C.M. 1990. *Principles of visual perception.* New York: Design Press.

Boacnin, D., & Ventura, D.F. 1995. Detection of shapes and illusory contours by bees. *Investigative Ophthalmology and Visual Science, ARVO Abstracts, 36*, 477.

Boff, K.R., Kaufman, L., & Thomas, J.P. (Eds.) 1986. *Handbook of perception and human performance.* New York: Wiley.

Bohm, D. 1952. A suggested interpretation of quantum theory in terms of "hidden variables," parts I and II. *Physical Review, 85*, 166-193.

Bonaiuto, P., Giannini, A.M., & Bonaiuto, M. 1991. Visual illusory productions with or without amodal completion. *Perception, 20*, 243–257.

Bonato, F., & Gilchrist, A.L. 1994. The perception of luminosity on different backgrounds and in different illuminations. *Perception, 23*, 991–1006.

Bonnet, C. 1760. *Essai analytique sur les facultes de l'ame.* Geneva: Philibert.

Boring, E.G. 1942. *Sensation and perception in the history of experimental psychology.* New York: Appleton-Century-Crofts.

Borjesson, E., & Ahlstrom, U. 1993. Motion structure in five-dot patterns as a determinant of perceptual grouping. *Perception & Psychophysics, 53,* 2–12.

Bower, G.H., & Glass, A.L. 1976. Structural units and the red-integrative power of picture fragments. *Journal of Experimental Psychology, 2,* 456–466.

Braddick, O. 1974. A short-range process in apparent motion. *Vision Research, 25,* 839–847.

Braddick, O. 1980. Low-level and high-level processes in apparent motion. *Philosophical Transactions of the Royal Society of London, B, 290,* 137–151.

Bradley, D.R. 1987. Cognitive contours and perceptual organization. In Petry & Meyer, 1987, pp. 201–212.

Bradley, D.R., Dumais, S.T., & Petry, H.M. 1976. Reply to Cavonius. *Nature, 261,* 77–78.

Bradley, D.R., & Petry, H.M. 1977. Organizational determinants of subjective contour: The subjective Necker cube. *American Journal of Psychology, 90,* 253–262.

Brainard, D.H., & Freeman, W.T. 1994. Bayesian method for recovering surface and illuminant properties from photosensor responses. *Proceedings of the SPIE Symposium on Human Vision, Visual Processing, and Digital Display V, Volume 2179,* 364–376.

Braunstein, M.L. 1976. *Depth perception through motion.* New York: Academic Press.

Braunstein, M.L., Hoffman, D.D., & Pollick, F.E. 1990. Discriminating rigid from nonrigid motion. *Perception & Psychophysics, 47,* 205–214.

Braunstein, M.L., Hoffman, D.D., & Saidpour, A. 1989. Parts of visual objects: An experimental test of the minima rule. *Perception, 18,* 817–826.

Bressan, P. 1993a. Revisitation of the luminance conditions for the occurrence of the achromatic neon color spreading illusion. *Perception & Psychophysics, 54,* 55–64.

Bressan, P. 1993b. Neon colour spreading with and without its figural prerequisites. *Perception, 22,* 353–361.

Bressan, P. 1995. A closer look at the dependence of neon colour spreading on wavelength and illuminance. *Vision Research, 35,* 375–379.

Bressan, P., & Vallortigara, G. 1991. Illusory depth from moving subjective figures and neon colour spreading. *Perception, 20,* 637–644.

Brigner, W.L., & Gallagher, M.B. 1974. Subjective contour: Apparent depth or simultaneous brightness contrast. *Perceptual and Motor Skills, 38,* 1047–1053.

Brindley, G., & Lewin, W. 1968. The visual sensations produced by electrical stimulation of the medial occipital cortex. *Journal of Physiology, 194,* 54–55.

Brindley, G., & Lewin, W. 1971. The sensations produced by electrical stimulation of the visual cortex. In T. Sterling, E. Bering, S. Pollack, and H. Vaughan (Eds.), *Visual prosthesis* 21–40. New York: Academic Press.

Brooks, R.A. 1981. Symbolic reasoning among 3-D models and 2-D images. *Artificial Intelligence, 17,* 205–244.

Brown, J.F. & Voth, A.C. 1937. The path of seen movement as a function of the vector field. *American Journal of Psychology, 49,* 543–563.

Bruce, V. 1988. *Recognising Faces.* Hillsdale, N.J.: Lawrence Erlbaum.

Bruce, V., & Morgan, M.J. 1975. Violations of symmetry and repetitions in visual patterns. *Perception, 4,* 239–249.

Bruner, J. 1973. On perceptual readiness. In J. Anglin (Ed.), *Beyond the information given.* New York: W. W. Norton.

Bülthoff, H., Little, J., & Poggio, T. 1989. A parallel algorithm for real-time computation of optical flow. *Nature, 337,* 549–553.

Burnham, R.W., Hanes, R.M., & Bartelson, C.J. 1963. *Color: A guide to basic facts and concepts.* New York: Wiley.

Burns, D. 1989. *The feeling good handbook.* New York: Plume.

Burton, H.E. 1945. The optics of Euclid. *Journal of the Optical Society of America, 35,* 357–372.

Button, J., & Putnam, T. 1962. Visual responses to cortical stimulation in the blind. *Journal of the Iowa State Medical Society, 52,* 17–21.

Campenhausen, C. von & Schramme, J. 1995. 100 years of Benham's top in colour science. *Perception, 24,* 695–717.

Campion, J. 1987. Apperceptive agnosia: The specification and description of constructs. In Humphreys & Riddoch, 1987, pp. 197–232.

Canny, J. 1986. A computational approach to edge detection. *IEEE Transactions on Pattern Analysis and Machine Intelligence, 8*, 679–698.

Capgras, J., & Reboul-Lachaux, J. 1923. L'illusion des "sosies" dans un délire systé-matise chronique. *Bull. Soc. Clinique Med. Mentale, 2*, 6–16.

Carey, S. 1978. The child as word-learner. In M. Halle, J. Bresnan, & G.A. Miller (Eds.), *Linguistic theory and psychological reality*. Cambridge, Mass.: MIT Press.

Carman, G.J., & Welch, L. 1992. Three-dimensional illusory contours and surfaces. *Nature, 360*, 585–587.

Carterette, E.C., & Friedman, M.P. (Eds.). 1978. *Handbook of perception, Volume 10: Perceptual ecology*. New York: Academic Press.

Cataliotti, J., & Gilchrist, A.L. 1995. Local and global processes in lightness per-ception. *Perception & Psychophysics, 57*, 125–135.

Cavanagh, P., & Mather, G. 1989. Motion: The long and short of it. *Spatial Vision, 4*, 103–129.

Cavanagh, P., Tyler, C.W., & Favreau, O.E. 1984. Perceived velocity of moving chro-matic gratings. *Journal of the Optical Society of America, A, 1*, 893–899.

Cave, C.B., & Kosslyn, S.M. 1993. The role of parts and spatial relations in object identification. *Perception, 22*, 229–248.

Chalmers, D.J. 1996. *The conscious mind*. Oxford: Oxford University Press.

Cholewiak, R.W., & Collins, A.A. 1991. Sensory and physiological bases of touch. In Heller & Schiff, 1991, pp. 21–60.

Chomsky, N. 1975. *Reflections on language*. New York: Pantheon.

Chubb, C., & Sperling, G. 1988. Drift-balanced random stimuli: a general basis for studying non-Fourier motion perception. *Journal of the Optical Society of America, A, 5*, 1986–2007.

Churchland, P.M. 1984. *Matter and consciousness*. Cambridge, Mass.: MIT Press.

Churchland, P.M. 1988. Perceptual plasticity and theoretical neutrality: a reply to Jerry Fodor. *Philosophy of Science, 55*, 167–187.

Churchland, P.M. 1995. *The engine of reason, the seat of the soul: A philosophical journey into the brain*. Cambridge, Mass.: MIT Press.

Churchland, P.S. 1986. *Neurophilosophy*. Cambridge, Mass.: MIT Press.

Cicerone, C.M., & Hoffman, D.D. 1991. Dynamic neon colors: Perceptual evidence for parallel visual pathways. *University of California, Irvine, Mathematical Behavior Sciences Memo 91–22*.

Cicerone, C.M., & Hoffman, D.D. 1992. Dynamic neon colors: Perceptual evidence for parallel visual pathways. *Advances in Color Vision Technical Digest, 1992* (Optical Society of America, Washington, D.C.), 4, 66–68.

Cicerone, C.M., Hoffman, D.D., Gowdy, P.D., & Kim, J.S. 1995. The perception of color from motion. *Perception & Psychophysics, 57*, 761–777.

Clark, J.J., & Yuille, A.L. 1990. *Data fusion for sensory information processing systems.* Boston: Kluwer Academic.

Clement, R.A. 1993. *Introduction to vision science.* Hillsdale, N.J.: Lawrence Erlbaum.

Cohen, J. 1964. Dependency of the spectral reflectance curves of the Munsell color chips. *Psychonomic Science, 1*, 369–370.

Cohen, J., & Gordon, D.A. 1949. The Prevost-Fechner-Benham subjective colors. *Psychological Bulletin, 46*, 97–136.

Collins, M. 1925. *Colour-blindness.* New York: Harcourt, Brace & Co.

Collon, D. 1987. *First impressions: Cylinder seals in the ancient near east.* British Museum, London. WA 104486.

Corballis, M.C., & Roldan, C.E. 1974. On the perception of symmetrical and repeated patterns. *Perception & Psychophysics, 16*, 136–142.

Cornford, F.M. (Translator). 1937. *Plato's cosmology: The Timaeus of Plato.* With a running commentary by Cornford. London: Routledge & Kegan Paul.

Cornilleau-Peres, V., & Droulez, J. 1989. Visual perception of surface curvature: Psychophysics of curvature detection induced by motion parallax. *Perception & Psychophysics, 46,* 351–364.

Cortese, J.M., & Andersen, G.J. 1991. Recovery of 3-D shape from deforming contours. *Perception & Psychophysics, 49,* 315–327.

Cowey, A., 1994. Cortical visual areas and the neurobiology of higher visual processes. In Farah & Ratcliff, 1994, pp. 3–31.

Cowey, A. & Heywood, C.A. 1997. Cerebral achromatopsia: Colour blindness despite wavelength processing. *Trends in Cognitive Sciences, 1*, 133–139.

Cramer, J. 1986. The transactional interpretation of quantum mechanics. *Reviews of Modern Physics, 58,* 647.

Craton, L., & Yonas, A. 1988. Infants' sensitivity to boundary flow information for depth at an edge. *Child Development, 59,* 1522–1529.

Craton, L., & Yonas, A. 1990. Kinetic occlusion: Further studies of the boundary flow cue. *Perception & Psychophysics, 47,* 169–179.

Crick, F.H.C. 1994. *The astonishing hypothesis: The scientific search for the soul.* New York: Scribner.

Critchley, M. 1965. Acquired anomalies of colour perception of central origin. *Brain, 88,* 711–724.

Cronholm, L.B. 1951. Phantom limbs in amputees. A study of changes in the integration of centripetal impulses with special reference to referred sensations. *Acta psychiatrica et neurologica Scandinavica, Supplementum, 72,* 1–310.

Cronin, T.W., & Marshall, N.J. 1989. A retina with at least ten spectral types of photoreceptors in a stomatopod crustacean. *Nature, 339,* 137–140.

Cronin, T.W., Marshall, N.J., & Land, M.F. 1994. The unique visual system of the mantis shrimp. *American Scientist, 82,* 4, 356–365.

Cronly-Dillon, J.R. (Ed.). 1991. *Vision and visual dysfunction.* Boca Raton: CRC Press.

Cumming, R., & Porter, T. 1990. *The colour eye.* London: BBC Books.

Cunningham, D.W., Shipley, T.F., & Kellman, P.J. 1996. The perception of surface qualities in dynamic scenes: Spatiotemporally defined boundaries and surfaces. *Submitted.*

Curcio, C.A., Millican, C.L., Allen, K.A., & Kalina, R.E. 1993. Aging of the human photoreceptor mosaic: Evidence for selective vulnerability of rods in central retina. *Investigative Ophthalmology & Visual Science, 34,* 3278–3296.

Cutting, J.E., & Kozlowski, L.T. 1977. Recognizing friends by their walk: Gait perception without familiarity cues. *Bulletin of the Psychonomic Society, 9,* 353–356.

Cutting, J.E., & Proffitt, D.R. 1981. Gait perception as an example of how we may perceive events. In R.D. Walk & H.L. Pick (Eds.), *Intersensory perception and sensory integration.* New York: Plenum, pp. 249–273.

Cutting, J.E., & Proffitt, D.R. 1982. The minimum principle and the perception of absolute, common, and relative motions. *Cognitive Psychology, 14,* 211–246.

Cutting, J.E., Proffitt, D.R., & Kozlowski, L.T. 1978. A biomechanical invariant for gait perception. *Journal of Experimental Psychology: Human Perception and Performance, 4*, 357–372.

Cytowic, R.E. 1989. *Synesthesia: A union of the senses.* New York: Springer Verlag.

Cytowic, R.E. 1993. *The man who tasted shapes.* New York: Putnam.

Cytowic, R.E., & Wood, R.B. 1982a. Synesthesia I: A review of theories and their brain basis. *Brain and Cognition, 1,* 23–35.

Cytowic, R.E., & Wood, R.B. 1982b. Synesthesia II: Psychophysical relationships in the synesthesia of geometrically shaped taste and colored hearing. *Brain and Cognition, 1,* 36–49.

Damasio, A., Yamada, T., Damasio, H., Corbett, J., & McKee, J. 1980. Central achromatopsia: Behavioral, anatomic, and physiologic aspects. *Neurology, 30,* 1064–1071.

Damas-Mora, J., Skelton-Robinson, M., & Jenner, F.A. 1982. The Charles Bonnet syndrome in perspective. *Psychological Medicine, 12,* 251–261.

Dancy, J. (Ed.). 1988. *Perceptual knowledge.* Oxford: Oxford University Press.

Davidoff, J. 1991. *Cognition through color.* Cambridge, Mass.: MIT Press.

da Vinci, Leonardo. 1956. *Treatise on painting.* Translated by A.P. McMahon. Princeton: Princeton University Press.

da Vinci, Leonardo. ca. 1500/1939/1958. *Notebooks.* Arranged, rendered into English, and introduced by Edward McCurdy. New York: G. Braziller.

da Vinci, Leonardo. ca. 1500/1970. *The literary works of Leonardo da Vinci.* Translated by J.P. Richter. 2nd ed. 2 vols. London: Phaidon, and New York: Dover.

Dawkins, R. 1987. *The blind watchmaker.* New York: W. W. Norton.

Day, R.H. 1983. Neon color spreading, partially delineated borders, and the formation of illusory contours. *Perception & Psychophysics, 34,* 488–490.

Day, R.H., & Jory, M.K. 1978. Subjective contours, visual acuity, and line contrast. In Armington et al., 1978, pp. 331–340.

Dekker, T., & de Groot, J. 1956. Decompositions of a sphere. *Fundamenta Mathematica, 43,* 185–194.

Deng, W.A., & Lyengar, S.S. 1996. A new probabilistic relaxation scheme and its application to edge detection. *IEEE Transactions on Pattern Analysis and Machine Intelligence, 18,* 4, 432–437.

Dennett, D.C. 1991. *Consciousness explained.* Boston: Little, Brown.

Derrington, A.M., Krauskopf, J., & Lennie, P. 1984. Chromatic mechanisms in lateral geniculate nucleus of macaque. *Journal of Physiology, 357,* 241–265.

Desimone, R., & Schein, S.J. 1987. Visual properties of neurons in area V4 of the macaque: sensitivity to stimulus form. *Journal of Neurophysiology, 57,* 835–868.

Desimone, R., Schein, S.J., Moran, J., & Ungerleider, L.G. 1985. Contour, color and shape analysis beyond the striate cortex. *Vision Research, 25,* 441–452.

DeValois, R.L. 1965a. Behavioral and electrophysiological studies of primate vision. In S.D. Neff (Ed.), *Contributions to sensory perception.* New York: Academic Press, pp. 137–177.

DeValois, R.L. 1965b. Analysis and coding of color vision in the primate visual system. *Cold Spring Harbor Symposia on Quantitative Biology, 30,* 565–579.

DeValois, R.L., Abramov, I., and Jacobs, G.H. 1966. Analysis of response patterns of LGN cells. *Journal of the Optical Society of America, 56,* 966–977.

DeValois, R.L., & DeValois, K.K. 1988. *Spatial vision.* New York: Oxford University Press.

DeValois, R.L., Smith, C.J. Karoly, A.J., & Kitai, S.T. 1958a. Electrical responses of primate visual system. I. Different layers of macaque lateral geniculate nucleus. *Journal of Comparative Physiology and Psychology, 51,* 662–668.

DeValois, R.L., Smith, C.J., Kitai, S.T., & Karoly, A.J. 1958b. Responses of single cells in different layers of the primate lateral geniculate nucleus to monochromatic light. *Science, 127,* 238–239.

Devlin, K.J. 1994. *Mathematics: The science of patterns.* New York: Freeman.

Dewdney, D. 1973. A specific distortion of the human facial percept in childhood schizophrenia. *Psychiatric Quarterly, 47,* 82–94.

de Weert, C.M.M. & van Kruysbergen, N.A.W.H. 1987. Subjective contour strength and perceptual superimposition: Transparency as a special case. In Petry & Meyer, 1987, pp. 165–170.

DeYoe, E.A., & Van Essen, D.C. 1988. Concurrent processing streams in monkey visual cortex. *Trends in Neuroscience, 11,* 219–226.

Diamond, A. 1953. Foveal simultaneous brightness contrast as a function of inducing- and test-field luminances. *Journal of Experimental Psychology, 45,* 304–314.

Diamond, A. 1955. Foveal simultaneous brightness contrast as a function of inducing- and test-field luminances. *Journal of Experimental Psychology, 50,* 144–152.

Diogenes Laertius. *Lives of eminent philosophers.* Translated by R.D. Hicks. 2 volumes. London: Loeb Classical Library, 1925.

Dmytryk, E. 1984. *On film editing: An introduction to the art of film construction.* London: Focal Press.

Dmytryk, E. 1986. *On filmmaking.* Boston: Focal Press.

Dobkins, K.R., & Albright, T.D. 1993a. Color, luminance, and the detection of visual motion. *Current Directions in Psychological Science, 2,* 189–193.

Dobkins, K.R., & Albright, T.D. 1993b. What happens if it changes color when it moves? Psychophysical experiments on the nature of chromatic input to motion detectors. *Vision Research, 33,* 1019–1036.

Dobkins, K.R., Stoner, G.R., & Albright, T.D. 1992. Oculomotor responses to perceptually coherent and non-coherent plaids. *Society of Neuroscience Abstracts, 18,* 1034.

Do Carmo, M. 1974. *Differential geometry of curves and surfaces.* New York: Prentice-Hall.

Dowling, J.E. 1987. *The retina: An approachable part of the brain.* Cambridge, Mass.: Harvard University Press.

Dörr, S., & Neumeyer, C. 1996. The goldfish—a colour-constant animal. *Perception, 25,* 243.

Dretske, F. 1995. *Naturalizing the mind.* Cambridge, Mass.: MIT Press.

Dufort, P.A., & Lumsden, C.J. 1991. Color categorization and color constancy in a neural network model of V4. *Biological Cybernetics, 65,* 293–303.

Duncker K., 1929. Über induzierte Bewegung (Ein Beitrag zur Theorie optisch wahrgenommener Bewegung). *Psychologische Forschung, 12,* 180–259. Reprinted in Ellis, 1937, pp. 161–172.

Dunlea, A. 1989. *Vision and the emergence of meaning : blind and sighted children's early language.* New York: Cambridge University Press.

Dürer, A. 1525. *Unterweisung der Messung.* Nuremberg.

D'Zmura, M. 1992. Color constancy: surface color from changing illumination. *Journal of the Optical Society of America A, 9,* 490–493.

D'Zmura, M., & Iverson, G. 1993a. Color constancy. 1. Basic theory of 2-stage linear recovery of spectral descriptions for lights and surfaces. *Journal of the Optical Society of America A, 10,* 2148–2163.

D'Zmura, M., & Iverson, G. 1993b. Color constancy. 2. Results for 2-stage linear recovery of spectral descriptions for lights and surfaces. *Journal of the Optical Society of America A, 10,* 2166–2180.

Edelman, G. 1989. *The remembered present: A biological theory of consciousness.* New York: Basic Books.

Edelman, G. 1992. *Bright air, brilliant fire: On the matter of the mind.* New York: Basic Books.

Efron, R. 1968. What is perception? *Boston Studies Philosophy Science, 4,* 137–173.

Ehrenstein, W. 1941. Über Abwandlungen der L. Hermannschen Helligkeitserscheinung. *Zeitschrift für Psychologie, 150,* 83–91. [Modifications of the brightness phenomenon of L. Hermann; translated by A. Hogg, in Petry & Meyer, 1987, pp. 35–39.]

Ehrenstein, W. 1954. *Probleme der ganzheitspsychologischen Wahrnehmungslehre.* Leipzig: Barth.

Einstein, A. 1956. *The meaning of relativity.* Princeton: Princeton University Press.

Ejima, Y., Redies, C., Takahashi, S., & Akita, M. 1984. The neon color effect in the Ehrenstein pattern: Dependence on wavelength and illuminance. *Vision Research, 24,* 1719–1726.

Ellis, H.D., & Young, A.W. 1990. Accounting for delusional misidentifications. *British Journal of Psychiatry, 157,* 239–248.

Ellis, S.R. (Ed.). 1993. *Pictorial communication in virtual and real environments.* Washington, D.C.: Taylor & Francis.

Ellis, W.D. (Ed.). 1937. *A Source Book of Gestalt Psychology.* London: Routledge & Kegan Paul.

Emmett, K., & Machamer, P.M. 1976. *Perception: an annotated bibliography.* New York: Garland.

Enroth-Cugell, C., & Robson, J.G. 1966. The contrast sensitivity of retinal ganglion cells of the cat. *Journal of Physiology, 187,* 517–552.

Epstein, W., & Rogers, S. (Eds.). 1995. *Perception of space and motion.* New York: Academic Press.

d'Espagnat, B. 1995. *Veiled reality: An analysis of present-day quantum mechanical concepts.* Reading, Mass.: Addison-Wesley.

Euclid. c. 300 B.C. *Optics. See* Burton, 1945.

Evans, R.M. 1948. *An introduction to color.* New York: Wiley.

Evarts, E.V. 1966. Methods for recording activity of individual neurons in moving animals. *Methods in Medical Research, 11,* 241–250.

Everson, S. (Ed.). 1991. *Psychology (Companions to Ancient Thought 2).* Cambridge: Cambridge University Press.

Ewert, J.-P. 1987. Neuroethology of releasing mechanisms: Prey-catching in toads. *Behavioral and Brain Sciences, 10,* 337–405.

Exner, S. 1875. Über das Sehen von Bewegungen und die Theorie des zusammengesetzen Auges [On the perception of movements and the theory of the integrative eye]. *Sitzungsberichte Akademie Wissenschaft Wien, 72,* 156–190.

Exner, S. 1888. Über optische Bewegungsempfindungen. *Biologisches Centralblatt, 8,* 437–448.

Faber, B. 1963. *Color: a survey in words and pictures, from ancient mysticism to modern science.* New Hyde Park, N.Y.: University Books.

Faber, B. 1976. *Color perception in art.* New York: Van Nostrand Reinhold.

Faber, B. 1978. *Color and human response.* New York: Van Nostrand Reinhold.

Faber, B. 1980. *Color psychology and color therapy: A factual study of the influence of color on human life.* Secaucus, N.J.: Citadel Press.

Farah, M.J. 1990. *Visual agnosia: Disorders of object recognition and what they tell us about normal vision.* Cambridge, Mass.: MIT Press.

Farah, M.J., & Ratcliff, G. 1994. *The neuropsychology of high-level vision: Collected tutorial essays.* Hillsdale, N.J.: Lawrence Erlbaum.

Fennema, C.I., & Thompson, W.B. 1979. Velocity determination in scenes containing several moving images. *Computer Graphics and Image Processing, 9,* 301–315.

von Fieandt, K. 1938. Über Sehen von Tiefengebilden bei wechselnder Beleuchtungsrichtung [The visual perception of depth under changing direction of illumination]. *Report of the Psychology Institute, University of Helsinki.*

von Fieandt, K., & Moustgaard, I.K. 1977. *The perceptual world.* London: Academic Press.

Finkel, L.H., & Edelman, G.M. 1989. Integration of distributed cortical systems by reentry: A computer simulation of interactive functionally segregated visual areas. *Journal of Neuroscience, 9,* 3188–3208.

Fiorentini, A., Baumgartner, G., Magnussen, S., Schiller, P.H., & Thomas, J.P. 1990. The perception of brightness and darkness: Relations to neuronal receptive fields. In Spillman & Werner, 1990, pp. 129–161.

Fodor, J. 1979. *The language of thought.* Cambridge, Mass.: Harvard University Press.

Fodor, J. 1983. *Modularity of mind.* Cambridge, Mass.: MIT Press.

Fodor, J. 1984. Observation reconsidered. *Philosophy of Science, 51,* 23–43.

Fodor, J. 1987. *Psychosemantics.* Cambridge, Mass.: MIT Press.

Fodor, J. 1988. A reply to Churchland's "Perceptual plasticity and theoretical neutrality." *Philosophy of Science, 55,* 188–198.

Fodor, J., & Pylyshyn, Z. 1981. How direct is visual perception?: Some reflections on Gibson's "Ecological Approach." *Cognition, 9,* 139–196.

Fox, R., Aslin, R.N., Shea, S.L., & Dumais, S.T. 1980. Stereopsis in human infants. *Science, 207,* 323–324.

Freedman, L., & Costa, L. 1992. Pure alexia and right hemiachromatopsia in posterior dementia. *Journal of Neurology, Neurosurgery, and Psychiatry, 55,* 500–502.

Freeman, W.T. 1994. The generic viewpoint assumption in a framework for visual perception. *Nature, 368,* 542–545.

Freeman, W.T. 1996. The generic viewpoint assumption in a Bayesian framework. In Knill & Richards, 1996.

Frisby, J.P., & Buckley, D. 1995. The role of contour in lightness illusion *Investigative Ophthalmology and Visual Science, ARVO Abstracts, 36,* 640.

Frisby, J.P., & Clatworthy, J.L. 1975. Illusory contours: Curious cases of simultaneous brightness contrast? *Perception, 4,* 349–357.

von Fritz, K. 1953. Democritus' theory of vision. In E. A. Underwood (Ed.), *Science, medicine, and history: Essays on the evolution of scientific thought and medical practice, written in honour of Charles Singer.* New York: Oxford University Press, pp. 83–99.

Galen. *On the Usefulness of the Parts of the Body.* Translated by Margaret T. May. Ithaca, 1968.

Gaze, R.M., & Jacobson, M. 1963. "Convexity detectors" in the frog's visual system. *Journal of Physiology, 169,* 1-30.

Geldard, F.A. 1975. *Sensory saltation: Metastability in the perceptual world.* Hillsdale, N.J.: Lawrence Erlbaum.

Geldard, F.A. 1977. Cutaneous stimuli, vibratory and saltatory. *Journal of Investigative Dermatology, 69,* 83–87.

Geldard, F.A., & Sherrick, C.E. 1972. The cutaneous "rabbit": A perceptual illusion. *Science, 178,* 178–179.

Geldard, F.A., & Sherrick, C.E. 1983. The cutaneous saltatory area and its presumed neural base. *Perception & Psychophysics, 33,* 299–304.

Geldard, F.A., & Sherrick, C.E. 1986. Space, time and touch. *Scientific American, 255,* July, 90–95.

Geman, S., & Geman, D. 1984. Stochastic relaxation, Gibbs distribution, and the Bayesian restoration of images. *IEEE Transactions on Pattern Analysis and Machine Intelligence, 6,* 721–741.

Gibson, J.J. 1950. *The perception of the visual world.* Boston: Houghton Mifflin.

Gibson, J.J. 1966. *The senses considered as perceptual systems.* Boston: Houghton Mifflin.

Gibson, J. J. 1979. *The ecological approach to visual perception.* Boston: Houghton Mifflin.

Gibson, J., & Gibson, E. 1957. Continuous perspective transformations and the perception of rigid motion. *J. Exp. Psych.,* 54, 2, 129–138.

Gigerenzer, G., & Murray, D.J. 1987. *Cognition as intuitive statistics.* Hillsdale, N.J.: Lawrence Erlbaum.

Gilbert, W. 1976. *Modern algebra with applications.* New York: Wiley.

Gilchrist, A.L. (Ed.). 1994. *Lightness, brightness, and transparency*. Hillsdale, N.J.: Lawrence Erlbaum.

Gilchrist, A.L., Kossyfidis, C., Bonatok, F., Agostino, T., Cataliotti, J., Li, X., Spehar, B., & Szura, J. 1996. A new theory of lightness perception. Unpublished manuscript.

Gilford, J.P. 1929. Illusory movement from a rotating barber pole. *American Journal of Psychology, 41,* 686–687.

Ginsburg, A.P. 1975. Is the illusory triangle physical or imaginary? *Nature, 257,* 219–220.

Ginsburg, A.P. 1987. The relationship between spatial filtering and subjective contours. In Petry & Meyer, 1987, pp. 109–115.

Girotti, F., Milanese, C., Casazza, M., Allegranza, A., Corridori, F., & Avanzini, G. 1982. Oculomotor disturbances in Balint's syndrome: Anatomoclinical findings and electrooculographic analysis in a case. *Cortex, 18,* 603–614.

Godwin-Austen, R.B. 1965. A case of visual disorientation. *Journal of Neurology, Neurosurgery and Psychiatry, 28,* 453–458.

Golomshtok, E.A. 1938. *The old stone age in European Russia*. Transactions of the American Philosophical Society, New series, vol. XXIX, pt. IIb, Philadelphia.

Gombrich, E.H. 1977. *Art and Illusion*. London: Phaidon.

Goodman, N. 1984. *Of mind and other matters*. Cambridge, Mass.: Harvard University Press.

Gorea, A. (Ed.). 1991. *Representations of vision: Trends and tacit assumption in vision*. Cambridge: Cambridge University Press.

Gould, S.J. 1991. *Bully for brontosaurus*. London: Hutchinson Radius.

Gouras, P. 1968. Identification of cone mechanisms in monkey ganglion cells. *Journal of Physiology, 199,* 533–547.

Gowers, W.R. 1887. *Lectures on the diagnosis of diseases of the brain*. London: J. & A. Churchill.

Gowers, W.R. 1888. *A manual of diseases of the brain*. London: J. & A. Churchill.

Granrud, C.E., Haake, R.J., & Yonas, A. 1985. Infants' sensitivity to familiar size: The effect of memory on spatial perception. *Perception & Psychophysics, 37,* 459–466.

Granrud, C.E. & Yonas, A. 1984. Infants' perception of pictorially specified inter-position. *Journal of Experimental Child Psychology, 37,* 500–511.

Granrud, C.E., Yonas, A., & Opland, E.A. 1985. Infants' sensitivity to the depth cue of shading. *Perception & Psychophysics, 37,* 415–419.

Granrud, C.E., Yonas, A., Smith, I.M., Arterberry, M.E., Glicksman, M.L., & Sorknes, A. 1984. Infants' sensitivity to accretion and deletion of texture as infor-mation for depth at an edge. *Child Development, 55,* 1630–1636.

Green, B. 1961. Figure coherence in the kinetic depth effect. *Journal of Experimental Psychology, 62,* 3, 272–282.

Green, G.J., & Lesell, S. 1977. Acquired cerebral dyschromatopsia. *Archives of Ophthalmology, 95,* 121–128.

Greenberger, D. 1986. *New techniques and ideas in quantum measurement theory.* New York: New York Academy of Sciences.

Gregory, R.L. 1966. *Eye and brain.* New York: McGraw-Hill.

Gregory, R.L. 1970. *The intelligent eye.* New York: McGraw-Hill.

Gregory, R.L. 1972. Cognitive contours. *Nature, 238,* 51–52.

Gregory, R.L. 1974. *Concepts and mechanisms of perception.* London: Duckworth.

Gregory, R.L. 1987. Illusory contours and occluding surfaces. In Petry & Meyer, 1987, pp. 81–89.

Gregory, R.L., & Gombrich, E.H. (Eds.). 1973. *Illusion in nature and art.* London: Duckworth.

Gregory, R.L., & Harris, J.P. 1974. Illusory contours and stereo depth. *Perception & Psychophysics, 15,* 411–416.

Gribbin, J. 1995. *Schrödinger's kittens and the search for reality: Solving the quantum mys-teries.* New York: Little, Brown.

Grosof, D.H., Shapley, R.M., & Hawken, J.J. 1993. Macaque V1 neurons can sig-nal illusory contours. *Nature, 365,* 550–552.

Grossberg, S., 1994. 3-D vision and figure-ground separation by visual cortex. *Perception & Psychophysics, 55,* 48–120.

Grossberg, S., & Mingolla, E. 1985a. Neural dynamics of form perception:

Boundary completion, illusory figures, and neon color spreading. *Psychological Review, 92,* 173–211.

Grossberg, S., & Mingolla, E. 1985b. Neural dynamics of perceptual grouping: Textures, boundaries, and emergent segmentations. *Perception & Psychophysics, 38,* 141–171.

Grossberg, S., & Mingolla, E. 1987. The role of illusory contours in visual segmentation. In Petry & Meyer, 1987, pp. 116–125.

Grüsser, O-J., & Landis, T. 1991. *Visual agnosias and other disturbances of visual perception and cognition.* Volume 12 of the series *Vision and visual dysfunction,* J.R. Cronly-Dillon (Ed.). Boca Raton: CRC Press.

Guillemin, V., & Pollack, A. 1974. *Differential topology.* Englewood Cliffs, N.J.: Prentice-Hall.

Hagen, M.A. (Ed.). 1980. *The perception of pictures.* Two volumes. New York: Academic Press.

Halligan, P.W., Marshall, J.C., & Ramachandran, V.S. 1994. Ghosts in the machine: A case description of visual and haptic hallucinations after right hemisphere stroke. *Cognitive Neuropsychology, 11,* 459–477.

Hanson, A.R., & Riseman, E.M. (Eds.). 1978. *Computer vision systems.* Orlando: Academic Press.

Hapgood, M.O. 1992. *Wallpaper and the artist: From Dürer to Warhol.* New York: Abbeville Press.

Hardin, C.L. 1990. Perception and physical theory. In W.C. Lycan (Ed.), *Mind and cognition: A reader.* Oxford: Blackwell.

Harth, E. 1993. *The creative loop: How the brain makes a mind.* New York: Addison-Wesley.

Hay, C. 1966. Optical motions and space perception—an extension of Gibson's analysis. *Psychological Review, 73,* 550–565.

Hayek, F.A. 1952/1976. *The sensory order.* London: Routledge.

Hecaen, H., & Ajuriaguerra, J. 1956. Agnosie visuelle pour les objets inanimes par lesion unilaterale gauche. *Revue Neurologique, 94,* 222–233.

Herbert, N. 1992. *Elemental mind.* New York: Dutton.

Heinemann, E.G. 1955. Simultaneous brightness induction as a function of inducing- and test-field luminances. *Journal of Experimental Psychology, 50,* 89–96.

Heitger, F., & von der Heydt, R. 1993. A computational model of neural contour processing: Figure-ground segregation and illusory contours. *Fourth International Conference on Computer Vision,* 32–40. Los Alamitos, California: IEEE Computer Society Press.

Held, R., Birch, E.E., & Gwiazda, J. 1980. Stereoacuity in human infants. *Proceedings of the National Academy of Sciences of the USA, 77,* 5572–5574.

Heller, M.A., & Schiff, W. (Eds.). 1991. *The psychology of touch.* Hillsdale, N.J.: Lawrence Erlbaum.

von Helmholtz, H.L.F. 1910. *Treatise on physiological optics.* Translated by J. Southal, 1925. New York: Dover.

Helson, H. 1943. Some factors and implications of color constancy. *Journal of the Optical Society of America, 33,* 555–567.

Helson, H. 1964. *Adaptation-level theory.* New York: Harper & Row.

Helson, H., & Joy, V. 1962. Domains of lightness, assimilation and contrast effects in vision. *Psychol. Beitr., 6,* 405–415.

Helson, H., & Rohles, F.H. 1959. A quantitative study of reversal of classical lightness contrast. *American Journal of Psychology, 72,* 530–538.

Herbert, N. 1993. *Elemental mind: Human consciousness and the new physics.* New York: Dutton.

Hering, E. 1905. Grundzuge der Lehre vom Lichtsinn. In *Handbuch der gesammter Augenheilkunde, Vol. 3, Ch. 13.* Berlin.

Hering, E. 1964. *Outlines of a theory of the light sense,* Translated by L.M. Hurvich & D. Jameson. Cambridge, Mass.: Harvard University Press.

Herschberger, W. 1970. Attached-shadow orientation perceived as depth by chickens reared in an environment illuminated from below. *Journal of Comparative Physiology and Psychology, 73,* 407–411.

Hess, E.H. 1950. Development of the chick's response to light and shade cues of depth. *Journal of Comparative Physiology and Psychology, 43,* 112–122.

Hess, E.H. 1961. Shadows and depth perception. *Scientific American, 204,* 139–148.

Hess, R.H., Baker, C.L., & Zihl, J. 1989. The "motion-blind" patient: Low-level spatial and temporal filters. *Journal of Neuroscience, 9,* 1628–1640.

von der Heydt, R., Peterhans, E., & Baumgartner, G. 1984. Illusory contours and cortical neuron responses. *Science, 224,* 1260–1262.

Heywood, C.A., Cowey, A., & Newcombe, F. 1994. On the role of parvocellular (P) and magnocellular (M) pathways in cerebral achromatopsia. *Brain, 117,* 245–254.

Heywood, C.A., Gadotti, A., & Cowey, A. 1992. Cortical area V4 and its role in the perception of color. *Journal of Neuroscience, 12,* 4056–4065.

Hewyood, C.A., Gaffan, D., & Cowey, A. 1995. Cerebral achromatopsia in monkeys. *European Journal of Neuroscience, 7,* 1064–1073.

Hildreth, E.C. 1982. The integration of motion information along contours. *Proceedings of the IEEE Workshop on Computer Vision: Representation and Control.* Rindge, N.H., August, 83–91.

Hildreth, E.C. 1984. *The measurement of visual motion,* Cambridge, Mass.: MIT Press.

Hildreth, E.C., Ando, H., Andersen, R.A., & Treue, S. 1995. Recovering three-dimensional structure from motion with surface reconstruction. *Vision Research, 35,* 117–137.

Hinton, H.E. 1973. Natural deception. In Gregory & Gombrich, 1973, pp. 97–159.

Hirsch, J., & Curcio, C.A. 1989. The spatial resolution capacity of human foveal retina. *Vision Research, 29,* 1095–1101.

Hirstein, W., & Ramachandran, V.S. 1997. Capgras syndrome: A novel probe for understanding neural representation of the identity and familiarity of persons. *Proceedings of the Royal Society of London, B, 264,* 1380, 437–444.

Hochberg, J. Art and perception. In Carterette & Friedman, 1978.

Hochberg, J., & Brooks, V. 1962. Picture perception is an unlearned ability. *American Journal of Psychology, 75,* 337–354.

Hochberg, J. 1964. *Perception.* Englewood Cliffs, N.J.: Prentice-Hall.

Hoffman, D.D. 1983a. *Representing shapes for visual recognition.* Doctoral Dissertation, Massachusetts Institute of Technology.

Hoffman, D.D. 1983b. The interpretation of visual illusions. *Scientific American, 249,* 6, 154–162.

Hoffman, D.D., & Bennett, B. 1985. Inferring the relative three-dimensional positions of two moving points. *Journal of the Optical Society of America A, 2,* 350–353.

Hoffman, D.D., & Bennett, B. 1986. The computation of structure from fixed-axis motion: rigid structures. *Biological Cybernetics, 54,* 71–83.

Hoffman, D.D., & Cicerone, C.M. 1992. Dynamic color spreading. Poster and demonstration. Advances in Vision, Optical Society of America, Irvine, Calif., 30 January–1 February.

Hoffman, D.D., & Cicerone, C.M. 1996. Dynamic color spreading and the opercular problem: A computational theory. *Zentrum für interdisziplinäre Forschung der Universität Bielefeld, Memo 12/96.*

Hoffman, D.D., & Flinchbaugh, B. 1982. The interpretation of biological motion. *Biological Cybernetics, 42,* 195–204.

Hoffman, D.D., & Richards, W.A. 1982. Representing smooth plane curves for recognition: Implications for figure-ground reversal. *Proceedings of the National Conference of the American Association for Artificial Intelligence,* 5–8.

Hoffman, D.D., & Richards, W.A. 1984. Parts of recognition. *Cognition, 18,* 65–96.

Hoffman, D.D., & Singh, M. 1997. Salience of visual parts. *Cognition,* in press.

Holmes, G. 1918. Disturbances of visual orientation. *British Journal of Ophthalmology, 2,* 449–468 and 506–518.

Holmes, G., & Horrax, G. 1919. Disturbances of spatial orientation and visual attention with loss of stereoscopic vision. *Archives of Neurology and Psychiatry, 1,* 385–407.

Home, D., & Gribbin, J. 1991. What is light? *New Scientist, 2.*

Horn, B. 1974. Determining lightness from an image. *Computer Graphics and Image Processing, 3,* 277–299.

Horn, B. 1975. Obtaining shape from shading information. In P. Winston (Ed.), *The Psychology of Computer Vision,* 115–155. New York: McGraw-Hill.

Horn, 1977. Understanding image intensities. *Artificial Intelligence, 21,* 201–231.

Horn, B. 1986. *Robot vision.* New York: McGraw-Hill.

Horn, B., & Brady, J.M. (Eds.). 1989. *Shape from shading.* Cambridge, Mass.: MIT Press.

Horn, B., & Schunck, B. 1981. Determining optical flow. *Artificial Intelligence, 17,* 185–203.

Horridge, G.A. 1991. Evolution of visual processing. In J.R. Cronly-Dillon & R.L. Gregory (Eds.), *Evolution of the eye and visual system.* Boca Raton: CRC Press.

Horridge, G.A., Zhang, S.W., & O'Carroll, D. 1992. Insect perception illusory contours. *Philosophical Transactions of the Royal Society of London, B, 337,* 59–64.

Howard, I., Bergström, S.S., & Ohmi, M. 1990. Shape from shading in different frames of reference. *Perception, 19,* 523–530.

Huang, T., & Lee, C. 1989. Motion and structure from orthographic projections. *IEEE Transactions on Pattern Analysis and Machine Intelligence, 11,* 536–540.

Hubel, D.H., & Wiesel, T.N. 1959. Receptive fields of single neurons in the cat's striate cortex. *Journal of Physiology, 148,* 574–591.

Hubel, D.H., & Wiesel, T.N. 1961. Integrative action in the cat's lateral geniculate body. *Journal of Physiology, 155,* 385–398.

Hubel, D.H., & Wiesel, T.N. 1962. Receptive fields, binocular interaction and functional architecture in the cat's visual cortex. *Journal of Physiology, 160,* 106–154.

Hubel, D.H., & Wiesel, T.N. 1965. Receptive fields and functional architecture in two non striate visual areas (18 and 19) of the cat. *Journal of Neurophysiology, 28,* 289–299.

Hubel, D.H., & Wiesel, T.N. 1968. Receptive fields and functional architecture of monkey striate cortex. *Journal of Physiology, 195,* 215–243.

Hubel, D.H., & Wiesel, T.N. 1977. The Ferrier Lecture: Functional architecture of macaque monkey visual cortex. *Proceedings of the Royal Society of London, B, 198,* 1–59.

Huffman, D.A. 1971. Impossible objects as nonsense sentences. In B. Meltzer & D. Michie (Eds.), *Machine Intelligence 6.* Edinburgh: Edinburgh University Press.

Humphrey, N. 1992. *A history of the mind.* New York: HarperCollins.

Humphreys, G.W., & Riddoch, M.J. 1987. *Visual object processing: A cognitive neuropsychological approach.* London: Erlbaum.

Hurlbert, A. 1986. Formal connections between lightness algorithms. *Journal of the Optical Society of America A, 3,* 1684–1693.

Hurvich, L.M. 1981. *Color vision.* Sunderland, Mass.: Sinnauer Associates.

Ikeuchi, K., & Horn, B. 1981. Numerical shape from shading and occluding boundaries. *Artificial Intelligence, 17,* 141–184.

Iverson, G., & D'Zmura, M. 1994. Criteria for color constancy in trichromatic bilinear models. *Journal of the Optical Society of America A, 11,* 1970–1975.

Jackendoff, R. 1987. *Consciousness and the computational mind.* Cambridge, Mass.: MIT Press.

Jacobi, J. (Ed.). 1988. *Paracelsus, 1493-1541. Selected writings.* Translated by N. Guterman. Princeton, N.J.: Princeton University Press.

James, W. 1887. The consciousness of lost limbs. *Proceedings of the American Society for Psychical Research, 1,* 249–258.

Jameson, D., & Hurvich, L.M. 1955. Some quantitative aspects of an opponent-colors theory. I. Chromatic responses and spectral saturation. *Journal of the Optical Society of America, 45,* 546–552.

Jameson, D., & Hurvich, L.M. 1959. Perceived color and its dependence on focal surrounding, and preceding stimulus variables. *Journal of the Optical Society of America, 49,* 890–898.

Jansson, G., Bergström, S.S., & Epstein, W. 1994. *Perceiving events and objects.* Hillsdale, N.J.: Lawrence Erlbaum.

Jepson, A.D., & Richards, W.A. (1993). What makes a good feature? In L. Harris & M. Jenkin (Eds.), *Spatial vision in humans and robots.* New York: Cambridge University Press.

Johansson, G. 1950. *Configuration in event perception.* Uppsala, Sweden: Almqvist & Wiksell.

Johansson, G. 1973. Visual perception of biological motion and a model for its analysis. *Perception & Psychophysics, 14,* 201–211.

Johansson, G. 1975. Visual motion perception. *Scientific American, 232,* 6, 76–88.

Johnson, M.H., & Morton, J. 1991. *Biology and cognitive development: The case of face recognition.* Oxford: Blackwell.

Johnson, P.E. 1993. *Darwin on trial.* Downers Grove, Ill.: InterVarsity Press.

Jory, M.K., & Day, R.H. 1979. The relationship between brightness contrast and illusory contours. *Perception, 8,* 3–9.

Judd, D.B., MacAdam, D.L., & Wyszecki, G.W. 1964. Spectral distribution of typical daylight as a function of correlated color temperature. *Journal of the Optical Society of America, 54,* 1031–1040.

Kaihara, T., Takahashi, S., Takemoto, A., & Ejima, Y. 1994. A linkage of chromatic and achromatic cues in neon color effect. Special Issue: Gestalt perception: I. *Japanese Psychological Research, 36,* 138–148.

Kanizsa, G. 1955. Margini quasi-percettivi in campi con stimolazione omogenea. *Rivista di Psicologia, 49,* 7–30. [Quasiperceptual margins in homogeneously stimulated fields; translated by W. Gerbino, in Petry & Meyer, 1987, pp. 40–49.]

Kanizsa, G. 1974. Contours without gradients or cognitive contours? *Italian Journal of Psychology, 1,* 93–113.

Kanizsa, G. 1976. Subjective contours. *Scientific American, 234,* 48–52.

Kanizsa, G. 1979. *Organization in vision.* New York: Praeger.

Kanisza, G., & Gerbino, W. 1976. Convexity and symmetry in figure-ground organization. In M. Henle (Ed.), *Art and artefacts.* New York: Springer, pp. 25–32.

Kase, C.S., Troncoso, J.F., Court, J.E., Tapia, F.J., & Mohr, J.P. 1977. Global spatial disorientation. *Journal of the Neurological Sciences, 34,* 267–278.

Kaufmann-Hayoz, R., Kaufmann, F., & Stucki, M. 1986. Kinetic contours in infants' visual perception. *Child Development, 57,* 292–299.

Kellman, P.J. 1984. Perception of three-dimensional form by human infants. *Perception & Psychophysics, 36,* 353–358.

Kellman, P.J. 1995. Ontogenesis of space and motion perception. In Epstein, W. & Rogers, S., 1995, pp. 327–364.

Kellman, P.J., & Shipley, T.F. 1991. A theory of visual interpolation in object perception. *Cognitive Psychology, 23,* 141–221.

Kellman, P.J., & Shipley, T.F. 1992. Perceiving objects across gaps in space and time. *Current Directions in Psychological Science, 1,* 193–199.

Kellman, P.J., & Short, K.R. 1987. Development of three-dimensional form perception. *Journal of Experimental Psychology: Human Perception and Performance, 13,* 545–557.

Kennedy, J.M. 1978. Illusory contours not due to completion. *Perception, 7,* 187–189.

Kennedy, J.M. 1979. Subjective contours, contrast, and assimilation. In Nodine & Fisher, 1979, pp. 167–195.

Kennedy, J.M. 1987. Lo, perception abhors not a contradiction. In Petry & Meyer, 1987, pp. 253–261.

Kennedy, J.M. 1988. Line endings and subjective contours. *Spatial Vision, 3,* 151–158.

Kennedy, J.M. 1993. *Drawings and the blind: Pictures to touch.* New Haven, Conn.: Yale University Press.

Kepler, J. 1904/1939. *Ad Vitellionem paralipomena, quibus astronomiae pars optica traditur.* Edited by Franz Hammer. In Gesammelte *werke.* Herausgegeben im auftrag der Deutschen forschungsgemeinschaft und der Bayerischen akademie der wissenschaften, unter der leitung von Walther von Dyck und Max Caspar. Munich: C.H. Beck, 1937-90.

Kersten, D., Bülthoff, H.H., Schwartz, B.L., & Kurtz, K.J. 1992. Interaction between transparency and structure from motion. *Neural Computation, 4,* 573–589.

Kersten, D., Mamassian, P., Bülthoff, I., Knill, D., & Bülthoff, H. 1994. *Cast shadows and the perception of depth, shape and rigidity* [Film]. Tübingen, Germany: Max Planck Institute for Biological Cybernetics.

Kleffner, D.A., & Ramachandran, V.S. 1992. On the perception of shape from shading. *Perception & Psychophysics, 52,* 18–36.

Knill, D.C., & Kersten, D. 1991. Apparent surface curvature affects lightness perception. *Nature, 351,* 228–230.

Knill, D.C., & Richards, W.A. (Eds.). 1996. *Perception as Bayesian inference.* Cambridge: Cambridge University Press.

Koenderink, J.J. 1984. What does the occluding contour tell us about solid shape? *Perception, 13,* 321–330.

Koenderink, J.J. 1990. *Solid shape.* Cambridge, Mass.: MIT Press.

Koenderink, J., & van Doorn, A. 1975. Invariant properties of the motion parallax field due to the movement of rigid bodies relative to an observer. *Optica Acta, 22,* 773–791.

Koenderink, J.J., & van Doorn, A.J. 1976. The singularities of the visual mapping. *Biological Cybernetics, 24,* 51–59.

Koenderink, J.J., & van Doorn, A.J. 1976. Geometry of binocular vision and a model for stereopsis. *Biological Cybernetics, 21,* 29–35.

Koenderink, J., & van Doorn, A. 1976. Local structure of movement parallax of the plane. *Journal of the Optical Society of America, 66,* 717–723.

Koenderink, J.J., & van Doorn, A.J. 1979. The internal representation of solid shape with respect to vision. *Biological Cybernetics, 32,* 211–216.

Koenderink, J., & van Doorn, A. 1980. Photometric invariants related to solid shape. *Optica Acta, 22,* 773–791.

Koenderink, J.J., & van Doorn, A.J. 1981. Exterospecific component of the motion parallax field. *J. Opt. Soc. Am.,* 71, 8, 953–957.

Koenderink, J.J., & van Doorn, A.J. 1982. The shape of smooth objects and the way contours end. *Perception, 11,* 129–137.

Koenderink, J.J., & van Doorn, A.J. 1986. Depth and shape from differential perspective in the presence of bending deformations. *Journal of the Optical Society of America A, 3,* 242–249.

Koenderink, J.J., & van Doorn, A.J. 1986. Optic flow. *Vision Research, 26,* 161–180.

Koenderink, J.J., & van Doorn, A.J. 1991. Affine structure from motion. *Journal of the Optical Society of America, A, 8,* 377–385.

Koffka, K. 1931. Die Wahrnehmung von Bewegung. In A. Bethe, G. v. Bergmann, G. Embden, & A. Ellinger (Eds.), *Handbuch der normalen und pathologischen Physiologie: Receptionsorgane II.* Berlin: Springer, pp. 1166–1214.

Koffka, K. 1935. *Principles of gestalt psychology.* New York: Harcourt, Brace and World.

Kohler, I. 1962. Experiments with goggles. In R. Held & W. Richards (Eds.), *Perception: Mechanisms and models.* San Francisco: Freeman Press, pp. 299–309.

Kojo, I.V., Liinasuo, M.E., & Rovamo, J.M. 1995. Neon colour spreading in three-dimensional illusory objects. *Investigative Ophthalmology and Visual Science, ARVO Abstracts, 36,* 665.

Kooi, F.L., de Valois, K.K., Switkes, E., & Grosof, D.H. 1992. Higher-order factors influencing the perception of sliding and coherence of a plaid. *Perception, 21,* 583–598.

Kopfermann, H. 1930. Psychologische Untersuchungen über die Wirkung zweidimensionaler Darstellungen Körperlicher Gebilde. *Psychologische Forschung, 13,* 293–364.

Kosslyn, S.M., and Koenig, O. 1992. *Wet mind: The new cognitive neuroscience.* Free Press.

Kozlowski, L.T., & Cutting, J.E. 1977. Recognizing the sex of a walker from a dynamic point-light display. *Perception & Psychophysics, 21,* 575–580.

Krause, C.L., & Mishler, C. 1986. *Standard catalog of world coins.* Iola, Wis.: Krause Publications.

Krauskopf, J., & Farrell, B. 1990. Influence of color on the perception of coherent motion. *Nature, 348,* 328–331.

Kubovy, M., & Pomerantz, J. (Eds.). 1981. *Perceptual organization.* Hillsdale, N.J.: Lawrence Erlbaum.

Kuffler, S.W. 1953. Discharge patterns and functional organization of mammalian retina. *Journal of Neurophysiology, 16,* 37–68.

Kulpa, Z. 1983. Are impossible figures possible? *Signal Processing, 5,* 201–220.

Lamme, V.A.F., Dijk, B.W. van, Spekreijse, H. 1993. Contour from motion processing occurs in primary visual cortex. *Nature, 363,* 541–543.

Land, E.H. 1959. Experiments in color vision. *Scientific American, 200,* 84–99.

Land, E.H. 1977. The retinex theory of color vision. *Scientific American, 237,* 108–128.

Land, E.H. 1983. Recent advances in retinex theory and some implications for cortical computations: color vision and the natural image. *Proceedings of the National Academy of Sciences U.S.A., 80,* 5163–6169.

Land, E.H. 1986a. Recent advances in retinex theory. *Vision Research, 26,* 7–21.

Land, E.H. 1986b. An alternative technique for the computation of the designator in the retinex theory of color vision. *Proceedings of the National Academy of Sciences U.S.A., 83,* 3078–3080.

Land, E.H., & McCann, J.J. 1971. Lightness theory. *Journal of the Optical Society of America, 61,* 1–11.

Landesman, C. 1993. *The eye and the mind: Reflections on perception and the problem of knowledge.* Dordrecht: Kluwer.

Larimar, J., Krantz, D.H., & Cicerone, C.M. 1975. Opponent-process additivity. II. Yellow/blue equilibria and nonlinear models. *Vision Research, 15,* 723–731.

Law, T., Itoh, H., & Seki, H. 1996. Image filtering, edge detection, and edge tracing using fuzzy reasoning. *IEEE Transaction on Pattern Analysis and Machine Intelligence, 18,* 5, 481–491.

Lee, E.N. 1978. The sense of an object: Epicurus on seeing and hearing. In Machamer & Turnbull, 1978, pp. 27–59.

Leeman, Fred. 1976. *Hidden images: Games of perception, anamorphic art, illusion: From the Renaissance to the present.* Text by Fred Leeman, concept, production, and photos by Joost Elffers and Mike Schuyt. New York: H.N. Abrams.

Leibowitz, H., Mote, F.A., & Thurlow, W.R. 1953. Simultaneous contrast as a function of separation between test and inducing fields. *Journal of Experimental Psychology, 46,* 453–456.

Lejeune, A. 1948. *Euclide et Ptolémée. Deux stades de l'optique géométrique grecque.* Université de Louvain, Recueil de travaux d'histoire et de philologie, ser. 3, fasc. 31. Louvain.

Lennie, P. 1980. Parallel pathways: A review. *Vision Research, 20,* 561–594.

Lennie, P. 1984. Recent developments in the physiology of color vision. *Trends in Neurosciences, 7,* 243–248.

Lennie, P., Krauskopf, J., and Sclar, G. 1990. Chromatic mechanisms in striate cortex of macaque. *Journal of Neuroscience, 2,* 649–669.

Leroi-Gourhan, A. 1967. *Treasures of prehistoric art.* New York: H. N. Abrams.

Lesher, G.W. 1995. Illusory contours: Toward a neurally based perceptual theory. *Psychonomic Bulletin & Review, 2* (3), 279–321.

Liebmann, S. 1927. Über das Verhalten farbiger Formen bei Helligkeitsgleichheit von Figure und Grund [On the behavior of colored forms with equality of brightness of figure and ground]. *Psychologische Forschung, 9,* 300–353.

Lindberg, D.C. 1976. *Theories of vision from al-Kindi to Kepler.* Chicago: University of Chicago Press.

Linke, P.E. 1907. Die stroboskopischen Täuschungen und das Problem des Sehens von Bewegungen. *Psychologische Studien, 3,* 393–545.

Livingstone, M.S., & Hubel, D.H. 1987. Psychophysical evidence for separate channels for the perception of form, color, movement, and depth. *Journal of Neuroscience, 7,* 3416–3468.

Liter, J., Braunstein, M., & Hoffman, D.D. 1993. Inferring structure from motion in two-view and multi-view displays. *Perception, 22,* 1441–1465.

Locke, J. 1690/1975. *An essay concerning human understanding.* P.H. Nidditch (Ed.). Oxford: Oxford University Press.

Locke, J. 1694. *An essay concerning human understanding.* 2 volumes. A.C. Fraser (Ed.) from the 3rd edition. Oxford: Clarendon, 1894. Reprinted, New York: Dover, 1959.

London, F., & Bauer, E. 1983. The theory of observation in quantum mechanics. In Wheeler & Zurek, 1983, pp. 217–259. Original: 1939. La théorie de l'observation en mécanique quantique. *Actualités scientifiques et industrielles: Exposés de physique générale,* publiés sous la direction de Paul Langevin. Paris: Hermann.

Longuet-Higgins, H.C. 1982. The role of the vertical dimension in stereoscopic vision. *Perception, 11,* 377–386.

Longuet-Higgins, H.C., & Prazdny, K. 1980. The interpretation of a moving retinal image. *Proceedings of the Royal Society of London, B208,* 385–397.

Lorenz, K. 1965. *Evolution and modification of behavior.* Chicago: University of Chicago Press.

Lorge, I., & Chall, J. 1963. Estimating the size of vocabularies of children and adults: An analysis of methodological issues. *Journal of Experimental Education, 32,* 147–157.

Lowe, D.G. 1985. *Perceptual organization and visual recognition.* Boston: Kluwer.

Lowe, D.G., & Binford, T.O. 1981. The interpretation of three-dimensional structure from image curves. *Proceedings of the International Joint Conference on Artificial Intelligence 7, Vancouver,* 613–618.

Lueck, C.J., Zeki, S., Friston, K.J., Deiber, M.-P., Cope, P., Cunningham, V.J., Lammertsma, A.A., Kennard, C., & Frackowiak, R.S.J. 1989. The colour centre in the cerebral cortex of man. *Nature, 340,* 386–389.

Luria, A.R. 1959. Disorders of "simultaneous perception" in a case of bilateral occipitoparietal brain injury. *Brain, 83,* 437–449.

Luria, A.R. 1968. *The mind of a mnemonist.* New York: Basic Books.

Luria, A.R., Pravdina-Vinarskaya, E.N., & Yarbuss, A.L. 1963. Disorders of ocular movement in a case of simultanagnosia. *Brain, 86,* 219–228.

Lythgoe, J.N. 1979. *The ecology of vision.* Oxford: Clarendon Press.

Mach, E. 1885/1959. *The analysis of sensations, and the relation of the physical to the psychical.* Translated by C.M. Williams. New York: Dover.

Machamer, P.K., & Turnbull, R.G. (Eds.). 1978. *Studies in perception: Interrelations in the history of philosophy and science.* Columbus: Ohio State University Press.

MacKay, G., & Dunlop, J.C. 1899. The cerebral lesions in a case of complete acquired colour-blindness. *Scot. Med. Surg. J., 5,* 503–512.

MacNichol, E.F., Jr. 1964. Three-pigment color vision. *Scientific American, 211,* 48–56.

Malebranche, N. *The search after truth* and *Elucidations of the search after truth.* Translated by T.P. Lennon & P.J. Olscamp. Columbus: Ohio State University Press.

Malik, J. 1987. Interpreting line drawings of curved objects. *International Journal of Computer Vision, 1,* 73–103.

Maloney, L.T. 1985. Computational approaches to color constancy. Ph.D. dissertation, Stanford University (Applied Psychological Laboratory Technical Report 1985-01).

Maloney, L.T. 1986. Evaluation of linear models of surface spectral reflectance with small numbers of parameters. *Journal of the Optical Society of America A, 3,* 1673–1683.

Maloney, L.T., & Wandell, B.A. 1986. Color constancy: A method for recovering surface spectral reflectance. *Journal of the Optical Society of America A, 3,* 29–33.

Marcel, A.J., and Bisiach, E. (Eds.). 1988. *Consciousness in contemporary science.* Oxford: Oxford University Press.

Marimont, D., & Wandell, B.A. 1992. Linear models of surface and illuminant spectra. *Journal of the Optical Society of America, A, 9,* 1905–1913.

Marr, D. 1982. *Vision.* San Francisco: Freeman.

Marr, D., & Hildreth, E.C. 1980. Theory of edge detection. *Proceedings of the Royal Society of London, B, 207,* 187–217.

Marr, D., & Nishihara, H.K. 1978. Representation and recognition of three-dimensional shapes. *Proceedings of the Royal Society of London, Series B, 200,* 269–294.

Marr, D., & Poggio, T. 1979. A computational theory of human stereo vision. *Proceedings of the Royal Society of London, B, 204,* 301–328.

Marr, D., & Ullman, S. 1981. Directional selectivity and its use in early visual processing. *Proceedings of the Royal Society of London, B, 211,* 151–180.

Martin, W.N., & Aggarwal, J.K. (Eds.). 1988. *Motion understanding: Robot and human vision.* Boston: Kluwer.

Mass, J.B., Johansson, G., Janson, G., & Runeson, S. 1971. *Motion perception I and II* [Film]. Boston: Houghton Mifflin.

Mausfeld, R., & Niederée, R. 1993. An inquiry into relational concepts of colour, based on incremental principles of colour coding for minimal relational stimuli. *Perception, 22,* 427–462.

Mayhew, J. 1982. The interpretation of stereo-disparity information: the computation of surface orientation and depth. *Perception, 11,* 387–403.

McCann, J.J. 1987. Local/global mechanisms for color constancy. *Die Farbe, 34,* 275–283.

Meadows, J. 1974. Disturbed perception of colours associated with localized cerebral lesions. *Brain, 97,* 615–632.

Merbs, S.L., & Nathans, J. 1992. Absorption spectra of human cone pigments. *Nature, 356,* 433–435.

Messiaen, O. 1956. *Technique de mon Language Musicale.* Paris: Alphonse Leduc.

Metelli, F. 1970. An algebraic development of the theory of perceptual transparency. *Ergonomics, 13,* 59–66.

Metelli, F. 1975a. The perception of transparency. In G.B. Flores d'Arcais (Ed.), *Studies in perception: Festschrift for Fabio Metelli.* Milano: Martello-Giunti, pp. 445–487.

Metelli, F. 1975b. Shadows without penumbra. In Ertel, Kemmler, & Stadler (Eds.), *Gestaltheorie in der modernen Psychologie {Gestalt theory in modern psychology}.* Darmstadt: Steinkopff, pp. 200–209.

Metelli, F. 1976. What does "more transparent" mean? A paradox. In M. Henle (Ed.), *Vision and artifact.* New York: Springer, pp. 19–24.

Metelli, F. 1985. Stimulation and perception of transparency. *Psychological Research, 7,* 185–202.

Metelli, F., Da Pos, O., & Cavedon, A. 1985. Balanced and unbalanced, complete and partial transparency. *Perception & Psychophysics, 38,* 354–366.

Metzger, W. 1953/1975. *Gesetze des Sehens.* Frankfurt: Waldemar Kramer.

Meyering, T.C. 1989. *Historical roots of cognitive science: The rise of a cognitive theory of perception from antiquity to the nineteenth century.* Dordrecht: Kluwer Academic Publishers.

Michael, C.R. 1968. Receptive fields of single optic nerve fibres in a mammal with an all-cone retina. I. Contrast-sensitive units. *Journal of Neurophysiology, 31,* 249–256.

Michotte, A., Thines, G., and Crabbe, G. 1964. *Les complements amodaux des structure perceptives.* Louvain: Publications Universitaires de Louvain.

Miller, D.T., Williams, D.R., Morris, G.M., & Liang, J. 1996. Images of cone photoreceptors in the living human eye. *Vision Research, 36,* 1067–1079.

Miller, G.A. 1991. *The science of words.* New York: Freeman.

Miller, G.A., & Licklider, J.C.R. 1950. The intelligibility of interrupted speech. *Journal of the Acoustical Society of America, 22,* 167–173.

Mitchell, S.W. 1871. *Lippincott's Magazine of Popular Literature and Science, 8,* 563–569.

Mizobuchi, Y., & Ohtake, Y. 1992. An experiment to throw more light on light. *Physics Letters A, 168,* 1–5.

Mollon, J.D. 1990. The tricks of colour. In Barlow, Blakemore, & Weston-Smith, 1990, pp. 61–78.

Mollon, J.D. 1992. Worlds of difference. *Nature, 356,* 378–379.

Mollon, J.D., Newcombe, F., Polden, P.G., & Ratcliff, G. 1980. On the presence of three cone mechanisms in a case of total achromatopsia. In G. Verriest (Ed.), *Colour vision deficiencies.* Bristol: Hilger, pp. 130–135.

Mollon, J., & Sharpe, L.T. (Eds.). 1983. *Colour vision: physiology and psychophysics.* New York: Academic Press.

de Monasterio, F.M. 1978. Properties of concentrically organized X and Y ganglion cells of macaque retina. *Journal of Neurophysiology, 41,* 1394–1417.

de Monasterio, F.M. & Schein, S.J. 1982. Spectral bandwidths of color-opponent cells of geniculo-cortical pathway of macaque monkeys. *Journal of Neurophysiology, 47,* 214–223.

Morinaga, S. 1941. Beobachtungen über Grundlagen und Wirkungen anschaulich gleichmässiger Breite. *Arch. Psychol., 110.*

Morsier, G. 1936. Les hallucinations. Les automatismes visuels. Hallucinations retrochiasmatiques. *Schweizer medizinische Wochenschrift, 66,* 700–708.

Motter, B.C. 1994. Neural correlates of attentive selection for color or luminance in extrastriate area V4. *Journal of Neuroscience, 14,* 2178–2189.

Mundy, J.L., & Zisserman, A. (Eds.). 1992. *Geometric invariance in computer vision.* Cambridge, Mass.: MIT Press.

Mundy, J.L., Zisserman, A., & Forsyth, D. (Eds.). 1994. *Applications of invariance in computer vision: Second joint European-U.S. workshop, Ponta Delgada, Azores, Portugal, October 9–14, 1993: Proceedings.* New York: Springer-Verlag.

Murray, D.J. 1995. *Gestalt psychology and the cognitive revolution.* London: Harvester Wheatsheaf.

Mycielski, J. 1955. On the paradox of the sphere. *Fundamenta Mathematica, 42,* 348–355.

Nabokov, V. 1966. *Speak, memory: An autobiography revisited.* New York: Dover.

Nagel, H.H., & Enkelmann, W. 1986. An investigation of smoothness constraints for the estimation of displacement vector fields for image sequences. *IEEE Transactions on Pattern Analysis and Machine Intelligence, 8,* 565–593.

Nakayama, K., Shimojo, S., & Ramachandran, V.S. 1990. Transparency: Relation to depth, subjective contours, luminance, and neon color spreading. *Perception, 19,* 497–513.

Nakayama, K., Shimojo, S., & Silverman, G.H. 1989. Stereoscopic depth: Its relation to image segmentation, grouping, and the recognition of occluded objects. *Perception, 18,* 55–68.

Narayan Bhat, U. 1984. *Elements of applied stochastic processes.* New York: Wiley.

Nathans, J. 1987. Molecular biology of visual pigments. *Annual Review of Neuroscience, 10,* 163–194.

Nathans, J. 1989. The genes for color vision. *Scientific American, 260,* 28–35.

Nathans, J., Piantanida, T.P., Eddy, R.L., Shows, T.B., & Hogness, D.S. 1986a. Molecular genetics of inherited variation in human color vision. *Science, 232,* 203–210.

Nathans, J., Thomas, D., & Hogness, D.S. 1986b. Molecular genetics of human color vision: the genes encoding blue, green, and red pigments. *Science, 232,* 193–202.

Necker, L.A. 1832. Observations on some remarkable phaenomena seen in Switzerland; and an optical phaenomenon which occurs on viewing of a crystal or geometrical solid. *Phil. Mag., 3,* 329–337.

Neitz, J., & Jacobs, G.H. 1986. Polymorphism of the long-wave-length cone in normal human color vision. *Nature, 323,* 623–635.

Nelson, E. 1985. *Quantum fluctuations.* Princeton: Princeton University Press.

Neuer, R., Liebertson, H., & Yoshida, S. 1981. *Ukiyo-e: 250 years of Japanese art.* New York: Mayflower Books.

von Neumann, J. 1929. Zur allgemeinen Theorie des Masses. *Fundamenta Mathematica, 34,* 73–116.

von Neumann, J. 1955. *Mathematical foundations of quantum mechanics.* Translated by R.T. Beyer. Princeton: Princeton University Press. Original: 1932. *Mathematische Grundlagen der Quantenmechanik.* Berlin: Springer.

Neumeyer, C. 1980. Simultaneous color contrast in the honeybee. *Journal of Comparative Physiology A, 139,* 165–176.

Neumeyer, C. 1981. Chromatic adaptation in the honeybee: Successive color contrast and color constancy. *Journal of Comparative Physiology A, 144,* 543–553.

Neumeyer, C. 1985. An ultraviolet receptor as a fourth receptor type in goldfish color vision. *Naturwissenschaften, 72,* 162–163.

Neumeyer, C. 1986. Wavelength discrimination in the goldfish. *Journal of Comparative Physiology A, 158,* 203–213.

Neumeyer, C. 1988. *Das Farbensehen des Goldfisches: Eine verhaltensphysiologische Analyse.* Stuttgart: Thieme.

Neumeyer, C. 1991. Evolution of colour vision. In J.R. Cronly-Dillon & R.L. Gregory (Eds.), *Evolution of the eye and visual system: Vision and visual dysfunction, Volume 2.* London: Macmillan.

Neumeyer, C. 1992. Tetrachromatic color vision in goldfish: Evidence from color mixture experiments. *Journal of Comparative Physiology A, 171,* 639–649.

Newton, I. 1730/1952. *Opticks, or a treatise of the reflections, refractions, inflections and colours of light,* based on the fourth edition of 1730. New York: Dover.

Nodine, C.F., & Fisher, D.F. 1979. *Perception and pictorial representation.* New York: Praeger.

Norman, J.F., & Lappin, J.S. 1992. The detection of surface curvatures defined by optical motion. *Perception & Psychophysics, 51,* 386–396.

Norman, J.F., & Todd, J.T. 1993. The perceptual analysis of structure from motion for rotating objects undergoing affine stretching transformations. *Perception & Psychophysics, 53,* 279–291.

Oppel, J.J. 1856. Über ein Anaglyptoskop [On the stereoscope]. *Annalen der Physik und Chemie, 175,* 466–469.

Orban, G.A., & Nagel, H.-H. 1992. *Artificial and biological vision systems.* New York: Springer-Verlag.

O'Reilly, J. 1983. *Observers for linear systems.* New York: Academic Press.

Oross, S., Francis, E., Mauk, D., & Fox, R. 1987. The Ames window illusion: Perception of illusory motion by human infants. Special Issue: The Ontogenesis of Perception. *Journal of Experimental Psychology: Human Perception and Performance, 13,* 609–613.

Pallis, C.A. 1955. Impaired identification of faces and places with agnosia for colors. *Journal of Neurology, Neurosurgery and Psychiatry, 18,* 218–224.

Palmer, S.E. 1977. Hierarchical structure in perceptual representation. *Cognitive Psychology, 9,* 441–474.

Pantle, A.J., & Picciano, L. 1976. A multistable display: Evidence for two separate motion systems in human vision. *Science, 193,* 500–502.

Paré, Ambroise. 1551. La maniere de traicter les playes faictes tāt par hacquebutes, que par fleches: . . . Paris: Par la vefue Iean de Brie.

Park, D.J., Nam, K.M., & Park, R.H. 1995. Multiresolution edge detection techniques. *Pattern Recognition, 28,* 2, 211–229.

Parks, T.E. 1980. Letter to the Editor. *Perception, 9,* 723.

Pastore, N. 1971. *Selective history of theories of visual perception: 1650–1950.* New York: Oxford University Press.

Patzelt, Otto 1991. *Faszination des Scheins: 500 Jahre Gesichte der Perspektive.* Berlin: Verlag für Bauwesen GmbH.

Paulson, H.L., Galetta, S.L., Grossman, M., & Alavi, A. Hemiachromatopsia of unilateral occipitotemporal infarcts. *American Journal of Ophthalmology, 118,* 518–523.

Penfield, W., & Boldrey, E. 1937. Somatic motor and sensory representation in the cerebral cortex of man as studied by electrical stimulation. *Brain, 60,* 389–443.

Penfield, W., & Rasmussen, T. 1950. *The cerebral cortex of man.* New York: Macmillan.

Penrose, R. 1989. *The emperor's new mind.* Oxford: Oxford University Press.

Penrose, R. 1994. *Shadows of the mind.* Oxford: Oxford University Press.

Pentland, A.P. 1984. Local shading analysis. *IEEE Transactions on Pattern Analysis and Machine Intelligence, 6,* 170–187.

Pentland, A.P. 1986. Perceptual organization and the representation of natural form. *Artificial Intelligence, 28,* 293–331.

Perrett, D.I., Harries, M., Mistlin, A.J., and Chitty, A.J. 1989. Recognizing objects and actions: frameworks for neuronal computation and perceptual experience. In D.M. Guthrie (Ed)., *Higher Order Sensory Processing. Studies in Neuroscience Series.* Manchester, England: Manchester University Press, pp. 94–108.

Peterhans, E., & von der Heydt, R. 1989. Mechanisms of contour perception in monkey visual cortex. II: Contours bridging gaps. *Journal of Neuroscience, 9,* 1749–1763.

Peterhans, E., & von der Heydt, R. 1991. Subjective contours—bridging the gap between psychophysics and physiology. *Trends in Neuroscience, 14,* 112–119.

Peterhans, E., von der Heydt, R., & Baumgartner, G. 1986. Neuronal responses to illusory contour stimuli reveal stages of visual cortical processing. In J.D. Pettigrew, K.J. Sanderson, & W.R. Levick (Eds.), *Visual neuroscience.* Cambridge: Cambridge University Press, pp. 343–351.

Petermann, B. 1932. *The gestalt theory and the problem of configuration.* London: Routledge.

Petersik, J.T., & Pantle, A. 1979. Factors controlling the competing sensations produced by a bistable stroboscopic motion display. *Vision Research, 19,* 143–154.

Peterson, M.A., & Gibson, B.S. 1993. Shape recognition inputs to figure-ground organization in three-dimensional display. *Cognitive Psychology, 25,* 383–429.

Peterson, M.A., & Gibson, B.S. 1994. Must figure-ground organization precede object recognition? An assumption in peril. *Psychological Science, 5,* 253–259.

Petrig, B., Julesz, B., Kropfl, W., Baumgartner, G., & Anliker, M. 1981. Development of stereopsis and cortical binocularity in human infants: Electrophysiological evidence. *Science, 213,* 1402–1405.

Petry, S., & Meyer, G.E. (Eds.). 1987. *The perception of illusory contours.* New York: Springer.

Pinker, S. 1994. *The language instinct.* London: Penguin.

Pirenne, M.H. 1967. *Vision and the eye.* London: Chapman & Hall.

Pirenne, M.H. 1970. *Optics, painting & photography.* London: Cambridge University Press.

Poggio, T., & Reichardt, W. 1976. Visual control of orientation behavior in the fly. Part II. Towards the underlying neural interactions. *Quarterly Review of Biophysics, 9,* 377–438.

Poggio, T., Torre, V., & Koch, C. 1985. Computational vision and regularization theory. *Nature, 317,* 314–319.

Popper, K.R., and Eccles, J.C. 1985. *The self and its brain.* New York: Springer-Verlag.

Prazdny, K. 1983. Illusory contours are not caused by simultaneous brightness contrast. *Perception & Psychophysics, 34,* 403–404.

Prazdny, K. 1985. On the nature of inducing forms generating perceptions of illusory contours. *Perception & Psychophysics, 37,* 237–242.

Prevost, B. 1826. Sur une apparence de décomposition de la lumière blanche par le mouvement du corps qui la réfléchit. *Mémoires de la Société de Physique et d'Histoire naturelle de Genéva, 3,* 121.

Price, D.B., & Twombly, N.J. 1978. *The phantom limb phenomenon: A medical, folkloric, and historical study.* Washington, D.C.: Georgetown University Press.

Prinzmetal, W. 1990. Neon colors illuminate reading units. *Journal of Experimental Psychology: Human Perception & Performance, 16,* 584–597.

Prinzmetal, W., & Keysar, B. 1989. Functional theory of illusory conjunctions and neon colors. *Journal of Experimental Psychology: General, 118,* 165–190.

Proffitt, D.R., & Bertenthal, B.I. 1988. Recovering connectivity from moving point-light displays. In Martin & Aggarwal, 1988, pp. 297–328.

Proffitt, D.R., & Cutting, J.E. 1980. An invariant for wheel-generated motions and the logic of its determination. *Perception, 9,* 435–449.

Proffitt, D.R., & Kaiser, M.K. 1995. Perceiving events. In Epstein & Rogers, 1995, pp. 227–261.

Ptolemy. 2nd century A.D. *Optics.* Available as *Ptolemy's theory of visual perception: An English translation of the Optics* with introduction and commentary [by] A. Mark Smith. Philadelphia: American Philosophical Society, 1996.

Purghe, F. 1991. Is amodal completion necessary for the formation of illusory figures? *Perception, 20,* 623–636.

Purghe, F., & Katsaras, P. 1991. Figural conditions affecting the formation of anomalous surfaces: Overall configuration versus single stimulus part. *Perception, 20,* 193–206.

Ramachandran, V.S. 1987. Visual perception of surfaces: A biological theory. In Petry & Meyer, 1987, pp. 93–108.

Ramachandran, V.S. 1988. Perceiving shape from shading. *Scientific American, 259,* 58–65.

Ramachandran, V.S. 1993a. Behavioral and magnetoencephalographic correlates of plasticity in the adult human brain. *Proceedings of the National Academy of Sciences, USA, 90,* 10413–10420.

Ramachandran, V.S. 1993b. Filling in gaps in perception: Part II. Scotomas and phantom limbs. *Current Directions in Psychological Science, 2,* 56–65.

Ramachandran, V.S. 1994. Phantom limbs, neglect syndromes, repressed memories, and Freudian psychology. In Sporns & Tononi, 1994, pp. 291–333.

Ramachandran, V.S. 1996. What neurological syndromes can tell us about human nature: Some lessons from phantom limbs, Capgras syndrome, and anosognosia. *Cold Spring Harbor Symposia on Quantitative Biology, 61,* 115–134.

Ramachandran, V.S., & Anstis, S.M. 1985. Perceptual organization in multistable apparent motion. *Perception, 14,* 135–144.

Ramachandran, V.S., & Gregory, R.L. 1978. Does colour provide an input to human motion perception? *Nature, 275,* 55–56.

Ramachandran, V.S., Rogers-Ramachandran, D., & Stewart, M. 1992. Perceptual correlates of massive cortical reorganization. *Science, 258,* 1159–1160.

Ramachandran, V.S., Stewart, M., & Rogers-Ramachandran, D. 1992. Perceptual correlates of massive cortical reorganization. *NeuroReport, 3,* 583–586.

Redies, C., Crook, J.M., & Creutzfeldt, O.D. 1986. Neuronal responses to borders with and without luminance gradients in cat visual cortex and dorsal lateral geniculate nucleus. *Experimental Brain Research, 61,* 469–481.

Redies, C., & Spillmann, L. 1981. The neon color effect in the Ehrenstein illusion. *Perception, 10,* 667–681.

Reed, C.L., & Caselli, R.J. 1994. The nature of tactile agnosia: A case study. *Neuropsychologia, 32,* 527–539.

Reed, C.L., Caselli, R.J., & Farah, M.J. 1996. Tactile agnosia: Underlying impairment and implications for normal tactile object recognition. *Brain, 119,* 875–888.

Reed, S.K. 1974. Structural descriptions and the limitations of visual images. *Memory and Cognition, 2,* 329–336.

Reichardt, W., & Poggio, T. 1976. Visual control of orientation behavior in the fly. Part I. A quantitative analysis. *Quarterly Review of Biophysics, 9,* 311–375.

Reichardt, W., & Poggio, T. 1981. Visual control of flight in flies. In W.E. Reichardt & T. Poggio (Eds.), *Recent theoretical developments in neurobiology.* Cambridge, Mass.: MIT Press, pp. 135–150.

Restle, F. 1979. Coding theory of the perception of motion configurations. *Psychological Review, 86,* 1–24.

Reutersvärd, O. 1984. *Unmögliche Figuren: Vom Abenteuer Der Perspektiven.* Munich: Verlag Moos & Partner KG.

Revuz, D. 1984. *Markov chains.* Amsterdam: North-Holland.

Rheingold, H. 1991. *Virtual reality.* New York: Simon & Schuster.

Richards, W.A. 1983. Structure from stereo and motion. *Artificial Intelligence Laboratory Memo, 731.* Cambridge, Mass.: MIT.

Richards, W.A., & Ullman, S. (Eds.). 1987. *Image understanding 1985–1986.* New York: Ablex.

Rittenhouse, D. 1786. Explanation of an optical deception. *Transactions of the American Philosophical Society, 2,* 37–42.

Rizzo, M., Nawrot, M., & Zihl, J. 1995. Motion and shape perception in cerebral akinetopsia. *Brain, 118,* 1105–1127.

Rizzo, M., Smith, V., Pokorny, J., & Damasio, A.R. 1993. Color perception profiles in central achromatopsia. *Neurology, 43,* 995–1001.

Roberts, L.G. 1965. Machine perception of three-dimensional solids. In J.T. Tippett et al. (Eds.), *Optical and electrooptical information processing*. Cambridge, Mass.: MIT Press, pp. 211–217.

Robinson, H. 1994. *Perception*. London: Routledge.

Robinson, R.M. 1947. On the decomposition of spheres. *Fundamenta Mathematica, 34,* 246–260.

Rock, I. 1973. *Orientation and Form.* New York: Academic Press.

Rock, I. 1983. *The logic of perception*. Cambridge, Mass.: MIT Press.

Rock, I. 1984. *Perception*. New York: Scientific American Library: Distributed by W.H. Freeman.

Rock, I. 1987. A problem-solving approach to illusory contours. In Petry & Meyer, 1987, pp. 62–70.

Rock, I., and DiVita, J. 1987. A case of viewer-centered object perception. *Cognitive Psychology, 19,* 280–293.

Rogers, B.J. 1986. The perception of surface curvature from disparity and motion parallax cues. *Investigative Ophthalmology and Visual Sciences, 27,* 181.

Rogers, B.J., & Cagenello, R. 1989. Disparity curvature and the perception of three-dimensional surfaces. *Nature, 339,* 135–137.

Rogers, B.J., & Collett, T.S. 1989. The appearance of surfaces specified by motion parallax and binocular disparity. *The Quarterly Journal of Experimental Psychology, 41,* 697–717.

Rogers, B.J., & Graham, M.E. 1983. Anisotropies in the perception of three-dimensional surfaces. *Science, 221,* 1409–1411.

Rosenthal, D.M. (Ed.). 1991. *The nature of mind.* Oxford: Oxford University Press.

Rossel, S. 1986. Binocular spatial localization in the praying mantis. *Journal of Experimental Biology, 120,* 265–281.

Rossotti, II. 1983. *Colour: Why the world isn't grey.* New York: Penguin.

Rubin, E. 1915/1958. Figure and ground. In D.C. Beardslee & M. Wertheimer (Eds.), *Readings in perception*. New York: D. Van Nostrand, 1958. Based on an abridged translation by M. Wertheimer of pp. 35–101 of E. Rubin, *Visuell wahrgenommene Figuren,* translated by P. Collett into German from the Danish *Synsoplevede Figurer* (Copenhagen: Gyldendalske, 1915).

Rubin, E. 1927. Visuell wehrgenommene wirkliche Bewegungen [Visually perceived actual motion]. *Zeitschrift für Psychologie, 103,* 384–392.

Rubin, J.M., & Richards, W.A. 1982. Color vision and image intensities: When are changes material? *Biological Cybernetics, 45,* 215–226.

Rubin, J.M., & Richards, W.A. 1987. Spectral categorization of materials. In W. Richards & S. Ullman (Eds.), *Image Understanding 1985-1986.* New York: Ablex, pp. 20–44.

Rubin, J.M., & Richards, W.A. 1988. Visual perception of moving parts. *Journal of the Optical Society of America, A, 5,* 2045–2049.

Rudinsky, M. 1931. Bone industry of the Palaeolithic site of Mezine in interpretation of T. Volkov. *Ukrainian Academy of Sciences; Anthropological Laboratory of T. Volkov, Kiev,* 1–65.

Sabra, A.I. 1978. Sensation and inference in Alhazen's theory of visual perception. In Machamer & Turnbull, 1978.

Sacks, O. 1991. To see and not see. *The New Yorker,* May 10, 59–72.

Sacks, O., 1995. *An anthropologist on Mars.* New York: Vintage Books.

Sacks, O., & Wasserman, R. 1987. The case of the colorblind painter. *New York Review of Books.* November 19.

Saidpour, A., & Braunstein, M.L. (1994). Curvature and depth judgments of the same simulated shape from motion parallax and structure from motion. *Investigative Ophthalmology and Visual Sciences*, 35.

Saint-Pierre, B. 1972. *La physique de la vision dan l'antiquité: Contribution à l'établissement des sources anciennes de l'optique médiévale.* Ph.D. Dissertation, University of Montreal.

Scharf, A. 1974. *Art and photography.* Baltimore: Penguin.

Schein, S.J., & Desimone, R. 1990. Spectral properties of V4 neurons in the macaque. *Journal of Neuroscience, 10,* 3369–3389.

Schein, S.J., Marrocco, R.T., & de Monasterio, F.M. 1982. Is there a high concentration of color-selective cells in area V4 of monkey visual cortex? *Journal of Neurophysiology, 47,* 193–213.

Schier, F. 1986. *Deeper into pictures: An essay on pictorial representation.* Cambridge: Cambridge University Press.

Schiller, P.H. 1986. The central visual system. *Vision Research, 26,* 1351–1386.

Schiller, P. v. 1933. Stroboskopische Alternativversuche. *Psychologische Forschung, 17,* 179–214.

Schneider, G.E. 1969. Two visual systems. *Science, 163,* 895–902.

Schreber, D.P. 1903. *Denkwürdigkeiten einer Nervenkranken.* Reprint in P. Heiligenthal & R. Volk (Eds.), *Bürgerliche Wahnwelt um 1900.* Wiesbaden: Focus, 1973, pp. 1–246.

Schröder, H. 1858. Über eine optische Inversion bei Betrachtung verkehrter, durch optische Vorrichtung entworfener physischer Bilder [On an optical inversion produced by viewing reversed stereoscopic images]. *Annalen der Physik und Chemie, 181,* 298–311.

Schumann, F. 1900. Beiträge zur Analyse der Gesichtswahrnehmungen. Erste Abhandlung. Einige Beobachtungen über die Zusammenfassung von Gesichtseindrücken zu Einheiten. *Zeitschrift für Psychologie und Physiologie der Sinnesorgane, 23,* 1–32. [Contribution to the analysis of visual perception: First paper: Some observations on the combination of visual impressions into units. Translated by A. Hogg, in Petry & Meyer, 1987, pp. 21–34.]

Schumann, F. 1904. Einige Beobachtungen über die Zusammenfassung von Gesichtseindrücken zu Einheiten. *Psychologische Studien, 1,* 1–32. [Reprint of Schumann, 1900.]

Schwartz, R.J. (Ed.). 1965. *Perceiving, sensing, and knowing.* Berkeley: University of California Press.

Schyns, P.G., & Murphy, G.L. 1994. The ontogeny of part representation in object concepts. *The Psychology of Learning and Motivation, 31,* 305–349.

Scott, T.R., & Noland, J.H. 1965. Some stimulus dimensions of rotating spirals. *Psychological Review, 72,* 344–357.

Searle, J. 1984. *Minds, brains, and science.* Cambridge, Mass.: Harvard University Press.

Searle, J. 1992. *The rediscovery of the mind.* Cambridge, Mass.: MIT Press.

Sekuler, R., Anstis, S.M., Braddick, O.J., Brandt, T., Movshon, J.A., & Orban, G. 1990. The perception of motion. In Spillmann & Werner, 1990, pp. 205–230.

Senden, Marius von. 1960. *Space and sight; the perception of space and shape in the congenitally blind before and after operation.* Translated by Peter Heath. Glencoe, Ill.: Free Press.

Sereno, M.E. 1987. Implementing stages of motion analysis in neural networks. *Proceedings of the Ninth Annual Conference of the Cognitive Science Society, 405–416.*

Sereno, M.I. 1989. Learning the solution to the aperture problem for pattern motion with a Hebb rule. *Advances in neural information processing systems.* San Mateo, Calif.: Morgan-Kaufmann.

Setala, K., & Vesti, E. 1994. Acquired cerebral achromatopsia—a case report. *Neuro-Ophthalmology, 14,* 31–36.

Shepard, R.N. 1981. Psychophysical complementarity. In Kubovy & Pomerantz, 1981, pp. 279–341.

Shepard, R.N. 1984. Ecological constraints on internal representation: Resonant kinematics of perceiving, imagining, thinking, and dreaming. *Psychological Review, 91,* 417–447.

Shepard, R.N. 1990. *Mind sights.* New York: Freeman.

Shepard, R.N., & Zare, S. 1983. Path-guided apparent motion. *Science, 220,* 632–634.

Shepherd, G.M. 1983. *Neurobiology.* New York: Oxford University Press.

Shimojo, S., Silverman, G.H., & Nakayama, K. 1988. An occlusion-related mechanism of depth perception based on motion and interocular sequence. *Nature, 333,* 265–268.

Shimojo, S., Silverman, G.H., & Nakayama, K. 1989. Occlusion and the solution to the aperture problem. *Vision Research, 29,* 619–626.

Shipley, T.F., & Kellman, P.J. 1990. The role of discontinuities in the perception of subjective figures. *Perception & Psychophysics, 48,* 259–270.

Shipley, T.F., & Kellman, P.J. 1992. Strength of visual interpolation depends on the ratio of physically specified to total edge length. *Perception & Psychophysics, 52,* 97–106.

Shipley, T.F., & Kellman, P.J. 1993. Optical tearing in spatiotemporal boundary formation: When do local element motions produce boundaries, form, and global motion? *Spatial Vision, 7,* 323–339.

Shipley, T.F., & Kellman, P.J. 1994. Spatiotemporal boundary formation: Boundary, form, and motion perception from transformations of surface elements. *Journal of Experimental Psychology: General, 123,* 3–20.

Siegel, R.M., & Andersen, R.A. 1988. Perception of three-dimensional structure from motion in monkey and man. *Nature, 331,* 259–261.

Silverman, I.E., & Galetta, S.L. 1995. Partial color loss in hemiachromatopsia. *Neuro-Ophthalmology, 15,* 127–134.

Singh, M., Seyranian, G., & Hoffman, D.D. 1997. Cuts for parsing visual shapes. (Under review.)

Skrzypek, J., & Ringer, B. 1992. Neural network models for illusory contour perception. *Proceedings of Computer Vision and Pattern Recognition 1992, Champaign, IL,* 586–591.

Skyrms, B. 1975. *Choice and chance.* Belmont, Calif.: Wadsworth Publishing.

Soriano, M., Spillmann, L., and Bach, M. 1996. The abutting grating illusion. *Vision Research, 36,* 109–116.

Sperling, H.G., Crawford, M.L.J., & Espinoza, S. 1978. Threshold spectral sensitivity of single neurons in the lateral geniculate nucleus and of performing monkeys. *Modern Problems in Ophthalmology, 19,* 2–18.

Spillmann, L., & Werner, J.S. 1990. *Visual perception: The neurophysiological foundations.* New York: Academic Press.

Stevens, J.C. 1967. Brightness inhibition re size of surround. *Perception & Psychophysics, 2,* 189–192.

Stevens, K.A., & Brookes, A. 1988. The concave cusp as a determiner of figure-ground. *Perception, 17,* 35–42.

Stewart, E. 1959. The Gelb effect. *Journal of Experimental Psychology, 57,* 235–242.

Stiles-Davis, J., Kritchevsky, M., & Bellugi, U. (Eds.) 1988. *Spatial cognition: Brain bases and development.* Hillsdale, N.J.: Lawrence Erlbaum.

Stoner, G.R., & Albright, T.D. 1992. The influence of foreground/background assignment on transparency and motion coherence in plaid patterns. *Investigative Ophthalmology and Visual Science, 33,* 1050.

Stoner, G.R., & Albright, T.D. 1993. Image segmentation cues in motion processing: Implications for modularity in vision. *Journal of Cognitive Neuroscience, 5,* 129–149.

Stoner, G.R., Albright, T.D., & Ramachandran, V.S. 1990. Transparency and coherence in human motion perception. *Nature, 344,* 153–155.

Stratton, G.M. 1896. Some preliminary experiments on vision without inversion of the retinal image. *Psychological Review, 3,* 611–617.

Stratton, G.M. 1897a. Vision without inversion of the retinal image. *Psychological Review, 4,* 341–360.

Stratton, G.M. 1897b. Vision without inversion of the retinal image (Concluded). *Psychological Review, 4,* 463–481.

Stuart, S., Wright, J.H., Thase, M.E., Beck, A.T. 1997. Cognitive therapy with inpatients. *General Hospital Psychiatry, 19,* 42–50.

Stumpf, P. 1911. Über die Abhängigkeit der visuellen Bewegungsempfindung und ihres negativen Nachbildes von den Reizvorgängen auf der Netzhaut. *Zeitschrift für Psychologie, 59,* 321–330.

Svaetichin, G. 1956. Spectral response curves from single cones. *Acta Physiologica Scandinavica, 134,* 17–46.

Szeliski, R. 1989. *Bayesian modeling of uncertainty in low-level vision.* Boston: Kluwer Academic.

Takeichi, H., Shimojo, S., & Watanabe, T. 1992. Neon flank and illusory contour: Interaction between the two processes leads to color filling-in. *Perception, 21,* 313–324.

Ternus, J. 1926. Experimentelle Untersuchung über phänomenale Identität. *Psychologische Forschung, 7,* 81–136. Reprinted as "The problem of phenomenal identity," in Ellis, 1937, pp. 149–160.

Thompson, E. 1995. *Colour vision.* New York: Routledge.

Tinbergen, N., & Kuenen, D.J. 1939. Über die auslösenden und richtungsgebenden Reizsituationen der Sperrbewegung von jungen Drosseln (*Turdus m. merula* L. und *T.e.ericetorum* Turdon*). Zeitschrift für Tierpsychologie, 3,* 37–60.

Todd, J.T. 1984. The perception of three-dimensional structure from rigid and non-rigid motion. *Perception & Psychophysics, 36,* 97–103.

Todd, J.T., & Bressan, P. 1990. The perception of 3-dimensional affine structure from minimal apparent motion sequences. *Perception & Psychophysics, 48,* 419–430.

Todd, J.T., & Norman, J.F. 1991. The visual perception of smoothly curved surfaces from minimal apparent motion sequences. *Perception & Psychophysics, 50,* 509–523.

Todorović, D. 1996. A gem from the past: Pleikart Stumpf's (1911) anticipation of the aperture problem, Reichardt detectors, and perceived motion loss at equiluminance. *Report 25/96 of the Center for Interdisciplinary Research, Bielefeld, Germany.*

Torii, S., & Uemura, Y. 1965. Effects of inducing luminance and area upon the apparent brightness of a test field. *Japanese Psychological Research, 7,* 86–100.

Treue, S., Andersen, R.A., Ando, H., & Hildreth, E.C. 1995. Structure-from-motion: Perceptual evidence for surface interpolation. *Vision Research, 35,* 139–148.

Trueswell, J.C., & Hayhoe, M.M. 1993. Surface segmentation mechanisms and motion perception. *Vision Research, 33,* 313–328.

Triesman, A., & Gormican, S. (1988). Feature analysis in early vision: Evidence from search asymmetries. *Psychological Review, 95,* 15–48.

Tye, M. 1995. *Ten problems of consciousness.* Cambridge, Mass.: MIT Press.

van Tuijl, H.F.J.M. 1975. A new visual illusion: neonlike color spreading and complementary color induction between subjective contours. *Acta Psychologica, 39,* 441–445.

Van Tuijl, H.F., & Leeuwenberg, E.L. 1979. Neon color spreading and structural information measures. *Perception & Psychophysics, 25,* 269–284.

Van Tuijl, H.F., & de Weert, C.M. 1979. Sensory conditions for the occurrence of the neon spreading illusion. *Perception, 8,* 211–215.

Turbayne, C.M. 1963. *Berkeley: Works on vision.* New York: Bobbs-Merrill.

Turton, W. 1819. *A conchological dictionary of the British Islands.* London: John Booth.

Tyler, H.R. 1968. Abnormalities of perception with defective eye movements (Balint's syndrome). *Cortex, 3,* 154–171.

Ullman, S. 1976. Filling in the gaps: The shape of subjective contours and a model for their generation. *Biological Cybernetics, 25,* 1–6.

Ullman, S. 1979. *The interpretation of visual motion.* Cambridge, Mass.: MIT Press.

Ullman, S. 1981. Analysis of visual motion by biological and computer systems. *IEEE Computer, 14,* 8, 57–69.

Ullman, S. 1983. Recent computational studies in the interpretation of structure from motion. In Beck & Rosenfeld, 1983, pp. 459–480.

Ullman, S. 1984. Maximizing rigidity: The incremental recovery of 3-D structure from rigid and rubbery motion. *Perception, 13,* 255–274.

Vaina, L.M. 1996. Akinetopsia, achromatopsia and blindsight: Recent studies on perception without awareness. *Synthese, 105,* 253–271.

Valenti, S.S., & Pittenger, J.B. (Eds.). 1993. *Studies in perception and action II.* Hillsdale, N.J.: Lawrence Erlbaum.

Vallortigara, G., & Bressan, P. 1991. Occlusion and the perception of coherent motion. *Vision Research, 31,* 1967–1978.

Valvo, A. 1971. *Sight restored after longterm blindness: The problems and behavior patterns of visual rehabilitation.* New York: American Foundation for the Blind.

Varin, D. 1971. Fenomeni di contrasto e diffusione cromatica nell'organizzazione spaziale del campo percettivo. *Rivista di Psicologia, 65,* 101–128.

Verrey, L. 1888. Hemiachromatopsie droite absolue. *Archs. Ophtalmol. (Paris), 8,* 289–301.

Wagon, S. 1985. *The Banach-Tarski Paradox.* Cambridge: Cambridge University Press.

Wallach H. 1935. Über visuell wahrgenommene Bewegungsrichtung. *Psychologische Forschung, 20,* 325–380.

Wallach, H. 1948. Brightness constancy and the nature of achromatic colors. *Journal of Experimental Psychology, 38,* 310–324.

Wallach, H. 1963. The perception of neutral colors. *Scientific American, 208,* 107–116.

Wallach, H. 1965. Visual perception of motion. In G. Keyes (Ed.), *The nature and the art of motion.* New York: George Braziller, pp. 52–59.

Wallach, H. 1976. *On perception.* New York: Quadrangle.

Wallach, H., & O'Connell, D. 1953. The kinetic depth effect. *Journal of Experimental Psychology, 45,* 205-217.

Waltz, D. 1975. Generating semantic descriptions from drawings of scenes with shadows. In P. Winston (Ed.), *The psychology of computer vision.* New York: McGraw-Hill, pp. 19–91.

Wandell, B.A. 1995. *Foundations of vision.* Sunderland, Mass.: Sinauer Associates, Inc.

Wang, H.T., Mathur, B., & Koch, C. 1989. Computing optical flow in the primate visual system. *Neural Computation, 1,* 92–103.

Wapner, W., Judd, T., & Gardner, H. 1978. Visual agnosia in an artist. *Cortex, 14,* 343–364.

Warren, R.M. 1984. Perceptual restoration of obliterated sounds. *Psychological Bulletin, 96,* 371–383.

Warren, R.M., & Warren, R.P. 1968. *Helmholtz on perception: Its physiology and development.* New York: Wiley.

Watanabe, T., & Sato, T. 1989. Effects of luminance contrast on color spreading and illusory contour in the neon color spreading effect. *Perception & Psychophysics, 45,* 427–430.

Watkins, C.D., Sadun, A., & Marenka, S. 1993. *Modern image processing; Warping, morphing, and classical techniques.* New York: Academic Press.

Webb, J., & Aggarwal, J. 1981. Visually interpreting the motion of objects in space. *IEEE Computer, 14,* 40–46.

Webb, J., & Aggarwal, J. 1982. Structure from motion of rigid and jointed objects. *Artificial Intelligence, 19,* 107–130.

Werner, A., Mensel, R., & Wehrhahn, C. 1988. Color constancy in the honeybee. *Journal of Neuroscience, 8,* 156–159.

Wertheimer, M. 1912. Experimentelle Studien über das Sehen von Bewegung. *Zeitschrift für Psychologie, 61,* 161–265.

Wheeler, J.A., & Zurek, W.H. 1983. *Quantum theory and measurement.* Princeton: Princeton University Press.

White, M. 1981. The effect of the nature of the surround on the perceived lightness of grey bars within square-wave test gratings. *Perception, 10,* 215–230.

Whitfield, R., & Farrer, A. 1990. *Caves of the thousand Buddhas: Chinese art from the silk route.* British Museum Exhibition catalogue, London.

Whitney, H. 1955. On singularities of mappings of Euclidean spaces. I. Mappings of the plane into the plane. *Annals of Mathematics, 62,* 374–410.

Whyte, L.L. 1968. *Aspects of form: a symposium on form in nature and art.* London: Lund Humphries.

Wiesel, T.N., & Hubel, D.H. 1966. Spatial and chromatic interaction in the lateral geniculate body of the rhesus monkey. *Journal of Neurophysiology, 29,* 1115–1156.

Wigner, E.P. 1961. Remarks on the mind-body question. In I.J. Good (Ed.), *The scientist speculates.* New York: Basic Books, pp. 284–302.

Williams, D.R. 1992. Photoreceptor sampling and aliasing in human vision. In D.T. Moore (Ed.), *Tutorials in optics.* Washington, D.C.: Optical Society of America, pp. 15–28.

Williams, M. 1970. *Brain damage and the mind.* Baltimore: Penguin Books.

Wilson, E. 1994. *Ornament: 8,000 years.* New York: H. N. Abrams.

Wilson, H.R., & Richards, W.A. 1985. Discrimination of contour curvature: data and theory. *Journal of the Optical Society of America, A, 2, 7,* 1191–1198.

Wilson, H.R., & Richards, W.A. 1989. Mechanism of contour curvature discrimination. *Journal of the Optical Society of America, A, 6, 1,* 1006–1115.

Winderickx, J., Lindsey, D.T., Sanocki, E., Teller, D.Y., Motulsky, A.G., & Deeb, S.S. 1992. Polymorphism in red photopigment underlies variation in colour matching. *Nature, 356,* 431–433.

Winston, P.A. 1975. Learning structural descriptions from examples. In P.H. Winston (Ed.), *The psychology of computer vision.* New York: McGraw-Hill, pp. 157–209.

Wishart, K., Frisby, J., & Buckley, L. 1995. The role of contour in a lightness illusion. *Investigative Ophthalmology & Visual Science, 36,* 4, S640.

Witkin, A.P. 1981. Recovering surface shape and orientation from texture. *Artificial Intelligence, 17,* 17–45.

Witkin, A.P. 1982. Intensity-based edge classification. *Proceedings of the National Conference on Artificial Intelligence,* 36–41.

Witkin, A.P., & Tenenbaum, J.M. 1983. On the rule of structure in vision. In J. Beck, B. Hope, & A. Rosenfeld (Eds.), *Human and machine vision.* New York: Academic Press.

Wittgenstein, L. 1977. *Remarks on colour.* Translated by L.L. McAlister & M. Schättle; ed. G.E.M. Anscombe. Berkeley: University of California Press.

Wolfe, J.M., Yee, A., & Friedman-Hill, S.R. 1992. Curvature is a basic feature for visual search tasks. *Perception, 21,* 465–480.

Wright, Lawrence. 1983. *Perspective in perspective.* London: Routledge & Kegan Paul.

Yang, T.T., Gallen, C.C., Ramachandran, V.S., Cobb, S., Schwartz, B.J., & Bloom, F.E. 1994. Noninvasive detection of cerebral plasticity in adult human somatosensory cortex. *NeuroReport, 5,* 701–704.

Yonas, A. 1981. Infants' responses to optical information for collision. In R.N. Aslin, J.R. Alberts, & M.R. Peterson (Eds.), *Development of perception: Psychobiological perspectives: Vol. 2. The visual system.* New York: Academic Press, pp. 313–334.

Yonas, A., Arterberry, M.E., & Granrud, C.E. 1987. Space perception in infancy. In R. Vasta (Ed.), *Annals of child development.* Greenwich, Conn.: JAI Press.

Yonas, A., Cleaves, W., & Pettersen, L. 1978. Development of sensitivity to pictorial depth. *Science, 200,* 77-79.

Yonas, A., & Granrud, C.E. 1985. Development of visual space perception in young infants. In J. Mehler & R. Foxs (Eds.), *Neonate cognition: Beyond the blooming buzzing confusion.* Hillsdale, N.J.: Lawrence Erlbaum.

Yonas, A., Pettersen, L., & Granrud, C.E. 1982. Infants' sensitivity to familiar size as information for distance. *Child Development, 3,* 1285–1290.

Yonas, A., Pettersen, L., & Lockman, J. 1979. Young infants' sensitivity to optical information for collision. *Canadian Journal of Psychology, 33,* 268–276.

Yoshioka, T., & Dow, B.M. 1996. Color, orientation and cytochrome oxidase reactivity in areas V1, V2, and V4 of macaque monkey visual cortex. *Behavioural Brain Research, 76,* 71–88.

Yoshioka, T., Dow, B.M., & Vautin, R.G. 1996. Neuronal mechanisms of color categorization in areas V1, V2, and V4 of macaque monkey visual cortex. *Behavioural Brain Research, 76,* 51–70.

Young, T. 1802. The Bakerian Lecture: On the theory of lights and colours. *Philosophical Transactions of the Royal Society of London, 92,* 12–48.

Yuille, A.L., & Grzywacz, N.M. 1988. A computational theory for the perception of coherent visual motion. *Nature, 333,* 71–74.

Zeki, S. 1973. Colour coding in rhesus monkey prestriate cortex. *Brain Research, 53,* 422–427.

Zeki, S. 1980. The representation of colours in the cerebral cortex. *Nature, 284,* 412–418.

Zeki, S. 1983a. Colour coding in the cerebral cortex: the reaction of cells in monkey visual cortex to wavelengths and colours. *Neuroscience, 9,* 741–765.

Zeki, S. 1983b. Colour coding in the cerebral cortex: the responses of wavelength-sensitive cells in monkey visual cortex to changes in wavelength composition. *Neuroscience, 9,* 767–781.

Zeki, S. 1985. Colour pathways and hierarchies in the cerebral cortex. In D. Ottoson & S. Zeki (Eds.), *Central and peripheral mechanisms of colour vision.* London: Macmillan.

Zeki, S. 1990. A century of cerebral achromatopsia. *Brain, 113,* 1721–1777.

Zeki, S. 1993. *A vision of the brain.* Boston: Blackwell Scientific Publications.

Zeki, S., Watson, J.D.G., Lueck, C.J., Friston, K.J., Kennard, C., & Frackowiak, R.S.J. 1991. A direct demonstration of functional specialization in human visual cortex. *Journal of Neuroscience, 11,* 641–649.

Zihl, J., Cramon, D. von, & Mai, N. 1983. Selective disturbance of movement vision after bilateral brain damage. *Brain, 106,* 313–340.

Zihl, J., Cramon, D. von, Mai, N., & Schmid, C.H. 1991. Disturbance of movement vision after bilateral posterior brain damage: Further evidence and follow up observations. *Brain, 114,* 2235–2252.

Zurek, W.H. 1990. *Complexity, entropy and the physics of information.* New York: Addison-Wesley.

ILLUSTRATION CREDITS

Figures 2, 81, 83, 84, 85, 89b, 94, 99, 100, and 101 adapted from *Cognition* 18: 65–69 (figures 2, 4, 5, 6, and 14), D. Hoffman and W. Richards, "Parts of Recognition," and from *Cognition* 63: 29–78 (figures 2, 24, 25, and 27), D. Hoffman and M. Singh, "Salience of Visual Parts," ©1984, 1996 with kind permission from Elsevier Science—NL, Sara Burgerhartstraat 25, 1055 KV Amsterdam, The Netherlands.

Figure 35 reprinted by permission of Museum Catharijneconvent, Utrecht, The Netherlands.

Figure 39 reprinted by permission of the Estate of Pablo Picasso / Artists Rights Society (ARS), New York ©1998.

Figures 48, 53b, 63, 73, and 74 adapted from the paper "Quasi-percettivi in campi con stimolazione omogenea," *Rivista di Psicologia* 49: 7–30 ("Kanizsa triangle" and "black crosses" figures), Gaetano Kanizsa, © 1955 Giunti Gruppo Editoriale, Florence, Italy.

Figure 50a ("Parks's illusory disk") adapted from "Letter to the editor," *Perception* 9: 723 (only figure), Theodore E. Parks, ©1980 by permission of Pion Limited, London.

Figure 50c ("Prazdny's illusory square") adapted from *Perception and Psychophysics* 37: 237–42 (figure 1a), "On the Nature of Inducing Forms Generating Perceptions of Illusory Contours," K. Prazdny, ©1985 by permission of Psychonomic Society, Inc., Austin, Tex.

Figure 50d adapted from *The Perception of Illusory Contours* (figure 28.2), Petry and Meyers, eds., Springer-Verlag, New York ©1987, by permission of the publisher and John M. Kennedy.

Figure 51a reprinted from *The Old Stone Age in European Russia*, E. A. Golomshtok, Transactions of the American Philosophical Society, New Series, vol. XXIX, pt. Iib, Philadelphia, Pa., by permission of the American Philosophical Society.

Figure 51b detail by permission of Madame Yvonne Vertut.

Figures 53, 54, and 58c-d adapted from *Perception* 22: 589–95 (figs. 3a, 5, and 7), "Parallelism and the Perception of Illusory Contours," Marc Albert, ©1993, by permission of Pion Limited, London, and Marc Albert.

Figure 66 reprinted from *Investigative Ophthalmology and Visual Science* 34: 3291 (fig. 10a), Curcio, Millican, Allen, and Kalina, ©1993, by permission of Lippincott-Raven Publishers, Philadelphia, Pa.

Figure 71 reprinted from *Neurobiology* (first figure), Gordon Shepherd, Oxford University Press, New York ©1983, by permission of Dennis Landis and Thomas Reese.

Figure 75 reprinted from *American Journal of Psychology* 90: 253–62 (figure 1), "Organizational Determinants of Subjective Contour: The Subjective Necker Cube," Heywood Petry and Drake Bradley, ©1977 by permission of University of Illinois Press, Heywood Petry, and Drake Bradley.

Figure 80 adapted with permission from a rpint by Geralyn Souza.

Figure 97 reprinted from *Computer Vision, Graphics, and Image Processing* 32: 29–73 (figure 17), "Human Image Understanding: Recent Research and Theory," Irving Biederman, ©1985 by permission of Irving Biederman and Academic Press, Inc., Orlando, Fla.

Figures 110 and 111a reprinted from *Perception* 10: 667–81 (figure 5d), "The Neon Color Effect in the Ehrenstein Illusion," Christoph Redies and Lothar Spillmann, ©1981 by permission of Christoph Redies and Lothar Spillmann and Pion Limited, London.

Figure 118b adapted from *Perception* 10: 215–30 (figure 1a), "The Effect of the Nature of the Surround on the Perceived Lightness of Grey Bars Within Square-Wave Test Gratings," White, © 1981 by permission of Pion Limited, London, and Michael White.

Figures 119, 120a, 120b, 123, and 124 adapted from *Science* 262: 2042–44 (figures 3a and 4), "Perceptual Organization and the Judgment of Brightness," Edward H. Adelson, by permission of Edward H. Adelson and © 1993 the American Association for the Advancement of Science.

Figure 133 adapted from *Trends in Neurosciences* 7: 243–48 (figure 1b), "Recent

Developments in the Physiology of Color Vision," Peter Lennie, ©1984 by permission of Elsevier Science Ltd., The Boulevard, Langford Lane, Kidlington OX5 1GB, UK.

Figure 156 adapted from *Nature* 300: 523–25 (figure 1), "Phenomenal Coherence of Moving Visual Patterns," E. Adelson and J. Movshon, © 1984 by permission of Macmillan Magazines Ltd., Porters South, Crinan Street, London N1 9XW, UK.

Figures 163 and 164 reprinted from *Perception As Bayesian Inference* (figure 6.15), David Knill and Whiman Richard, Cambridge University Press, New York © 1996 by permission of the publisher.

Figure 166 reprinted from *Current Directions in Psychological Science* 2: 189–93 ("three frames from a movie" figure), "Color, Luminance, and the Detection of Visual Motion," K. Dobkins and T. Albright, ©1993 by permission of Cambridge University Press, New York.

Figures 168 and 169 adapted from *Perception* 26:1367–80 (figure 5), "Color from Motion: Dichoptic Activation and a Possible Role in Breaking Camouflage," Cicerone and Hoffman, © 1998 by permission of Pion Limited, London.

Figures 174 and 175 adapted from *Proceedings of the National Academy of Sciences, U.S.A.* 90: 10413–20 (figures 2 and 3), "Behavioral and Magnetoencephalographic Correlates of Plasticity in the Adult Human Brain," V. S. Ramachandran, ©1993 by permission of the National Academy of Sciences, U.S.A.